Statecraft
in the
Middle
East

Edited by

Eric Davis

Nicolas Gavrielides

Sponsored by the
Joint Committee on the Near and Middle East
Social Science Research Council
New York City

**Florida International University Press
Miami**

Statecraft in the Middle East

Oil, Historical Memory, and Popular Culture

Library of Congress Cataloging-in-Publication Data

The Florida International University Press is a member of University Presses of
Florida, the scholarly publishing agency of the State University System of Flor-
ida. Books are selected for publication by faculty editorial committees at each of
Florida's nine public universities: Florida A & M University (Tallahassee), Flor-
ida Atlantic University (Boca Raton), Florida International University (Miami),
Florida State University (Tallahassee), University of Central Florida (Orlando),
University of Florida (Gainesville), University of North Florida (Jacksonville),
University of South Florida (Tampa), and University of West Florida (Pensacola).

Orders for books published by all member presses should be addressed to University Presses of Florida, 15 Northwest 15th Street, Gainesville, FL 32603.

Statecraft in the Middle East: oil, historical memory, and popular culture / edited
   by Eric Davis and Nicolas Gavrielides: sponsored by the Joint Committee on
   the Near and Middle East, Social Science Research Council, New York City.
       p.   cm.
   Includes bibliographical references and index.
   ISBN 0-8130-1046-2 (cloth). — ISBN 0-8130-1058-6 (paper)
   1. Political culture—Arab countries—Congresses. 2. Politics and culture—
Arab countries—Congresses. 3. Politics and literature—Arab countries—Congresses. 4. Arab countries—Politics and government—Historiography—
Congresses. 5. Arab countries—Social conditions—Historiography—Congresses. 6. Arab countries—Popular culture—Congresses. I. Davis, Eric,
1946-. II. Gavrielides, Nicolas E. III. Joint Committee on the Near and
Middle East.
JQ1850.A91S73   1991   90-48024
306.2'0917'4927—dc20   CIP

To Muhammad Alwan
Richard Steiner
and Louise Sweet
who helped us understand
how to interpret the past

Contents

Contributors

LISA ANDERSON is associate professor of political science and assistant director of the Middle East Institute at Columbia University.

ERIC DAVIS is associate professor of political science at Rutgers University.

ASSEM DESSOUKI is professor of history and dean of the Faculty of Arts at Asyut University.

NOURA AL-FALAH is associate professor of sociology at Kuwait University.

NICOLAS GAVRIELIDES is associate professor of anthropology at the State University of New York at Cortland and an adjunct professor at the Southwest Asian and North African Studies Program at the State University of New York at Binghamton.

ABDEL-MALEK MORTAD is director of the Institute of Arabic Language at Oran University.

MUHSIN JASSIM AL-MUSAWI is professor of English and comparative literature at Baghdad University and editor-in-chief of *Afaq* ^c*Arabiya*.

MUHAMMAD RAJAB AL-NAJJAR is professor of Arabic language at Kuwait University.

KHALDOUN HASAN AL-NAQEEB is professor of sociology and dean of the Faculty of Arts at Kuwait University.

Foreword

During the Gulf crisis that erupted in 1990, President George Bush drew "a line in the sand," demarcating America's interests in the region. Lines drawn not in the sand but arbitrarily on maps were indeed a cause not only of the 1990 confrontation but also of the chronic political instability in the modern Middle East.

The Middle East historically is an old region and popularly is recognized as one of the cradles of civilization. However, the states of the modern Middle East are new, among the most recently founded in the world, and were created, more or less willy-nilly, by European diplomats when World War I ended in 1918.

At the beginning of the twentieth century, the Ottoman Empire, from its capital in Constantinople/Istanbul, had ruled virtually all of the Middle East (except for the territory of modern Iran). Following their conquest of the Middle East in the sixteenth century, Ottoman officials, for their administrative convenience, had divided the region into provinces and then districts and then subdistricts. These divisions became the political reality of the Middle East for centuries. The important provinces were Aleppo, Damascus, and Mosul in the Ottoman Syrian provinces and Baghdad and Basra in the Iraqi regions of the empire. At the end of the nineteenth century, Kuwait was an Ottoman subdistrict, officially part of the province of Basra. At the time, the subdistrict held approximately 2,000 houses, 14 mosques, and 500 shops. The Arabian Peninsula included the provinces of Hijaz and Asir and of the Yemen. Less important districts were Beirut, Mount Lebanon, and Jerusalem. Further west, the Ottomans' grasp fell lightly on the province of Tripoli in Africa (present-day Libya). The Ottoman organizational points of reference were the provincial capitals—Aleppo, Damascus, Mosul, Baghdad, Basra—that reported directly back to the imperial capital. These were the political boundaries of the Middle East in 1900, more or less as they had been since the Ottoman conquest of 1516–17.

By 1900, the Ottoman state was in the final stage of disintegration. Its Balkan provinces already were gone, thanks to the twin forces of nationalism and imperialism. In the Middle East, former Ottoman provinces in Egypt (and Cyprus) had de facto become part of the British Empire by 1882. The Ottomans' hold on territories at the head of the Persian Gulf was in jeopardy a few years later as a result of imperial Germany's scheme to build a railroad from Berlin to Baghdad. As this line began reaching closer toward the gulf, British anxiety mounted over the integrity of communications with its Indian possessions. To forestall a German takeover of the lands at the head of the Gulf, Britain accepted the clientage of the al-Sabah family, locally important in the area that later became Kuwait, who were seeking to break free of Ottoman suzerainty. Thus, in 1899, the region of Kuwait became an appendage of the British Empire. It acquired formal protectorate status in 1914 when the Ottomans declared war on Britain, France, and Russia.

In the aftermath of World War I, the Ottoman Empire disappeared from the face of the earth, as did the centuries-old administrative boundaries that it had drawn in the Middle East. These Ottoman realities vanished and in their stead new states literally were created by strokes of pens on treaties and on maps. The new lines on the maps were arbitrary and had little reference to then-current ethnic, economic, and cultural boundaries in the area. Nor, generally, did they reflect local sentiments that probably would have favored continuation of the Ottoman system. Instead, the lines were drawn to satisfy the imperial needs of the victorious British and French who, after much squabbling, made the political map of the modern Middle East more or less what it is today.

These places on the map were new states, to which few of their inhabitants then felt any loyalty or identity. As their borders were drawn after World War I, Syria, Iraq, Jordan, Kuwait, Palestine (and, to a lesser extent, Lebanon) were the creations of European imaginations and requirements. A major theme of Middle East history in the twentieth century has been the emergent reality of those fictive creations. Nation-state formation has competed successfully with rival ideologies, including Pan-Arabism as well as Pan-Islam. In the former Arab provinces of the Ottoman Empire, Pan-Arabism foundered on the realities of the new borders despite the numerous unification schemes that sought an overarching identity to deny them. As the failed efforts to export the 1979 Iranian Revolution have shown, Middle Eastern governments resist outside efforts to interfere. To varying degrees, residents of many states in the region, including Libya and Turkey as well as former Arab provinces, formed national identities as their governments acquired vested interests in maintaining the boundaries of the postwar treaties. The processes and mechanisms of this identity formation are an important focus of many of the chapters of this book, including those by al-Naqeeb, Anderson, al-Najjar, and al-Musawi. However, these state boundaries are open to challenge. Numerous disputes continue: on the Iraq–Kuwait–Iran–Saudi Arabia borders, on the very question of Lebanon and of Palestine and Israel, and, perhaps, even between Turkey and its Syrian and Iraqi neighbors.

As they existed in mid-1990, before the Iraqi invasion of Kuwait, the national boundaries of Middle Eastern states generally served Great Power interests. Comparatively weak individual states battled one another relentlessly, preventing the region from exercising its potential international influence and leaving it open to outside manipulation. The Arab Gulf states for their part, including Saudi Arabia, had provided petroleum under generally acceptable terms, for some of the reasons delineated by Davis in chapter 1. Saddam Husayn's invasion of 1990 challenged those arrangements and the existing political order and reopened border disputes, provoking exceptional responses from the Great Powers and the international community.

The chapters in this book treat a number of important topics, including the colonial heritage that molded a violent and distorted subsequent political development in many countries. There are several themes that seem at or near the center of most of the chapters, hence, the analyses by Davis and Gavrielides and by al-Najjar on identity formation in the new states and the mechanisms that worked to change self-perceptions within these boundaries. Similarly, other chapters, such as those by Anderson, Dessouki, al-Musawi and, again, by al-Najjar, explore the reshaping of the historical past—both written and folkloric—to fit emerging needs in the new societies. These studies, including the chapter by al-Falah and Mortad, altogether offer something that is rare in Middle Eastern studies, a view from within the society and culture. The perspectives presented here give us a unique opportunity for understanding the internal dynamics of this region with its varied cultures, societies, and political formations.

Donald Quataert,
Director, South West Asian and North African Studies Program,
State University of New York at Binghamton

Preface

The chapters in this volume are the result of a project that was conceived in late 1980 by Eric Davis and that was subsequently sponsored in January 1981 by the Joint Committee on the Near and Middle East (JCNME) of the Social Science Research Council and the American Council of Learned Societies. Between 1981 and 1984, the Social Science Research Council provided funds to sponsor a series of workshops. Funds were also allocated for travel to the Middle East to consult with a broad range of Arab scholars as well as Arabic collections in Europe and the United States. In May 1983 the JCNME authorized the creation of a Task Force on Social Change in Arab Oil-Producing Countries chaired by Eric Davis.

The activities of the task force resulted in the organization of a small conference in November 1984 and a much larger one in August 1985, both of which were held at Rutgers University. The November conference was funded by the Social Science Research Council, while the August conference was made possible by grants from the National Endowment for the Humanities and the Ford Foundation. Apart from the revised chapters by Khaldoun Hasan al-Naqeeb and Abdel-Malek Mortad, all the chapters contained in this volume were presented, in Arabic or English, at the conferences held at Rutgers University. Eric Davis and Nicolas Gavrielides translated the Arabic chapters into English.

In formulating the theme of the project in late 1980, Davis was reacting to the widespread belief in the West, especially the United States, that the rapid rise in oil prices during the 1970s had led to a dramatic increase in the strength of the state in Arab oil-producing countries. Davis's own research in Iraq during the spring and summer of 1980 indicated that oil wealth did not necessarily enhance the power and legitimacy of the central state. Indeed, the massive effort that he found underway at that time to rewrite the country's history suggested that the state enjoyed a much more precarious position.

Nicolas Gavrielides, who joined the project in late 1981, had taught at Kuwait University during the late 1970s. While there he had been struck by the state's efforts to reinterpret the country's history and popular culture. Gavrielides's research on the coffeehouses of former Kuwaiti pearl divers and on the social change reflected in Kuwaiti dress drew his attention to the state's efforts to influence two historical and cultural spheres that, at first glance, appeared to lack any political significance. A social anthropologist, Gavrielides added a critical cultural dimension to the project whose ultimate focus became the relationship among state formation, historical memory, and popular culture in Arab oil-producing countries. Influenced by Antonio Gramsci, particularly by his notion of hegemony, Davis and Gavrielides studied the manner in which the state was reinterpreting history and popular culture in ways intended to weaken active or potential opposition to its rule.

Trips to the Arab world during 1980, 1982, and 1984 helped to define the project's focus, establish contacts with Arab scholars, and expand research materials. Arab scholars responded enthusiastically to the idea that cultural materials such as history writing, literary texts, and folklore could be used as effective vehicles not only for understanding state formation but also social change more broadly defined. Scholarly monographs and articles, novels, short stories, poetry, folktales and folk proverbs as well as visual representation, such as reproductions of art in museum catalogs and "official" photographs, were gathered in order to establish a database from which to formulate a more thorough understanding of how the state was attempting to manipulate history and popular culture for its own ends.

In addition to using cultural materials to study state formation and social change, the project has tried to make other contributions as well. Reacting to the frequent assertion in the West that

Arab scholars produce relatively little in the way of social science literature, many of the chapters in this volume attempt to demonstrate the degree to which contemporary political and cultural discourse is encoded in debates over the nation's history and the origins of popular culture. In other words, the project suggests that the most appropriate sources for acquiring a better understanding of social change in Arab oil-producing countries (and non-oil-producing countries as well) may not be in social science journals but rather in debates in historical and cultural journals and in creative forms of expression, such as literature, art, photography, and film. As most Arab oil states are ruled by authoritarian regimes where overt political discourse is risky if not impossible, authors in this volume strongly encourage this avenue of research. Indeed, a number of the authors are currently working on larger monographs that expand upon the themes presented in their chapters in this volume.

As a final, but equally significant, goal, the project has sought to bring to Western audiences examples of contemporary writing by indigenous scholars in Arab oil-producing countries. Whether directly concerned with how the state in these countries is attempting to restructure historical memory and popular culture or more indirectly with the impact of these efforts, the authors seek to provide a voice for some of the most innovative Arab political and cultural discourse, especially the manner in which Arab scholars themselves conceptualize and study state formation and social change.

We would like to thank the Social Science Research Council for financial and administrative support that made the project leading to this volume possible. In particular, we would like to thank Peter von Sivers of the University of Utah and Roger Owen of Oxford University, the immediate past chairperson and the current chairperson respectively, of the Joint Committee on the Near and Middle East (JCNME) of the Social Science Research Council and the American Council of Learned Societies. The former staff associates of the committee, Robert Gates, Nikiforos Diamandouros, Stefan Tanaka, and the current staff associate, Tom Lodge, deserve our thanks also. We would also like to express our appreciation to the members of the JCNME who read the manuscript and provided helpful comments on it.

We would also like to thank the National Endowment for the Humanities and the Ford Foundation for funding a conference in August 1985 where the chapters contained in this volume were originally presented. We are also grateful to the Department of Political Science and International Programs at Rutgers University, the Department of Sociology-Anthropology at the State University of New York at Cortland, the Shelby Cullom Davis Center for Historical Studies at Princeton University, and the Hoover Institution on War, Revolution, and Peace at Stanford University for additional financial and administrative support.

Gilda Mason, Phyllis Moditz, and Sheila Friedlander provided invaluable assistance in typing the manuscript. Mazen Arafat and Emad Tinawi assisted in translating Khaldoun al-Naqeeb's chapter, and Muhammad Afrid assisted in translating Abdel-Malek Mortad's chapter. Professor Michael Mahoney of the Department of History at Princeton University provided essential computer programming that greatly facilitated preparation of the manuscript. Thanks also go to Dorothy Gavrielides for her editorial assistance.

1. Theorizing Statecraft and Social Change in Arab Oil-Producing Countries

Eric Davis

The recent Iraqi invasion of Kuwait underscores not only the importance of oil to the world economy but also the need for greater Western understanding of processes of social change in oil-producing countries themselves. Possessing the majority of the world's proven reserves and beset by continued political instability, an examination of Arab oil-producing countries seems particularly important.

If the crisis engendered by Iraq's seizure of Kuwait has increased interest in Arab oil states, the intellectual stimulus for this volume grew out of another oil crisis, namely the reaction of Western policy makers and social scientists to rapid price rises following the purported Arab oil boycott of 1973. The Western response centered around the notion that Arab oil states had greatly increased their power as players in the global political economy through the accumulation of large amounts of oil wealth. In a 1979 article, I challenged the idea that increased oil wealth led to a concomitant increase in the power of Arab oil-producing countries with respect to the West. Instead I argued that these countries were unable to absorb most of their "petrodollars." The investment of much of their oil wealth in the West, whether in bank deposits or fixed assets, the purchase of large amounts of Western capital goods, and the reliance on the West for increased military supplies and training to protect their newfound wealth, led most Arab oil-producing countries to greater, not lesser, dependence on the West.[1] Thus, one of the first questions posed in this project was to ask what in fact was the impact of oil wealth on Arab oil-producing countries.

1

If research conducted during the mid-1970s indicated that the oil wealth created as many social and political problems as it solved, my research in Iraq during 1980 pointed to a highly significant phenomenon that had heretofore been unexamined in the West. The Iraqi state was using a significant portion of its oil wealth to promote an ideologically mediated reexamination of the past, including the nation's history, national heritage (*al-turath*), and popular culture (*al-turath al-sha°bi*). Most striking was the fact that the country's president, Saddam Husayn, was head of a project entitled "The Rewriting of History Project" (*mashru° i°adat kitabat al-tarikh*). The fact that the Iraqi state felt the need to utilize its oil wealth to sponsor the establishment of research centers, publishing houses, museums, scholarly and popular journals, conferences and festivals, and programs in the mass media indicated that it did not feel immune from domestic challenges to its authority.

From the vantage point of either the global political economy or domestic sociopolitical considerations, the authority and legitimacy of the Iraqi, and other Arab oil states, seemed to be much more precarious than implied by the writings of Western social scientists. In short, the potential of oil wealth to increase political and social instability seemed to be as tenable a hypothesis as that which argued for an increase in the strength of the state.

Despite assertions that, after seizing Kuwait and hence controlling 20 percent of all proven oil reserves, Iraq is now the most powerful state in the Middle East, and indeed an emerging global power, it can also be argued that the August 1990 invasion was more a sign of Iraqi weakness rather than of its strength. First, lower oil prices presented Iraq with severe economic problems, foremost of which was meeting its war debts. The state found itself under pressure to compensate its populace for the extensive casualties and material sacrifices suffered between 1980 and 1988 during the war with Iran. Second, relations between the civilian leadership and the military had shifted during the war. In 1986, faced with possible defeat by Iran following a series of assaults on the southern port of Basra, the ruling Ba°th party was forced to cede greater freedom to the military to pursue the war. The subsequent campaign in which the Iraqi army decisively defeated Iranian forces, including successive human wave assaults, strengthened the military's hand. The end of the war found the state faced with an enormous military buildup. However, despite its accom-· plishments, the military faced a series of purges following the 1986 Basra campaign that continued after the 1988 truce with Iran. It is not surprising that there were a number of coup attempts prior to the invasion of Kuwait.[2]

The invasion of Kuwait can thus be seen as an effort by the Iraqi state both to rescue itself economically and to divert the military from domestic politics. Far from strengthening the state, the global condemnations of Iraq's actions and the United Nations sanctions suggest the potential for even greater future political instability. Indeed the reported execution of over 120 army officers who opposed the Kuwaiti invasion, expressions of doubt by troops in Kuwait as to the wisdom of the invasion, and defections of troops along the Turkish border may represent only the tip of the iceberg of opposition to recent events.[3] Appearances belie a more sobering reality for the state. Does the control of Kuwait's oil wealth, a million men under arms, possession of chemical and biological weapons and a repressive secret service indicate a strong state or one with a brittle legitimacy whose citizens reside in a "republic of fear"?[4]

Among Arab oil states, Iraq's bellicose actions have made it the most visible player on the global stage. However, while its invasion of Kuwait represents a more extreme example of the impact of oil wealth, do processes of social change in Iraq differ that much from those in other oil states? At first glance, the reasons for Iraq's invasion stem from Kuwait's thinly veiled attempt to weaken Iraq economically by exceeding, along with the United Arab Emirates, its OPEC quota and thereby driving down the world price of oil. Iraq was further angered by Kuwait's drawing oil from the Iraqi side of the Rumailia oil field that straddles the disputed Iraq-Kuwait border. Certainly Iraq's desire to become the dominant power both in the Persian Gulf and in setting world oil prices also played a role.

All of these factors constitute immediate causes for Iraq's military action. However, they ignore the deeper structural changes underlying the invasion that have affected not only Iraq but other Arab oil-producing countries as well. While these changes are discussed in greater detail in chapter 5, suffice it to mention here that the Iraqi invasions of Kuwait and Iran are both indicative of an incomplete process of nation building in which substantial segments of the populace have yet to be given the right of economic, political, and cultural participation. In other words, the state's resort to military action can be seen as part of its strategy to avoid seriously addressing the internal cleavages that beset Iraqi society and its refusal to recognize cultural difference and ideological diversity.

Oil Wealth, "Spectacle," and the Politics of Representation

One of the most interesting cartoons to emerge from the Iraqi invasion of Kuwait shows an American and an Iraqi television camera mounted on tanks facing one another in the desert with the caption, "Ready . . . Aim . . . Roll 'Em."[5] The cartoon is indicative of a central problem confronting any study of the contemporary Middle East which may be called the "problem of spectacle." While news concerning the Middle East has always suffered from distortion, in recent times the amount of news and information transmitted to Western audiences is steadily being replaced by a sensationalist caricature centered around a core of constantly repeated stereotypes. The Middle East as spectacle tells us more about the problems and insecurities of Western society than it enlightens us about the sociopolitical reality of the region.[6] Nor does the notion of spectacle apply only to the mass media. Terms such as "religious fundamentalism" or "revivalism" and monograph titles such as *The Sword of Islam* are indicative of the manner in which even Western intellectuals represent the Middle East as spectacle. These terms serve to reinforce the concept of the Middle East as "exotic," unique, and somehow always beyond complete comprehension by foreigners.[7] For many Western intellectuals, Arabs in particular seem encapsulated by simplistic concepts such as *jihad* ("holy war") and a "flowery" and rhetorical language that leads to theatrics and an avoidance of reality. No other region of the Third World is represented in the West in such a distorted manner. Given this prevailing image of the Middle East (and its Arab and Muslim inhabitants in particular), any study must be self-conscious about how it seeks to represent the region.

During the twentieth century, oil has become the major source of energy for the world economy. In the minds of many Westerners, oil production has come to be identified with the Arab world, a region containing the largest amount of proven reserves. Another cause for this identification, of which the Iraqi seizure of Kuwait is the most recent example, has been the perceived threat in the West that the supply of Arab oil might be disrupted as a result of political and social unrest in the region. Despite the Arab world's importance to the global economy and to international peace, comprehensive studies of social change in Arab oil-producing countries are relatively limited and largely informed by strategic considerations. As a result, it can be argued that the representation of Arab oil-producing countries is affected in at least two ways. First, Arab oil states are affected by the general problem of stereotyping and negative imagery that is attached to most things identified as Arab in Western, particularly American, culture. Second, these countries have acquired the additional opprobrium of being perceived to have the potential to harm Western interests through their control of the supply of oil. Indeed, it is probably not an exaggeration to say that, for many Westerners, "Arab" has become synonymous with "oil."

The fact that the supply and price of Arab oil are crucial to the continued economic prosperity of the advanced industrialized countries has served to accentuate a long history of conflict between the Middle East and the West. Indeed, hardly a day passes without the mass media presenting news that promotes an image of the region as inhabited by fanatic, irrational, and violence-prone peoples. In addition to the Iraqi invasion of Kuwait, other events— the Israeli-Palestinian dispute, the Iranian revolution and ensuing hostage crisis, the conflict in Lebanon, the Iran-Iraq war, attacks on civilian airliners, and the proliferation of nuclear and chemical weapons in the region—have served to shape a perception of the Middle East as threatening to Westerners and Western interests. It is little wonder that fears that hostile forces such as Iraq might seek to disrupt Arab oil supplies have prompted some influential Western scholars and policy makers to advocate military means to ensure the continued supply of oil to the West.[8] In short, super-imposing the economic and strategic importance of Arab oil on a long history of negative imagery of the Middle East has served to distort Western perceptions of the region still further.

If the state in Arab oil-producing countries is not as strong as implied by Western analysts, it raises further questions about its representation in the West. In line with the general image promoted by the Western, especially American, mass media, Arab states are alleged not only to possess potential power to harm Western inter-ests (such as during the purported 1973 Arab oil boycott led by Saudi Arabia and in the period following Iraq's 1990 invasion of Kuwait) but also to desire to do so. During the purported Arab oil embargo of 1973, Saudi Arabia was the enemy. Following the hostage crisis, Iran, which was non-Arab but continued to be per-ceived as such, replaced Saudi Arabia. Under the Reagan admin-istration, the mantle of premier terrorist state and archenemy of the West was bestowed on Libya and its leader, Muᶜammar al-Qadhdhaffi. Most recently, Saddam Husayn has assumed this role.

Are Arab oil states as powerful and malevolent as they are pur-ported to be? A more objective view than that presented either by Western policy makers or by the mass media suggests that they are not. Rather than assuming that the impact of oil wealth and the process of state formation in Arab oil-producing countries are objective realities the dimensions of which are waiting, in some positivist sense, to be discovered "out there," I am instead arguing that these categories are as much social constructions of Western policy makers and intellectuals. Thus they need not just to be stud-ied in the conventional sense but also to be ideologically decoded. It is hoped that the substance and approach of this volume serves both to avoid the problem of spectacle and to offer a more au-thentic conceptualization of social change in Arab oil-producing countries.

The Problematic of State Formation

The rapid rise in oil prices during the 1970s led many Western and Arab analysts to conclude that Arab oil-producing countries had dramatically increased their power as players within the global political economy. A competing and less influential hypothesis—one that was less apparent during the initial rise in the price of oil—held that the rapid influx of oil wealth had as much potential to undermine the social and political stability of the state in Arab oil-producing countries, by causing major social, political, and cultural disruption, as it did to strengthen it.

If the latter hypothesis is more valid than the former, then there are significant implications for the conceptualization and study of state formation. First, any period of rapid social change highlights the importance of the state, because the state is the key institution responsible for ensuring political and social stability. Furthermore, if periods of rapid social change do disrupt a society's political and sociocultural order, then the state often becomes a central arena of contestation among competing sociopolitical forces. Rather than assuming that increased oil wealth augments "state capacity" (to use a term currently in vogue), we can ask to what extent oil wealth has in fact strengthened the authority and legitimacy of oil-rich Arab states and to what extent has it undermined it.

The rapid rise in the global price of oil during the mid-1970s coincided with a renewed interest in Western social science in the importance of the state. The causes for this renewed interest are complex and cannot be discussed in detail here.[9] However, two points are important. First, the focus on the state was stimulated in part by what has been referred to as "the crisis of democracy."[10] The increased demands for social entitlements and political participation that the mass populace in advanced industrialized countries have placed upon the state, coupled with the inability of elected political bodies and capitalist economies to cope with these demands, has prompted calls for "demand reduction" and technocratic solutions to these problems. Strong state bureaucrats who are immune from electoral pressures are much better placed to confront the complexities of advanced industrial society than members of legislative bodies.[11] In asking why the state has become such a prominent point of analysis in recent years, the call to "bring the state back in" is perhaps less a result of its neglect by Western social scientists than a response to a growing crisis in the Western political economy.

Second, it is important to realize that the argument among Marxist theorists during the 1970s that the state should be reintegrated into Marxist theory strongly influenced Western social scientists. In the debate among "instrumentalist" and "structuralist" Marxists, many Western social scientists adopted the notion of the "relative autonomy of the state" propounded by the structuralists, often pushing it to an extreme. In many instances, the relative autonomy attributed to the state became almost complete autonomy from society.[12] In stressing the need to see "state actors" as having interests irreducible to those of social classes outside the state, many studies moved far in the other direction to place the state beyond the influence of social forces. The intellectual tendency to emphasize the relative autonomy of the state fit well with the underlying policy concern for the need for a strong state. As much of the Western social science literature focused on state intervention in the economy, it frequently represented itself as political economy—a paradigm whose purported attraction was its holistic approach. However, the end result of much research has led frequently to an ahistoricism and fragmentation of knowledge as state and society are no longer organically linked. Causal change emanating from the state was emphasized while societal constraints on state behavior were downplayed.[13]

This state-centered perspective for understanding state formation in Arab oil-producing countries (as well as in other Third World countries) promoted a notion of the state as situated beyond the constraints of indigenous sociopolitical forces. Oil wealth provided the conceptual foundation par excellence for transferring the notion of relative autonomy from advanced industrialized to oil states. Two important concepts derived from the notion of relative autonomy were the "distributive state" and the "rentier state."[14]

As oil states derived their surplus from the global economy rather than the indigenous society, it was argued that they were largely immune from domestic political and social constraints.

A number of theoretical shortcomings beset this tendency to "fetishize" the state by considering it to be situated beyond societal constraints.[15] First, the prevailing concern with the state should not blind us to the problem of reification. The concept of the state is largely a Western category that was socially constructed at a particular point in time in the context of the struggle between an emerging bourgeoisie and a declining feudal order. In the liberal tradition, the concept of the state is inextricably bound up with notions of law and order and hence is conservative in that it is tied more closely to ideas of stasis and social integration than to those of change and social conflict. In emphasizing stability and bureaucratic-technocratic as opposed to participatory solutions to societal problems, terms such as *state capacity* may, under certain circumstances, become ideological smokescreens for the domination of one or more sets of social groups or classes over an entire society. In other words, one must be careful that the more ideologically neutral concept of state formation does not in fact hide the reality of class or other forms of domination. In this volume, the study of state formation is less an end in itself than a process through which to understand broader dimensions of social conflict and change in Arab oil-producing countries as well as the manner in which Arab intellectuals interpret this transformation, particularly as reflected in interpretative texts that deal with history, tradition, and popular culture. In this sense, many of the chapters are less concerned with the institutional forms of power traditionally associated with the state, such as the military and the bureaucracy, than with how power is exercised in public and private space not always associated with the state (see the discussions of historiographical writing discussed in chapter 4 and the formulation of codes governing gender relations in chapter 6).

A second theoretical shortcoming of much contemporary literature on the state is its failure to situate the state within a historical perspective. In many Arab oil-producing countries—Iraq being perhaps the most notable example—the combined impact of integration into the world market, colonial rule, and the onset of oil production served to produce a powerful nationalist movement by the mid-twentieth century. Despite access to considerable wealth after 1952, the Iraqi state failed to translate this wealth into political legitimacy and hence political power and to prevent a bloody revolution in 1958. Oil wealth was likewise unable to protect the Libyan monarchy from a revolution in 1969. More recently, Arab oil states have not been immune from serious challenges to their authority. In Algeria, free elections produced a wholesale repudiation of the ruling National Liberation Front. Even before the Iraqi invasion, Kuwait faced attacks from religious radicals sympathetic to Iran and growing demands from the merchants and professional middle class for the reestablishment of an expanded parliament. To take a non-Arab example, the Shah of Iran was unable to preserve Pahlavi rule despite having employed oil wealth to amass one of the largest and most powerful armed forces in the world. As many have argued, it was precisely the cultural and ideological distance that separated the Shah's regime from the traditional middle and lower classes that prevented the mass populace from developing any loyalty to it.

As chapter 2 makes clear, one of the most significant shortcomings of "liberal" political systems that governed Arab oil-producing countries and non-oil-producing countries under monarchical rule earlier in this century was the cultural and ideological distance that separated them from the mass populace. This social distance assumed political significance as the lower middle class, workers and peasants became increasingly dissatisfied with deteriorating economic conditions following World War I. Oil wealth alone could not prolong the rule of these regimes. Only when, more recently, regimes realized the need to use oil wealth to create a national ideology to which the bulk of the populace could feel some affinity has the state been able to institutionalize a degree of stable rule. In other words, it was not the state's social and political distance from society but precisely its active involvement in mobilizing the masses around an ideology, be it Baʿthism, Algerian socialism, the "Third International Theory," or "Gulf Arabism" (for lack of a better term) that enabled it to begin to strengthen its power.

The problem of applying the notion of "relative autonomy" is not limited to the question of whether increased revenues derived from oil production did in fact strengthen the state in Arab oil-producing countries. Rather the question is how those who employ this concept explain the manner in which the state was strengthened. To simply posit that oil wealth engenders "relative autonomy" without specifying the historical processes by which this occurred raises more questions than it answers. Indeed, even on its own terms (i.e., removed from a historical context), the notion of the oil state as possessing relative autonomy is highly problematic. Even if the state were not dependent upon the indigenous populace for surplus, it is nevertheless dependent upon the world market. If the price of oil declines, as indeed it did during the 1980s, the state is placed in a difficult position. Indeed, both Algeria's and Iraq's main problem during the late 1980s resulted from a combination of dependence on the sale of hydrocarbons in the world market for the bulk of its foreign currency reserves, a massive foreign debt, and low oil prices. It is precisely under these circumstances that the state is forced to confront the society that it rules.

Each Arab oil-producing state possesses a different historical tradition and trajectory and has had to respond to a different set of sociohistorical forces. The notion of "relative autonomy" collapses the historical specificity of Arab oil states into a static conceptual framework that fails to indicate the genesis of particular types of state formation (e.g., the origins of the hereditary monarchies of the Arabian Peninsula and Arab Gulf as opposed to the populist single-party states in Iraq, Algeria, and Libya) or to suggest the future development of the state. The concept of relative autonomy is nowhere suggestive of many of the important dimensions of state formation discussed in this volume. It fails, for example, to explain the complex and multivaried historical development of the modern Arab state so comprehensively analyzed in chapter

2. In short, the "problematic of oil wealth" is not as self-evident as many Western scholars assumed initially. Oil wealth has not necessarily increased the power of Arab oil-producing countries within the global political economy, nor has it made the state immune from domestic challenges to its authority.

Statecraft and State Formation

In this volume, a distinction is made between the notions of *statecraft* and *state formation*. As we use the term, statecraft applies to the processes or mechanisms whereby a state enhances its power and authority. Put differently, statecraft entails the skills whereby political elites or ruling classes promote state formation. The notion of statecraft allows us to infuse the concept of state formation with a dynamic element. The key question posed here is how groups that control the state are able to increase its strength. Achieving this end may involve the use of formal institutions, such as the manipulation of legislative bodies, or more informal means. Statecraft always entails the effort of those who control the state to generalize their interests to the populace at large. While force, legislation, or law may all be employed to achieve this end, no state can persist and no group can rule without some effective bond with the ruled. Statecraft that is limited to the use of formal mechanisms of power is bound to be of limited efficacy in promoting state formation. This condition seems especially true in "new states" such as the Arab oil-producing countries, where formal state institutions are often not the arena in which real power is exercised.

In traditional studies of state formation, such as the important work by Tilly and his collaborators, the focus is largely on formal institution building. Parliaments, bureaucracies, the judiciary, the police, and the armed forces become the appropriate analytic foci.[16] The processes scrutinized here, on the other hand, are cultural and ideological and hence outside the formal institutional realm of the state. Here the boundaries of power and authority are somewhat more ambiguous. For example, the attempts of Arab Gulf states to use folklore to promote their legitimacy (discussed in chapter 7) do not have immediate institutional implications apart from the creation of state-sponsored research centers. In other words, these processes do not directly strengthen the state bureaucracy or the armed forces, to mention two central state institutions. Apart from references to the need for national pride and awareness of the past, those who control the state never make explicit the political rationale behind their reinterpretation of history and popular culture. To do so would render them ineffectual. Thus it is precisely the unspoken and subtle nature of these processes that gives them their power. Reinterpreting the past requires a strong sense of the factors that resonate emotionally with subaltern groups. It also entails an ability to reconstruct, synthesize, and even invent symbols that will touch a psychological nerve in the populace at large. A strong state is one that can exercise this craft and that continues to forge emotive links with the populace over which it rules. "Relative autonomy" fails to capture the nature of this relationship because it offers no dialectical notion of the links between ruler and ruled. A strong state is precisely one that is closely tied to its subjects. To look at a state from a largely economic perspective, as implied by a "rentier" or "distributive" state, does not necessarily imply power. Quite the opposite may be hypothesized; derivation of the surplus from the world market in the form of oil wealth may ultimately weaken the state by isolating it from the populace, as happened under the Shah's regime in Iran.

However, the construction of a particular form of historical memory, whether through the use of history writing or the reinterpretation of folklore, helps create a more favorable environment in which to exercise more overt, institutionalized forms of power and authority. As argued in chapter 5, the extensive campaign of the Baʿthist regime to rewrite Iraqi history may help explain why no significant domestic opposition has developed to the invasion of Kuwait despite the severe economic and military threats posed by the international community. Conversely, the fact that Kuwaitis both inside and outside Kuwait have rallied to support of the Sabah family may indicate a modicum of success in the regime's efforts to use folklore to create a modern national identity.[17] The ability of those who control the state to recast history and deploy culture, whether in its "high" or popular forms, requires a subtlety and finesse that differs from the exercise of overt force or the resort to codified forms of power, whether of a "traditional" or "rational-legal" nature. It entails the construction of hegemony in the Gramscian sense of the term. It is this form of statecraft that is addressed here.

The Socioeconomic Context of State Formation

State Formation and Nation-State

A central premise underlying the approach adopted in this volume is that state formation in Arab oil-producing countries can only be understood in a historical perspective. While it has its own causal influence, the development of oil production must be seen as part of a larger process of integration of the Arab world into the global capitalist economy. Rather than viewing processes of social change in these countries as unique, they should be seen as linked to processes of social transformation that were present prior to the onset of oil. Indeed, this is the thrust of chapters 2–4, which underscore the impossibility of assessing the impact of the period following the onset of oil production without a comprehensive understanding of its historical antecedents. Weak states, the lack of social and political integration among large sectors of the populace, and the maldistribution of income and political power were not caused by oil wealth. Prior to the onset of oil production, many Arab countries experienced major social upheaval in the form of massive migration from rural and desert hinterlands to urban areas. This social change involved both "push" and "pull" factors in the sense that the agricultural sector could no longer sustain large segments of the peasantry while urban areas offered them the only immediate hope of economic sustenance. In Iraq, for example, large-scale migration to urban centers such as Baghdad and Basra accompanied the deterioration of agricultural production in the Tigris-Euphrates Delta following World War I and continued throughout the century. A similar process occurred in Algeria both before and after the revolution of 1954–62. In Kuwait, and through-out the Gulf and the Arabian Peninsula, on the other hand, the onset of oil production had a more direct impact on major pro-cesses of social change. Many traditional artisan handicrafts, whether related to production organized around either the sea or the desert, became redundant. The social welfare systems enacted by the state as the result of oil wealth provided a major incentive for peasants and tribesmen—already experiencing economic hard-ship—to leave their traditional occupations and become employees of the state. For tribesmen in particular, this process entailed relo-cation to urban areas.

Despite the fact that it has been the primary initiator of impor-tant processes of social change, more often than not oil wealth has served as an "intrusion" into ongoing processes of that change. This consideration is important as the lack of a historical approach tends to promote the "fetishism" of oil wealth and hence to over-emphasize its impact on social change. Thus we seek here to ex-amine the manner in which oil wealth has promoted, distorted, or retarded already extant processes of social change. The complex and multifaceted nature of social change prior to the rise in oil prices that is documented in chapter 2 points to a conceptualiza-tion of the Arab world as "beginning with oil" as yet another mis-representation of the region. It is another example of how the Arab world is constructed as something "unique" and "exotic," thus providing yet additional encouragement for viewing the region in terms of political spectacle. Unfortunately, a considerable amount of Western social science writing, especially by political scientists, suffers from a "presentist" fallacy in which historical forces are given only cursory attention.

While the state in "premodern" or precapitalist Arab society was invariably despotic and broached no opposition, the state's power was limited for the most part to urban centers or garrison cities. It rarely exercised extensive control in rural areas or the hinterlands. This institutional weakness of the state reflected in large measure the weak social integration and diffuse political identity of the geographical area over which it ruled, a characteristic that existed at the onset of the Arab world's integration into the world market.

The state's lack of legitimacy manifested itself most clearly in the lack of acceptance by large segments of the populace of the national boundaries of which they were a part. The boundaries of such prominent Arab oil-producing states as Iraq, Kuwait, Algeria, and Libya, for example, were structured more by exogenous forces such as the Ottoman Empire, Great Britain, and France than by actions of the indigenous populaces. In many instances, this historical experience led to a lack of congruence between the nation-state, on the one hand, and the primordial commitments of various indigenous groups, on the other. These groups constitute "organic social formations" that are defined, objectively, by their relationship to agricultural production or pastoral nomadism and, subjectively, by the ethnic, sectarian and linguistic criteria that developed over time around their productive activities.[18] In Iraq and Algeria, groups representing subunits within the nation-state either challenged its very existence (such as the Kurds of northern Iraq), or they challenged its political and social orientation (as did elements of the shi'a of southern Iraq and the Kabyle-speaking Berbers of north-central Algeria). In Kuwait, Saudi Arabia, and some of the smaller gulf oil-producing countries, the lack of congruence between social formation and nation-state was somewhat the reverse of Iraq and Algeria. Here tribal groupings, such as the 'Anaza, Shamar, Mutayr, Bani Khalid, and others, sustained membership and affilial loyalties that transcended national boundaries. National boundaries often served to create artificial separations among tribal compatriots.

Tribalism

The dynamics of social class formation that emerge from this lack of congruence between nation-state and social formation are far more complex than Western theories—whether modernization theory or neo-Marxism—would allow. All of the ruling groups in the Arab oil-producing states of the Arabian Peninsula, in Kuwait, and in the states of the lower Gulf, for example, are drawn from tribal formations. Far from being a rigid structure, as is often thought, the tribe possesses a significant capacity for adaptation to

changing social conditions.[19] Indeed, oil wealth has allowed certain tribal values, such as those of hospitality and paterfamilias, to
be transferred from the tribal context to that of the nation-state as
a whole. Thus the position of leaders of states in the Arabian Peninsula and the Gulf as paramount shaykhs or tribal chieftains has
been fortified in the eyes of many sectors of the populace and
their legitimacy strengthened.[20] Far from undermining traditional
structures, oil wealth in this instance has reinforced them.

Nevertheless, the very cohesiveness and rigidity of the tribal
structure often excludes from political participation important social groups, such as the traditional merchant class and technocrats
(often themselves from tribal backgrounds), who are almost always educated abroad. As both these groups make substantial
contributions to the accumulation of social wealth, they often re-
sent their exclusion from the political decision-making process.
While oil wealth may foster state formation by strengthening the
bonds between ruler and tribal followers, it has also served to increase political and economic friction between ruler and merchants. The collapse of the Suq al-Manakh (the non-official stock
market), politically engineered by the Amir of Kuwait in 1983, that
led to the bankruptcy of many merchant families is just one indicator of this tension.[21]

In other cases, such as Iraq, a conscious effort has been made to
eliminate the category of tribe from national political discourse.
This suppression of the notion of tribalism has gone as far as banning of a prominent historical study by ʿAbbas al-ʿAzzawi, *ashaʿir
al-ʿiraq* [*The Tribes of Iraq*], the imprisonment of Iraqis who have
asserted that tribal criteria still influence recruitment within the state
bureaucracy, and the order by Saddam Husayn that all Iraqis with
the surname al-Takriti—derived from the hometown of the president and many other prominent Baʿthist officials—drop the name.

As a number of chapters indicate, the concept of tribe has undergone significant change in Arab oil-producing countries. As
shown in chapter 8, the thematic content of the Iraqi short story
reflects an increasing rejection of tribal values by educated and
urban sectors of the populace following the 1920 revolution. However, as pointed out in chapter 5, while the Iraqi state has eliminated the concept of tribe from contemporary political discourse,

it has promoted a number of historical studies in which the concept of tribe in society is reconstructed so as to reinforce its own ideological vision of society. Such actions on the part of the state represent an implicit recognition of the continued salience of tribalism.

If the Iraqi state seeks to downplay tribalism, the reverse is true of many of the Gulf states where tribalism provides an important component of the official conceptualization of state formation. In Kuwait and the Arab Gulf, the state has actively worked to foster the notion of the modern state as an extension of the traditional tribal structure of society. Why the relationship between tribalism and state formation differs among Arab oil-producing countries is an important question addressed in this volume.

Labor Dependency and State Formation

The rapid accumulation of oil wealth has produced considerable shortages of wage labor as Arab oil-producing countries have sought to industrialize in anticipation of the end of oil production, even in countries with relatively large populations. In Iraq, for example, the war with Iran placed heavy burdens on labor supplies, resulting in significant importation of expatriate labor from the Arab world and from South and East Asia. Following its invasion of Kuwait, Iraqi dependence on foreign labor became even more evident as thousands of expatriate workers fled the country. Egyptian, Syrian, and other Arab teachers have been used to bolster Algeria's state's Arabization policies. Thus it is necessary to differentiate between two types of labor dependency: the need for technical skills, such as in economic planning, in developing industrial production, in providing financial services, and in cultural development; and the need for manual labor.

In Saudi Arabia and the Arab Gulf states, the expatriate labor force, which often outnumbers the indigenous population, neither holds citizenship nor bears allegiance to the society in which it is employed. As this working class—comprised of Palestinians, Egyptians, Yemenis, Indians, Baluchis, Pakistanis, and East Asians—performs almost all of society's manual labor, it removes the indigenous populace from any involvement in such labor. This process creates a strong social cleavage between the state and its indigenous citizenry and expatriate workers. Often this cleavage makes it difficult for the state to respond to social and political crises— witness Kuwait's inability to deal with labor unrest during a 1984 strike by stevedores who had not been paid for several months following the decline of world oil prices. Expatriate strike leaders were simply deported. A recent rise in political activism among Islamic radicals loyal to Iran who tried to assassinate the Amir of Kuwait, for example, led to the rapid and wholesale deportation of Iraqi, Palestinian, Egyptian, and other Arab laborers. Following the invasion of Kuwait, the cleavage between citizens and noncitizens became even more evident when many Palestinian residents openly cooperated with the Iraqi forces providing labor services. Such developments not only underline the tenuous nature of economic development in those Arab oil-producing countries dependent upon expatriate labor but also point to yet another vulnerability of the state.

A similar argument could be made for more specialized occupations, as these countries are likewise dependent on Arab and Western technocrats to perform a wide variety of services. Banking and related financial services, for example, are largely controlled by foreign technocrats throughout the Gulf region. Prior to the Iraqi invasion, it was argued that, if foreign computer specialists were to leave Kuwait, access to data on bank accounts would be virtually impossible to achieve. The citizens of the Gulf states are not only divorced from manual labor; they are also prevented from developing an understanding of the productive forces and historical development of their own societies.

The problem of labor dependency has made the Arab Gulf countries extremely sensitive to the need for cultural and ideological solidarity, particularly a cohesive Gulf identity. As documented in chapter 7, these states have actively promoted the notion of Gulf folklore as a basis for forging a more explicit political consciousness centered around a Gulf Arab identity that could be used to offset the cultural and political influences of expatriate Arab and non-Arab labor. While oil wealth has brought greater material wealth to Arab oil-producing societies and has fostered a sense of

complacency among those sectors of society that have benefited
from that wealth, the material in chapter 7 underlines the sense of
alarm that has arisen that the indigenous culture will be uprooted
and destroyed.

Gender Relations, Family Structure, and Socialization

It has frequently been assumed that modernization in the form of
the development of a capitalist economy necessarily leads to an
improvement in the status of women. Studies of Saudi Arabia indicate that many women, especially those of the middle and lower
classes, find themselves *more* restricted as economic development
progresses. As large numbers of Saudi men return from education
abroad and enter posts with lucrative salaries, they often prevent
their wives from entering the workplace by arguing that added
family income is no longer necessary. Further, Saudi technocrats
with foreign education frequently become dissatisfied with their
spouses, who are often poorly educated or illiterate. As a result of
their interaction with Western society, Saudi males are frequently
unable to find wives whom they consider compatible. In many instances, this situation can lead to divorce. A divorced Saudi woman
may find herself ostracized and without a family of her own.[22]
Thus middle- and upper-class men can benefit from oil wealth by
raising their education and social status, while women from the
same social classes not only lack such benefits but often are even
negatively affected.

A different type of impact is being felt by lower-class women in
Algeria, an Arab oil-producing country that has an excess population in relation to employment possibilities and hence exports
labor, particularly to France and the Arab Gulf. Under these circumstances, women are often left as heads of households, which
places them in a role traditionally occupied by males. The skills
that women are forced to learn in order to protect their families
create a change in consciousness that can lead to conflict when the
males return and seek to reassert their traditional authority. This is
especially true if males who return from employment abroad seek
to use their accumulated savings to take more than one wife.[23]

A phenomenon that has received much attention from Western social scientists is the recent increase in the use of the veil in Arab and other Muslim societies. In Kuwait, however, it is males who have insisted upon retaining traditional garb (in order to differentiate themselves from expatriate labor) while the women often adopt Western dress. By having their wives wear expensive Western dress, Kuwaiti males have been able to demonstrate their own economic status, which they cannot do through their own daily garb, the white *dishdasha*.[24] Superficially at least, Kuwaiti women seemed to have gained more freedom during the oil era: many became wealthy by acquiring real estate, since the state has strictly enforced Islamic inheritance laws that award women one-half of the male's share of his father's wealth. Of course, the impact of the Iraqi invasion on gender relations in Kuwait has yet to be seen.

In Iraq, the state has expressed strong support for gender equality. This support led to the creation of Iraqi Federation of Women, which has been actively involved in fighting illiteracy among Iraqi women, especially those from the lower classes, and in providing child-care centers for working women.[25] Following the 1980 national assembly elections, Iraqi television played up President Saddam Husayn's visits to poor households to encourage women to exercise their right to vote. On the surface, state actions seem to constitute progressive reforms and to have furthered gender equality. While there is little doubt that state policies have affected the political and social consciousness of many Iraqi women, the more important question is whether they are leading to fundamental changes in gender relations in Iraqi society. The primary motivation for state policies seems to be the low productivity of Iraqi industry and the desire for a larger domestic work force. Women who are illiterate and forced to remain at home to rear children cannot contribute to industrial production or the service sector. While it would be unwarranted to reduce state policy on gender relations simply to the need for more workers, the Iraqi case raises the question of the outcomes of such policies. Is a purported commitment to gender equality serving to increase social tensions by raising expectations among women regarding social changes that do not in fact occur? Paralleling a situation in other industrialized and less developed countries, is the movement of women outside the home only placing more burdens on them, since traditional male patriarchal values have not changed?

This indeed is suggested in chapter 6 on gender relations in Kuwait. Education has raised women's expectations about what they should expect from society, but traditional patriarchal attitudes have prevented women from actually experiencing significant social change. The chapter indicates that the state may be forced to change historically institutionalized forms of domination such as gender inequality because of material needs which, in this instance, entail the need for more indigenous labor for the service sector. However, these changes may only replace the older, more blatant forms of oppression with more subtle forms. While the exigencies of labor shortages have served to undermine traditional concepts of women in "Arab patriarchal ideology," the material in chapter 6 also underscores a main theme of this volume—that much of the struggle over the form that gender relations in Kuwait and other Arab oil-producing countries will assume occurs within the sphere of representation. While Kuwaiti "traditionalists" have reluctantly agreed to allow women to acquire advanced educational degrees and to enter the labor force, efforts are still being made to represent women as incapable of equaling men in the performance of their new roles. Hence representation is part of a process whereby traditional frameworks of domination are recast to incorporate new material realities. Whether such efforts are successful is an important question raised in this volume.

These reflections on gender relations illustrate their diverse and multifaceted character in Arab oil-producing societies. They point to the need to study questions of gender and family structure from the perspective of social class and regional variation and to answer key questions. What is the impact of oil wealth on traditional Arab family structure and the socialization of children? Are children of the upper classes losing their links to traditional society when their daily supervision is more in the hands of expatriate women, such as Indians and East Asians, who do not speak Arabic and who are not conversant with Arab culture and traditions? Are middle- and upper-class women finding mechanisms of resistance to oppose the attempted extension of patriarchy? Are lower-class women whose husbands migrate abroad becoming more politicized? Are women who have benefited from oil wealth—whether in the form of greater access to wealth, education, professional careers, or travel—translating their financial resources into increased economic and political power? At the very least, the study of gender relations must transcend a facile reductionism that would equate the spread of capitalist market relations in Arab oil-producing countries with an improved status of women. What is clear is that the influx of oil wealth has placed severe strains on the traditional Arab family structure and that these strains contribute, if only indirectly, to the problem of state formation.

In terms of Western conceptualizations, and following the emphasis in this volume on power and representation, why has the concept of gender been largely limited to the study of women? How, for example, have conceptualizations of masculinity in the Arab world been affected by the impact of oil wealth and the larger social change of which it is a part? Bringing the issue closer to home, to what extent are Western conceptualizations of gender relations in Arab oil-producing countries, and less developed countries generally, influenced by changes in gender relations in the West? Just as greater awareness of how our understandings of the state in Arab oil-producing countries are affected by changing views of the state in the West, so too it behooves us to examine how questions of patriarchal domination are filtered through a prism that is structured by changes in gender relations in Western society.

The Ideological Bases of State Formation in Arab Oil-Producing Countries

One of the aims of this volume is to redress two shortcomings in the literature on state formation in Third World countries and in Arab oil-producing countries in particular. One tendency has been to assume that Third World states are already more or less fully formed and thus to take the present form of the state as given. If not placed in a historical context, categories such as the authoritarian state, the rentier state, or the distributive state are often more structural than processual. They describe more than they explain. A second tendency has viewed the state almost entirely from a narrow political or economic perspective. In one discourse, shaped by the liberal tradition in the social sciences, emphasis is placed upon institution building and the state's "search for legitimacy."[26] In the second discourse, largely shaped by neo-Marxist and dependency/world systems theories, the primary focus is the manner and ability of the state to extract surplus.

Both discourses neglect two important considerations. First, as mentioned, the state in the Third World often rules over a nation that is not congruent with what I have called an "organic social formation." Second, in approaching state formation, both discourses, reflecting the influence of traditional readings of Marx, Weber, and Lenin, have emphasized force and coercion as the primary means whereby the state asserts its authority. In both instances, the ideological bases of state formation are neglected. The fact that the state in Arab oil-producing countries has had to take an active role in reconciling a legacy of social cleavages—cleavages that were often exacerbated or even created by colonial rule—is precisely what has led it to take such an interest in culture and ideology. As the analysis in chapter 2 of the authoritarianism that pervades the Arab world makes clear, the continued need to resort to force is debilitating to the state as well as to the populace at large. Indeed, the belated recognition by groups controlling the state that ideological coercion through manipulating readings of history and popular culture is a potentially far more effective form of rule than physical coercion constitutes an important shift in state behavior.[27]

Existing social cleavages in Arab oil-producing countries point to the fact that the state finds its legitimacy tenuous among large sectors of the populace. Indeed, this is one of the conclusions to be derived from an analysis of elements of popular culture. While the analysis of Algerian folk proverbs in chapter 9 can be read as the author's attempt to demonstrate that a widely shared folk culture can form the basis for a unified political community, it can also be read as pointing to considerable latent discontent, among the mass populace, with existing social conditions. Although the short story writers discussed in chapter 8 support the secular, modernist ideology espoused by the Iraqi state, they also convey considerable discontent and alienation in society brought on by a disruption of the traditional rural social structure, the rapid growth of urban areas, and the spread of materialism and corruption, due in part to oil wealth. As these two chapters illustrate, an examination of popular culture and literary production can provide a more authentic method of understanding mass attitudes than more formal methods such as survey research.[28] Just as significantly, they point to culture and ideology as a domain of struggle and to the shortcomings of the concept of the "relative autonomy of the state." If it did enjoy such "relative autonomy" and was largely immune from societal pressures, then one is hard pressed to explain why the state in Arab oil-producing countries feels such a necessity to engage in the "invention of tradition."[29]

The desire to view state formation as a process and to incorporate the role of culture and ideology into the dynamics of that process is central to this volume. It is true, of course, that many Third World states, including oil states, have come into existence through violent revolutions and that ruling groups in these states often resort to violence as a centerpiece of public policy. However, the great wealth at the disposal of ruling groups that dominate Arab oil states has given them options not available to their counterparts in countries that lack substantial mineral wealth. One such option is the use of a portion of this wealth to coopt sections of the intelligentsia in order to employ their mental skills to create what Gramsci calls a "historical bloc" that is intended to generalize the ideology of the ruling group to that of the society at large.[30] The effort to promote state formation through the use of ideology and culture rather than coercion—that is, to create what Gramsci refers to as hegemony—is a process that still has not received adequate attention in Arab oil-producing countries or in other parts of the Third World.

The focus on "cultural" or "humanistic" writings is not meant to imply that Western social science concepts are irrelevant to the study of state formation in Arab oil-producing countries. Rather texts that, in the Western context, might not be as edifying may be more fruitful to the study of the state in the Arab context. The past, or more precisely its sociopolitical construction, is more salient to the state in Arab oil-producing countries than in advanced industrialized countries in two respects. First, with the exception of Saudi Arabia, all Arab oil-producing countries have been subject to colonial rule during the twentieth century. Many, such as the Gulf states and Algeria, only recently achieved independence from colonial rule. Even the Saudi state is "new" in the sense that it only came into existence in 1932. Second, the institutionalized historical memory of most Arab oil-producing countries—for example, in the form of archaeological remains and written texts—is much more developed than that of many Western societies, especially the United States. Arab oil states possess a rich symbolic past upon which to draw as a base for grounding modern civil society. Debates over whether Islam, Arabism, or some form of local nationalism (*al-qutriya*) should provide the basis of the modern state and social institutions, and how symbols drawn from the past interrelate with exogenously derived institutions and ideologies, represent the critical subtext of many historiographical and cultural debates that on the surface do not necessarily seem overtly political.

Given the challenges to state authority and legitimacy created by oil wealth, what have been some of the responses by the state or groups that control it? As indicated, when faced with threats to their authority, all Arab oil states have taken repressive measures. However, the resources available to these states have allowed them to channel large amounts of wealth into the establishment of government-controlled publishing houses, scholarly and popular journals, folkloric research centers, museums, local and international conferences and festivals, and mass media designed to encourage the citizenry to conform to an officially sanctioned vision of state and society. While not underestimating the role of force and coercion in the process of state formation, a number of chapters here indicate that one of the most important ways to understand the relationship between state and society in Arab oil-producing countries is through the manner in which the state seeks to reshape historical memory.

As chapters 3, 4, 5, 7 and 8 indicate, such efforts have been grafted onto or have attempted to co-opt ongoing intellectual tendencies whose roots go back to the rise of nationalism in the early part of this century and even back to the nineteenth century. This process is complex and cannot be reduced to a Machiavellian calculus in which the state seeks to manipulate historical symbols for predesigned ends. As pointed out in chapter 3, the Libyan state's promotion of a Libyan or Libyan Arab identity is, at one level, key to strenghthening Muʿammar al-Qadhdhaffi's rule. However, Libya lacks a historical tradition as a nation-state—a fact that assumes added significance when considered in light of the negative impact of Italian and British colonial rule on such a tradition. Thus the society at large (including the leaders of the state who are drawn from that society) needs a sense of national identity. This need is particularly acute in a nation-state such as Libya that achieved independence only in 1951, that is oil-rich, and that is dependent upon foreign capital and expatriate labor to reap the benefits of its oil production. Thus state efforts to manipulate historical and cultural symbols already have the advantage of speaking to the populace's felt need for a greater sense of social and political identity. If this were not the case, it would be difficult to explain the strong interest in cultural and historical writings, as well as in television and radio programs and films that deal with historical and cultural themes, in such oil-rich countries as Libya, Iraq, Kuwait, and Algeria.

While chapters 3 and 5 provide an analysis of the way in which Arab oil states have attempted to use oil wealth to manipulate historical memory and popular culture, chapter 4 presents an important case study of the role played by intellectuals in extending the hegemony of the state. Assem Dessouki describes the efforts of the *hawla*—an ethnic Arab migrant community that has sought to reintegrate itself into Arab Gulf society after residing for several centuries on the Iranian side of the Gulf—to reexamine the history and culture of the gulf in order to situate itself socially, culturally, and politically. Despite the implicit critique in *hawla* writings of the hereditary and corrupt rule of Arab Gulf states and their alliances with Western powers, the state has, ironically, used *hawla*

efforts to promote an Arab nationalist perspective by demonstrating the Arab character and cultural unity of the Gulf to enhance
its legitimacy and authority. If the Arab Gulf does indeed possess
a cultural unity that has evolved over many centuries, then it cannot be argued that the modern state is simply an outgrowth of
windfall profits derived from oil production.

One of the important ways in which the state has moved to co-
opt historical and cultural writings is by using its oil wealth so as
to appear as the "protector" of Arab historical tradition (*al-turath*)
and popular culture (*al-turath al-sha‘bi*). Having emerged from a
long period of Western colonial rule, Arab states continue to confront the legacy of Western "cultural imperialism." Western forms
of political administration, legal codes, financial enterprises, educational institutions, armed forces, and styles of living that accompanied colonial rule continue—subtly and not so subtly—to
"inform" colonized peoples of their "inferior" status in comparison
with the West. Even with political independence, large amounts
of Western technology, consumer goods, television programs, and
films continue to flow into Arab countries, often bringing with
them values, symbols, and beliefs that are considered alien by
large segments of the populace. One of the main problems facing
Arab countries, as well as most less developed ones, is how to
define their own distinctive national culture in the face of the onslaught of a global culture produced and dominated by the West.
This problem is especially large for Arab oil-producing countries
whose inhabitants have greater wealth to use to consume Western
culture. Empty Coca-Cola cans strewn along remote stretches of
the Arab Gulf are symbolic of the extent to which Western culture
has penetrated their lives. As pointed out in chapters 8 and 9, the
problems of alienation felt by large sectors of Iraqi and Algerian
society have dramatically increased with the emergence of a more
materially and consumer-oriented society. Chapter 7 is important
for documenting how oil revenues can be used to promote a massive revival of folkloric studies intended to counter the negative
effects of Western cultural imperialism. However, the chapter also
demonstrates how, on the surface, the state's concern with protecting the inhabitants of Arab Gulf states from cultural imperialism

and dislocation simultaneously contributes to enhancing its role as paterfamilias. As such, the state is building on a more traditional structure of the paramount shaykh as the provider and protector of his tribal followers. The key question raised in chapter 7 is the extent to which the state will be able to continue to overcome the potential contradiction between exclusionary rule, corruption, close financial and military ties with the West, and its proclaimed role as the protector of historic Gulf traditions and values.

While one concern of the contributions to this volume is to avoid a conceptual approach that removes the state from its social context through emphasizing its "relative autonomy," another is to avoid viewing state efforts to "invent tradition" as merely Machiavellian attempts to manipulate the populace to conform to narrowly defined ideological goals. Clearly this does constitute one of the central aims of state efforts to reexamine the past, as Saddam Husayn makes explicit in the introductory essay to *hawla kitabat al-tarikh* (*On the Writing of History*).[31] However, the voracious appetite with which literate and nonliterate sectors of the populace in Arab oil-producing countries consume officially sponsored histories and interpretations of popular culture—whether books, articles, folkloric exhibits, or poetry readings on radio or television—is indicative of a widespread desire to gain a better understanding of history, heritage, and popular culture. While the term is not without conceptual problems, what Abdallah Laroui and others have referred to as the search for "authenticity" (*al-asala*) points to yet another important process of social change affecting Arab oil-producing countries.[32]

Intellectuals and State Formation

The role of intellectuals in state formation in Arab oil-producing countries is complex. As in any nation-state, some opt to write according to the dictates of the ruling elite. Others choose to defend their integrity by going into exile. More interesting for our concerns are those intellectuals who remain in Arab oil-producing countries but do not allow themselves to be co-opted by the state and continue to write in a critical vein. Such intellectuals often stretch the boundaries of permissible political and social discourse, and it is from their studies that one is often able to decode critical political subtexts.[33]

Examples of such subtexts are evident in a number of chapters. While chapter 2 contains a compelling analysis of the pernicious impact of authoritarian rule on Arab political development, Khaldoun al-Naqeeb is simultaneously calling attention to the need for more liberal attitudes toward civil liberties and political organization in other Arab oil states, such as neighboring Iraq. He also can be seen as subtly supporting the state in his own country, Kuwait, by comparing it to other Arab states. Despite occasional lapses into authoritarianism, Kuwait, prior to the Iraqi invasion, did not have the history of violence, political instability, and use of physical repression that characterizes the other states discussed in chapter 2. The presentation in chapter 3 of the *hawla*'s critique of the state in the Arab Gulf can also be seen as reflecting an indirect critique of social and political injustice in the region by progressive intellectuals such as the author who are not indigenous to the Gulf. Although praising the state for its support for a revival of folkloric studies, chapter 7 also contains a subtle criticism. If the state fails to concern itself with the revival and promotion of folklore, particularly with folklore as a means of staving off Western cultural imperialism, then the leaders of Arab Gulf states are not living up to their responsibilities and must lose legitimacy in the eyes of the populace. Finally, the discussion of proverbs in chapter 9 and the author's somewhat literal style belie the strong underlying critique of the spread of materialism and avarice as well as his emphasis on the Arab nature of Algerian society. By not acting to counter the spread of consumerism, the desire for quick wealth, and increased dependence upon others, the state can be seen as an accomplice in the erosion of the traditional values that have provided Algerian society, particularly its less privileged sectors, with their sense of community and social solidarity. Abdel-Malek Mortad is also making a plea for greater cooperation among Algerians in order to foster social and economic development.

These chapters indicate that state formation is a multifaceted process of struggle, an important dimension of which is reflected in the realm of culture and ideology. The inhabitants of Arab oil-producing countries struggle to define themselves politically in relationship to an alien culture. The state, however, attempts to direct this process to benefit certain groups or classes that constitute its base of power. Looking at state formation from the vantage of ideology and culture stands on its head the notion of "relative autonomy" or bifurcation between state and society. Following Foucault, the state does not "inject" certain values into society but rather sits astride and derives its power from a society that already has a predilection toward precisely the processes of social change in which the state is engaged.[34]

> I don't want to say that the state isn't important; what I want to say is that relations of power, and hence the analysis that must be made of them, necessarily extend beyond the limits of the state. In two senses: first of all because the state, for all the omnipotence of its apparatuses, is far from being able to occupy the whole field of actual power relations, and further because the state can only operate on the basis of other existing power relations. The state is superstructural in relation to a whole series of power networks that invest the body, sexuality, the family, kinship, knowledge, technology and so forth. . . . I would say that the state consists in the codification of a whole number of power relations which render its functioning possible.

In other words, the state emerges from society and not the reverse. In a period of rapid social change, and a challenge from an alien culture, the past becomes crucial to a newly formed state, as well as to the inhabitants of society, in defining themselves in relation to an "other." While the populace may be searching for its roots in many disparate and often diffuse ways, the state is often able to give this search greater definition in the form of an officially sanctioned ideology. Nevertheless, in most instances a rigid distinction between the cultural proclivities of society at large and state ideology is difficult to draw. Even the most explicit and sharply defined ideology in an Arab oil-producing state, Iraqi

Ba'thism, is still vague in its approach to interpreting the past. The point remains that an examination of the ideological dimensions of state formation is not only of substantive but also of methodological significance, as it underlines the contention that the state cannot be understood in isolation from broader sociopolitical forces.

In summary, the five most significant characteristics that provide the context for understanding state formation in Arab oil-producing countries are (1) the rapid influx of oil wealth at various points throughout the twentieth century, especially during the mid-1970s, which had a significant impact on ongoing processes of social change; (2) large-scale migration from rural and desert areas to urban locales; (3) the recent independence of most Arab oil-producing states from colonial rule and hence the "newness" of the state; (4) the lack of congruence between the postcolonial nation-state and domestic social formations; and (5) the calling into question of "traditional" value systems as a result of extensive contact with Western culture, hence the perceived need of the state to promote an ideologically mediated reexamination of the past that reflects an overall recodification of power relations in society at large.

NOTES

1. Eric Davis, "The Political Economy of the Arab Oil-Producing Nations: Convergence with Western Interests," *Studies in Comparative International Development* 19, no. 2 (1979): 75–94. Of course, the idea that wealth alone does not necessarily increase a nation-state's economic and political power is not new, as Adam Smith argued over two centuries ago in his critique of mercantilism, *The Wealth of Nations.*

2. Efraim Karsh, "In Baghdad, Politics Is a Lethal Game," *New York Times Magazine,* September 30, 1990, 100.

3. *New York Times,* August 5, 13, October 25, 1990.

4. Samir al-Khalil, *Republic of Fear: The Politics of Modern Iraq* (Berkeley: University of California Press, 1990).

5. This cartoon originally appeared in the *Providence* (R.I.) *Journal-Bulletin* and was reprinted in the *Binghamton* (N.Y.) *Press & Sun-Bulletin,* September 30, 1990.

6. Laurence Michalak, *Cruel and Unusual: Negative Images of Arabs in*

American Popular Culture (Washington, D.C.: ADC Research Institute, 1988); Eric Davis, "Imagery of the Third World and the Construction of the Self in Contemporary American Society," Rutgers University, 1987 (mimeo); Murray Edelman, *Constructing the Political Spectacle* (Chicago: University of Chicago Press, 1988).

7. For a more extensive discussion, see Edward Said, *Orientalism* (New York: Pantheon Books, 1978).

8. See, for example, Robert W. Tucker, "Oil: The Issue of American Intervention," and "Further Reflections on Oil and Force," both in *Commentary* 59 (January 1975): 21, (March 1975): 45, respectively. Tucker's more recent article, "Using Force Against Libya?" (*New York Times*, January 11, 1989), indicates that force and intervention are still seen as appropriate foreign policy options in the Middle East. Of course, the Iraqi invasion of Kuwait brought a whole spate of op-ed articles calling for military action against Iraq even if it were to withdraw from Kuwait. A good example of this perspective is Richard Perle, "In the Gulf, the Danger of a Diplomatic Solution," *New York Times*, September 23, 1990. See also "Iraqi Pullout? Election in Kuwait? Prospect Worries Hawks," *New York Times*, October 8, 1990.

9. See my essay "Between Development and Underdevelopment: Knowledge, Power and the Study of the Third World," forthcoming in L. Cantori and I. Harik (eds.), *Critical Paradigms in the Study of Middle East Politics.*

10. Michel Crozier, Samuel Huntington and Joji Watanuki, *The Crisis of Democracy* (New York: New York University Press, 1975).

11. See Peter B. Evans, Dietrich Rueschemeyer, and Theda Skocpol (eds.), *Bringing the State Back In* (Cambridge: Cambridge University Press, 1985), especially the introductory essay by Theda Skocpol, "Bringing the State Back In: Strategies of Analysis in Current Research," 3–43.

12. Two examples of such writing are Stephen Krasner, *Defending the National Interest: Raw Materials Investments and U.S. Foreign Policy* (Princeton, N.J.: Princeton University Press, 1978), and Eric A. Nordlinger, *On the Autonomy of the Democratic State* (Cambridge, Mass.: Harvard University Press, 1981).

13. This is the main thrust of the essays contained in Evans et al., *Bringing the State Back In.*

14. On the notion of the distributive state, see Jacques Delacroix, "The Distributive State in the World System," *Studies in Comparative International Development* 15 (1980): 3–21, especially his discussion of Kuwait. For a discussion of the concept of the rentier state, see Hazem Beblawi and Giacomo Luciani (eds.), *The Rentier State* (London: Croom Helm, 1987). See also Theda Skocpol, "Rentier State and Shi'a Islam in the Iranian Revolution," *Theory and Society* 11 (1982): 265–83. Skocpol is more cautious than Delacroix and others in asserting that oil revenues necessarily produce state autonomy: "Windfall revenues from international oil sales, for example, can render states *both* more autonomous from

societal controls and, because social roots and political pacts are weak, more vulnerable in moments of crisis" (35, n. 44). For a more comprehensive discussion of the treatment of the state in writings on the Middle East, see Lisa Anderson, "The State in the Middle East and North Africa," *Comparative Politics* 20 (October 1987): 1–18.

15. For a useful "corrective" to the outpouring of recent studies that have adopted state-centered approaches, see Joel S. Migdal, *Strong Societies and Weak States: State-Society Relations and State Capabilities in the Third World* (Princeton, N.J.: Princeton University Press, 1988).

16. See Charles Tilly (ed.), *The Formation of National States in Western Europe* (Princeton, N.J.: Princeton University Press, 1975).

17. *New York Times*, Oct. 14, 16, 17, 1990.

18. For a more extensive theoretical discussion, see Talal Asad, "Equality in Nomadic Social Systems? Notes Towards the Dissolution of an Anthropological Category," in Equipe et anthropologie des societés pastorales, *Pastoral Production and Society* (Cambridge and Paris: Cambridge University Press and Maison des Sciences de l'Homme, 1979), 419–28.

19. For an excellent discussion of the adaptability of tribal forms of social organization, see Dale Eickelman, *The Middle East: An Anthropological Approach* (Englewood Cliffs, N.J.: Prentice-Hall; 1981), 85–104.

20. Nicolas Gavrielides, "Tribal Democracy: The Anatomy of Parliamentary Democracy in Kuwait," in L. Layne (ed.), *Elections in the Middle East* (Boulder, Col.: Westview Press, 1987), 157.

21. The manner in which the collapse was engendered by the state is discussed in *azmat suq al-manakh* [*The Crisis of the al-Manakh Market*] (Kuwait: n.p., 1984).

22. Hamid Muhammad al-Baadi, *Social Change, Education, and the Roles of Women in Arabia* (Ph.D. dissertation, Stanford University, 1982). It is significant that, while a Saudi citizen, al-Baadi refuses to use the term "*Saudi* Arabia," reflecting his own hostility to the existing royal family.

23. This phenomenon has also affected other Arab countries, such as Egypt and Jordan, that have also sent large numbers of expatriate laborers abroad.

24. Nicolas Gavrielides, "Islamic Fundamentalism and Tribalism in the State of Kuwait," paper delivered to the American Anthropological Association Annual Meeting, Washington, D.C., 1980.

25. Zahar Abdul-Karim Hadid, *Mass Communication and Social Change in Iraq: Changing the Attitudes of Women* (M.A. thesis, University of Durham, 1980), 83–85.

26. Michael Hudson, *Arab Politics: The Search for Legitimacy* (New Haven, Conn.: Yale University Press, 1977).

27. So as not to create a dichotomous view of Arab history, it is important to note that Arab states have attempted to use history and culture in the past to attempt to enhance their rule. However, it is only the modern Arab state (especially oil states with large amounts of revenue) with its access to new forms of

communications such as modern publishing facilities, mass circulation newspapers, radio, television, film, and photography that has really been able to promote hegemonic forms of domination based upon ideologically informed understandings of history and culture in such a comprehensive manner.

28. For cultural studies that provide a fertile avenue for a deeper understanding of social change in Arab oil states, see, for example, al-Tali bin al-Shaykh, *dawr al-shᶜir al-shaᶜbi al-jaza'iri fi-l-thawra, 1830–1945* [*The Role of Algerian Popular Poetry in the Revolution, 1830–1945*] (Algiers: al-Shirka al-Wataniya li-l-Nashr wa-l-Tawziᶜ [SNED], 1983); Muhammad Saᶜid al-Qashshat, *sada al-jihad al-libi fi-l-adab al-shaᶜbi* [*The Impact of the Libyan Struggle on Popular Literature*] (Beirut: Dar Lubnan li-l-Tibaᶜa wa-l-Nashr, 1970); and, Majid Muhammad al-Samara'i, *al-tayyar al-qawmi fi-l-shiᶜr al-ᶜiraqi al-hadith, 1939–1967* [*The Nationalist Tendency in Iraqi Poetry, 1939–1967*] (Baghdad: Ministry of Culture and Information, Dar al-Hurriya li-l-Nashr, 1983).

29. Eric Hobsbawm and Terence Ranger (eds.), *The Invention of Tradition* (Cambridge: Cambridge University Press, 1987).

30. Antonio Gramsci, *Selections from the Prison Notebooks* (London: Lawrence and Wishart, 1971), 137, 168, 366, 377, 418.

31. Saddam Husayn, *hawla kitabat al-tarikh* (Baghdad: Dar al-Hurriya li-l-Tibaᶜa, 1979). esp. 28–40.

32. See Abdallah Laroui, *The Crisis of the Arab Intellectual: Traditionalism or Historicism?* (Berkeley: The University of California Press, 1976).

33. The role of intellectuals in state formation in Iraq is the subject of my forthcoming monograph on historical memory and collective identity in modern Iraq.

34. Michel Foucault, "Power, Sovereignity and Discipline," in D. Held et al. (eds.), *States and Societies* (New York: New York University Press, 1983), 312.

2. Social Origins of the Authoritarian State in the Arab East

Khaldoun Hasan al-Naqeeb

In the aftermath of events in Lebanon during the summer of 1982, it became clear that the repeated defeats and crises that afflicted the Arabs could not be explained in a mechanical (*aliya*) fashion that focused only on causal factors drawn from the contemporary era. The phenomenon of crises is not simply a question of military or "cultural" impotence. Nor is the political fragmentation of the Arab world or the prevalence of despotic regimes sufficient to explain the Arabs' inability to experience progress since the beginning of their struggle for independence following World War I. How then are we to explain the historical development that began with revolutions in Egypt (1919), Syria (1920), and Iraq (1920) and that ended in the summer of 1982 in the dependency and subordination of the Arab world?[1]

Events following World War I created an almost unanimous agreement in the Arab East (*al-mashriq*) that independence, democracy, unity, and development were the Arabs' fundamental national aspirations (*al-ahdaf al-ʿarabiya al-ʿulya*). These goals represented the fundamental elements of the renaissance (*al-nahda*) to which they aspired. It was natural that these aspirations assumed different meanings depending on the stage of the national struggle and the level of political consciousness.

For example, in the Arab world, only after World War II did the notion of independence begin to mean complete freedom from formal colonial control. Similarly, the idea of unity did not imply the complete integration of the Arab world under one central government until the 1950s, when the expression "immediate integrative unity" (*al-wihda al-indimajiya al-fawriya*) became widespread. Likewise, until the 1940s the concept of development—which for the "pioneer" generation was signified by the term "renaissance" (al-nahda)—meant an emphasis on cultural and industrial progress. It was not until the 1950s that the emphasis shifted from "renaissance" to "revolution," and to the association of development with socialism. After 1967 there was a return to calls for a cultural renaissance and "comprehensive development." As for democracy as a national goal, its meaning was limited to the struggle for independence: parliamentary rule within the framework of a constitutional monarchy. However, during the 1930s and 1940s, doubt began to be cast upon the utility of parliamentary democracy, especially after the large landowners and merchants succeeded in corrupting it. Thereafter, a multiplication of characterizations, such as "centralism," "populism," and "socialism," expanded or modified the concept of democracy.[2]

In 1929 Amir Shakib Arslan summarized these concerns in a succinct question: Why were Muslims underdeveloped, and why did others progress?[3] Ever since, we have repeatedly asked the same question in different ways after each defeat and setback. Astonishingly, the same answers seem to recur.[4] We have not progressed because we have not achieved independence, have failed to create unity, are not developed, and are still under dictatorial rule. Muhammad Jabir al-Ansari describes the situation well when he says:

> One of the catastrophic phenomena of the modern Arab world is that its intellectual and social structure has not benefitted from past experiences, that is, it has not built upon past intellectual and social achievements. Rather, we observe that every new generation becomes disappointed with the convictions and beliefs of prior generations and therefore is forced to demolish these convictions and begin all over again. It does not take long, however, for the new generation to become tormented by its own convictions leaving nothing for coming generations but its bitter experience.[5]

During the summer of 1982, Arab nationalist aspirations encountered another setback that resulted from the same causes that had led to previous setbacks. Once again beliefs about the possibility of unity, democracy, liberation, and development were shattered. Moreover, the fall of Beirut after the Israeli invasion represented a new dimension of defeat. Most Arab countries lacked organized political opposition. No street demonstrations accompanied this latest setback, not even the usual outpouring of ritualistic speeches. The political arena appeared to be paralyzed.

The question now is, if there was an almost unanimous agreement on the nationalist aspirations that the Arabs were attempting to achieve (regardless of their ideological affiliations or regional origins), and if there was a consensus of sorts on what obstacles prevented the attainment of these aspirations, then why were the Arabs not able to overcome these obstacles in more than sixty years of struggle? Where did the defects and weaknesses lie? Why were we unable to benefit from our past experiences, as Ansari points out so vividly? Why did Arab nationalist aspirations lose their historical significance and become for our intellectuals and politicians a mere rearrangement of polemics? Every time one polemical formula failed, another one was substituted in its place. As al-Jabiri asks: "Why do our thinkers and intellectuals talk past one another and not to one another?"

There must be more than one essential reason for this defect. First, perhaps there are obstacles in Arab societies themselves that the Arabs have failed to comprehend and analyze, and consequently could not assess. For instance, we can point to the political parties that came to power during the 1930s and 1940s only to subvert the demands of the masses for democratic freedoms, or the military that came to power during the 1950s and 1960s and completely eliminated all democratic institutions and freedoms under the pretext of reforms, as if the problem were the democratic institutions themselves.

Perhaps a second source of Arab shortcomings lies in our proximity to Western imperialism. This impediment to Arab national aspirations would imply that their attainment presents a threat to the imperialists' strategic interests and, hence, explains their covert and overt attempts to undermine any realization of these goals.

Third, perhaps the source of the defect is the "Arab mind" itself, that is, the way the Arab thinks, which is characterized by "reconciliation" (*al-tawfiqiya*) (or "hypocrisy" [*al-talfiqiya*]), that is, by the attempt to reconcile irreconcilable contradictions. This type of thinking leads to unrealistic results and to problems that have no solutions.[6]

This chapter is concerned with the first type of defect, or internal sociological dynamics. Through a historical assessment of local sociopolitical forces, I will diagnose the general features of the political struggle of the Arab East since 1919 and those forces that led us to the complex situation we find ourselves in today. In applying this method, I will attempt to reveal the logic underlying the sequence of events and to delineate the key historical movements (*al-harakat al-tarikhiya al-kubra*), their turning points (*al-mun'atafat*), and their transformations (*al-tahawwulat*).

The Main Turning Points of
Contemporary Arab Political History

A serious reading of modern Arab history allows us to pinpoint two important watersheds. The first occurred around 1839 and continued through the era of reforms known as the *tanzimat*. The second period, beginning around 1920, represents the beginning of an era defined by organized political action to achieve independence. This second period also represents the beginning of contemporary Arab history.

The first watershed represented the intersection of a number of important events whose roots extend long before 1839. Those events, represented in the appearance of regional powers such as the Mamluk state (Iraq), Muhammad ʿAli (Egypt), Ibrahim Pasha (Syria), al-Jazzar (Palestine), and al-Shihabi (Lebanon), constituted the age of despotism in the Arab world.[7] This period was also represented by the gradual emergence of the notables and ʿulama in politics and economics and of the role of reformist associations in leading the political struggle within the Ottoman state.[8]

The second watershed of 1920 can be conceptualized as follows: 1920 to 1950, a period of struggle for independence and a gestation and crystallization of the social forces produced by this turning point; 1950 to 1970, the coming of the military to power and the beginning of the age of American domination in the region; 1970 to the present, characterized by the completion of dependency and the crystallization of the institutions of the modern authoritarian state.

This chapter deals mainly with the major eastern Arab countries (*al-mashriq al-ᶜarabi*) that are important due to their large populations and political-economic significance: Egypt, Syria, Lebanon, Iraq, and Palestine. Although occasional reference is made to the countries of the Arabian Peninsula and the Arab West (*al-maghrib*), such references pertain to the 1960s and after.

It should also be noted that there is a disparity among the major countries of the Arab East in their levels of politico-economic development and their cultural and ideological maturity. This disparity is obvious between Egypt, on the one hand, and the rest of the countries of the Arab East, on the other. Although this does not affect the validity of my conclusions, it must be taken into consideration. One of the results of this disparity is that all major events do not occur simultaneously in all the countries, but all are related and successive.

The Era of Struggle for Independence

The watershed of 1920 represented a succession of events that coincided with a number of significant historical processes following World War I which constitute the main background for contemporary Arab history. These include, first, the collapse of the Ottoman empire and the establishment of the contemporary division of Arab world; second, the Russian empire's collapse following the Bolshevik Revolution; third, Woodrow Wilson's Fourteen Point plan, which encouraged independence movements in colonized nations; and, fourth, the political and economic hegemony of the British (Pax Britannica) over the countries of the Arab East.[9]

Against this backdrop, the Arab revolt against the Ottomans broke out in 1916. It was followed by the Egyptian Revolution of March 1919 and, in July 1919, by the Syrian people's call for the National Conference that declared independence in March 1920.[10] After less than three months, the Iraqi people rose up in revolt in June 1920 (*thawrat al-ʿishrin*).[11]

These revolutions demanded independence, the right of self-determination, and the right to establish constitutional, representative monarchical regimes. Gradually these demands progressed from the call for decentralization and reform within the Ottoman State (as it crystallized in the First Arab Conference of 1913), to the call for complete independence, constitutional representative government, and protection of minority rights. The latter three demands constituted the common denominator of the revolutions in Egypt, Syria, and Iraq.

An examination of historical evidence reflects a number of issues, including inter-imperialist competition in the region among Britain, France, and the United States, which was resolved in favor of the British. The evidence also reflects the early coordination between the Sharifian officers in Syria and Iraq that continued even after the Sharifs came to power in those two countries.

Following these three revolutions, another extremely important phenomenon was the increased dominance of the large landowners and indigenous merchants over the political realm. In Egypt these social groups were prominent in the National party and later in the Wafd, after it gained momentum with the "Egyptianization" of the latifundia and the higher ranking administrative positions as a result of the ʿUrabi movement of 1882.[12] In Iraq these rising social groups were represented by the heads of tribes in the countryside (the tribes were in the process of being transformed into "feudalists" [*iqtaʿiyun*]) along with the Sharifian officers, the urban merchants, and the notables (*aʿyan*) who joined the ʿAhd, the National, and the Renaissance parties. In Syria these groups were recruited primarily from the merchants of Damascus and Aleppo, the landowners of other areas, and the Sharifian officers. This is reflected clearly in the composition of the Syrian ʿAhd party and the National Coalition.[13] The importance of this process in the Arab East is that the rise to power, or to a position of opposition, of the latifundia and the indigenous merchants occurred after a long hiatus that dates back to the fall of the ʿAbbasid empire to the Buwayhids during the mid-tenth century and the fall of the Fatimids to the Mamluks during the mid-eleventh century.

Those ruling groups came to power and influence after a long period of gestation, the roots of which can be found in the Ottoman Reform movement (*Tanzimat*) and the rule of Muhammad ʿAli in Egypt and Syria. It is possible to trace their socioeconomic background to the notables, ʿulama, and the tribal shaykhs who acquired political influence during the nineteenth and early twentieth centuries. To promote their nationalist credentials, they opposed the British and French colonial administrations and the comprador (local merchants who were agents of foreign interests), who in most cases were non-Arab.[14]

Thus, local landlords and merchants came to power as oppositional groups calling for reforms and demanding the achievement of Arab nationalist aspirations. Although these groups were armed with a relatively mature ideology, their political program was limited. Their ideology was characterized mainly by liberalism, compromise (*al-tawfiqiya*), and an ideal of an Arab nation or its regional derivatives, such as the Egyptian or Syrian nation, as an alternative to the existing forms of sociopolitical organization. The rise to power of these groups allowed their ideology to prevail.

It is important to realize that the three dominant ideological tendencies—the secular (Shibli Shumayyil, Salama Musa, Ismaʾil Mazhar, Jamil Sidqi al-Zahawi); the liberal (ʿAli ʿAbd al-Raziq, Taha Husayn, Ahmad Amin, Muhammad Husayn Haykal); and the national (al-Kawakibi, Rashid Rida and Satiʿ al-Husari)—dominated not because their ideologies represented the interests of landowners and merchants, but because their ideologies did not conflict with these interests.

Also, their rise to power coincided with the aspiration to emulate the West and the appearance of contemporary political entities (e.g., the nation-state and the political party) under the influence of the colonial mandate and the superpowers. Here the difference between the coincidental compatibility of ideologies with certain classes, on the one hand, and *the active support and representation* of them, on the other, should be borne in mind.

The political program of these ruling groups was limited, as it only provided solutions and alternatives for the "political question" (*al-mas'ala al-siyasiya*)—for example, independence and the organization of government—and did not go on to provide solutions and alternatives for the "socioeconomic question" (*al-mas'ala al-ijtima'iya al-iqtisadiya*), such as class differences, social justice, and distribution of national wealth. Many writers and researchers of this period claim that the preoccupation of the ruling groups, or old nationalists, with matters of independence, constitution and democracy diverted their "attention" from increasing class differences and the consolidation of power and authority in the hands of wealthy classes. However, in fact the landowners and merchants were not capable of addressing these issues, nor did it serve their interests to provide solutions and alternatives to the "socioeconomic question."

Therefore, in less than twenty years—that is, by the late 1930s—the ideological, political, and economic impotence of liberal Arab regimes had become clear. Ideological latitude was manifested in an early failure of the "accommodating liberalism" (*al-libaraliya al-tawfiqiya*)—that is, with imperialism—that opened the way for the strong appearance of radical currents of both the right and the left. Concomitantly, this failure clearly manifested itself in the retreat of most liberals to excessive accommodation with imperialism and to the return to traditional formulas that had previously been rejected, such as Muhammad 'Abduh's formula of the "just tyrant."[15] Political impotence was manifested in fraudulent democracy, the rigging of elections, the subordination of nationalism to party interests, and the monopolization of government by "professional" ministers who were chronically rotated among ministries. Furthermore, with the global economic stagnation during the 1930s, economic and financial accomplishments were unimpressive, and the standard of living improved very slowly, or even declined.

Economic, political, and ideological paralysis began to appear as three crises facing the Mashriq states. In Egypt the political process assumed a tripartite struggle for power among the British, the palace, and the Wafd party, none of whom was able to escape the status quo.[16] In Iraq an alliance arose between Sharifian officers and "feudal" tribal shaykhs in a unique political division of labor according to which the officers monopolized the government while the shaykhs dominated the parliament (in partnership with urban notables). This division of labor functioned until the mid-1930s, when cooperation and integration between these two groups led to the formation of a new ruling class. In Syria the Sharifian officers represented both landowners and merchants. Despite the fact that they were in a continuous struggle with the French-mandated administration following the fall of Faysal's government in 1920, the Sharifians were unable to reach a consensus as to how to fight the colonialists.[17]

The Arab state's impotence in confronting these three crises was reflected directly in the succession of cabinets or in the rapid rotation of cabinets among nearly the same people. This rotation occurred so quickly that the average term of a cabinet, during the first fifteen years of national rule in Egypt and Iraq, did not exceed one year. Although the cabinet did not enjoy the same authority in Syria as it did in Egypt and Iraq due to direct French rule, 52 percent of the cabinets between 1919 and 1959 were formed by the same eight people, who ruled on average for about twenty-four years.

As for national parliaments, their domination from their inception by an alliance of large landowners and powerful merchants jeopardized democratic elections. Following the Ottoman tradition, the elections of the 1920s and 1930s were not direct elections but occurred in stages. Overwhelmingly, victory was always for those nominated by the state, who were drawn from the landowning or merchant classes. From 1924 until the arrival of the military in 1958, large landowners, who were also at the time becoming a "feudalist" (*iqta°i*) class, dominated the Iraqi parliament. Independents occupied less than a tenth of the seats. Following World War II, the latifundist membership of the Iraqi parliament never fell below one third. As we shall see, this was a period of extensive crystallization of ideological differences and class antagonisms.

In Egypt one newspaper reported that in the parliament of 1950 (the last parliament prior to the coup of the Free Officers), 115 members of the 319 total were landowners whose property was no less than 100 faddans (a faddan is 4200.833 square meters). Forty-five members owned more than 500 faddans. Thus the situation in Egypt did not differ from that in Iraq. In fact, the proportion of large landowners in the Egyptian parliament exceeded the percentage in Iraqi parliaments, for twice during World War II landowners constituted more than half the membership. Even the leadership of the Wafd party saw an increase in the representation of large landowners from 15.7 percent to 39 percent in the span of a few years during the 1930s.[18]

Although due to direct French mandate the Syrian parliaments were only consultative assemblies, nevertheless, they do give us a good picture of the crystallization of social forces and the dominance of the latifundia and merchants over the political life of the country.[19] As a result, in Syria, Egypt, and Iraq, the "national" governments were satisfied or forced to be content with accomplishments that fell considerably short of the demands of 1920. Nonetheless, these achievements did not come without a bitter struggle. Iraq obtained its independence in 1932 under direct British guardianship and through the unfavorable Treaty of 1930. Egypt was granted only limited rights in the 1923 constitution and the Treaty of 1936 with Great Britain. Despite the many shortcomings of this treaty (especially since it constituted de facto recognition of the failure to obtain independence), it nevertheless allowed more freedom of movement than in the past. Syria was not able to obtain its independence until December 1939; prior to that time elected local assemblies were the only form of native Syrian political control allowed.

However, the period from the mid-1930s until the end of World War II can truly be considered the period of constellation (*tabalwur*) of the opposition to nationalist governments and the polarization of social forces. These forces would erupt into a political and social crisis paving the way for the momentous events of the early 1950s, which constituted a new turning point in contemporary Arab history.

The opposition in Egypt crystallized early, pitting the Wafd party (a majority party that became the representative of a vast coalition of national forces), on the one hand, against the king and the minority parties, on the other. In Syria the opposition centered in the national block and the ᶜAbd al-Rahman al-Shahabandar group, which were set against the mandate administration and its allies (the landowners and merchants drawn from the religious minorities and the compradors). In Iraq the emergence of the al-Ahali group and later the Popular Reform Organization served as a rallying point for opposition to the monarchy, the Sharifian officers, and merchants and "feudalists" represented in the parliamentary parties. Moreover, in this period regional leaderships and national independence movements also developed in Lebanon, Palestine, Bahrain, and Kuwait.

Several characteristics distinguish the opposition movements of this period (1935–1945) from preceding ones. First and foremost, they were directed at broad popular bases and supported by professional syndicates and labor unions, contrary to the earlier situation where opposition parties had worked within the parliamentary framework and with memberships that were confined to a number of influential actors and "chronic" ministers.

The second distinguishing characteristic is that the opposition movements had clear ideological and doctrinal affiliations. The earlier opposition groups were predominantly liberal reformists, with moderate nationalistic tendencies. During this period conservative religious parties, such as the Muslim Brotherhood, were formed as were chauvinist nationalist organizations such as Young Egypt (*misr al-fatat*) and the Syrian Nationalists (*hizb al-suri al-qawmi*). Also, leftist parties such as the communists and socialists became more visible. Furthermore, during the ferment of World War II, even the main opposition parties became divided internally according to ideological affiliations. For example, the Saᶜdiyun split from the Wafd in 1938. The Syrian National Bloc (*al-kutla*) splintered first into the People's party and then into the Baᶜth party in 1941. Ideological alternatives were brought to the fore when political parties were forced to face the "social question" (*al-mas'ala al-ijtimaᶜiya*) in constructing their platforms. However, it was only after World War II that these ideological alternatives became truly polarized.

The emerging role of minorities in political life is a third trait that distinguished these new movements. Religious and ethnic minorities made up a large part of the radical left opposition parties and also of the institutions of the state as patronage groups of the corporate system. Their presence paved the way for politicizing the issue of minorities, confessional affiliations, and their role in the nation-state.

A fourth distinguishing characteristic of the opposition movements was the beginning of the politicization of the army in favor of these movements, in order to disrupt the traditional balance of sociopolitical forces. As is well known, the military was already a political issue in the process of independence in Egypt, Syria, and Lebanon. One of the British conditions for Egyptian independence was the readiness of the Egyptian army and its ability to defend Egypt (from whom?). The Treaty of 1936, among others, was intended to correct this situation and to open the colleges and military academies for the first time to the local middle class. Sixteen years later graduates of these institutions were to take part in the coup of 1952.[20]

In Syria and Lebanon the question of the Special Forces (*troupes speciales*) was one of the issues that was not resolved until 1945. The French had already surrendered all governmental services and institutions to those countries in 1941 in preparation for the declaration of independence, except for the Special Forces over which they retained control. The public justification for retaining these troops was that they were comprised of religious and ethnic minorities (Kurds, Druze, Alawites, and Christians) and "were France's only remaining weapon to use as pressure for an agreement on its own terms, i.e. allowing France to continue its guardianship and dominance over the region." After independence in 1945 these troops became the nucleus of the modern Syrian and Lebanese armies.[21] Only four years later a group of officers seized power in Syria, virtually declaring a new era in our contemporary history.

The situation in Iraq was somewhat different. First, Iraq achieved its independence earlier than Egypt and Syria, and second, by

1921 the Iraqi army was already composed of members of the indigenous population. The military block in Iraq emerged as a political group during the early 1930s, and the entry of military
officers into politics culminated in the 1936 coup d'etat led by the
Kurdish officer Bakr Sidqi. The officers' intrusion into politics did
not end despite the failure of their coup one year later; rather their
involvement increased and became more organized. Four lieuten-
ant colonels, who were the leaders of the military block known as
the "golden square" (al-murabbaᶜ al-dhahabi), were behind at least
four changes in government: twice in 1938 and twice in 1940. They
also took direct part in the movement of Rashid ᶜAli al-Kaylani in
April 1941, which developed into a military-civil mutiny against
the British. However, the failure of the rebellion brought the return of the British occupation three months later and led to the
weakening of the Iraqi army. It was only after 1946 that the army
began to grow again. Contrary to what might be expected, this
growth was not as a consequence of the crisis in Palestine.[22]

During this period Palestine became one of the sources of popular turmoil. The failure of the revolt of 1936 to 1939 was, in effect,
a declaration of Arab impotence in resisting the British and the
Zionists and a foreshadowing of the loss of Palestine. In this
charged atmosphere, the issue of Arab unity was raised repeatedly in different forms: the Fertile Crescent (the Hashimi project
and al-Mufti al-Husayni project), Greater Syria (The National Syrian project), and the Arab Union (Prince ᶜAbdallah project).[23]
These calls for Arab unity played an important role in regional
political alliances and fueled much popular turmoil. In 1945 the
Arab League's charter was signed, effectively supplanting other
pan-Arabist projects. It was the product of a renewed regional alliance among Saudi Arabia, Syria (under the leadership of Shukri
al-Quwwatli), and Egypt (under the Wafd).[24] With the Arab
League project, the process of the "political Arabization of Egypt"
occurred. Several years later the 1948 war in Palestine firmly rooted
Egypt in the Arab world.

In the period immediately following World War II (1945–1956),
the social conflict in the Arab East became very deeply politicized
and radicalized. Before delineating the features of this process, the
political context in which it arose must be defined. First, the new

world order was characterized by the division of the world between the two superpowers and the consequent replacement of
British security concerns with American ones (Pax Americana).
Moreover, the division of the world between the superpowers in
the context of the Cold War furthered the ideological polarization
between the left and the right on a global level. The Baghdad
Pact of 1958, the internal situation in Syria between 1954 and 1958,
the Czechoslovak arms deals, the spread of the idea of "positive
neutrality," and the Suez war in 1956 are good examples of how
this process affected the Middle East.

A second issue was the relative improvement of the economic
situation in the region, especially in Syria and Iraq. In these two
countries improvement was partly due to the increase in agricultural production (in Iraq, this increase was augmented by income
generated by oil production). For Egypt, economic improvement
additionally can be attributed to the growth of the public sector
with the momentum of Bank Misr and its institutions in a manner
unequaled in other Arab countries. The growth of the industrial
sector occurred only because of the cooperation between Egyptian capital and "local" foreign capital, which is a phenomenon
that warrants further investigation.[25] The relative improvement in
this period of economic conditions led to a severe concentration
(*tarkiz*) of agricultural ownership in the countryside and to the
deepening of social class divisions in the cities. This eventually resulted in the social polarization between the ruling groups of large
landowners, merchants, and others who benefited from the state,
on the one hand, and the popular social forces, on the other.

The increase in structural mobility (*al-harak al-bina'i*)—that is,
social mobililty, as a result of the change in demand for labor due
to structural changes in society—is a third characteristic that defined the social context of the post–World War II era. The increase
in the average structural mobility is fundamentally related to, first,
the attempt to enhance the role of the public sector in the process
of development (i.e., the role of the centralized bureaucracy); and,
second, the abnormal expansion of the service sector. As a result,
there was a dramatic drop in the demand for traditional occupations and crafts and an increased demand for modern professions
that required a minimum of formal secular education. This led to

the spread of education, beginning in Egypt during the mid-1920s and then in Syria and Iraq after World War II. Consequently, the middle class, composed of civil servants (the effendis) and the self-employed (petty merchants and small landowners), absorbed socially both upwardly and downwardly mobile groups.

A fourth trait was the appearance on the political stage of the middle class. As mentioned earlier, the middle strata traditionally supported the major moderate opposition parties. However, at a time when the moderate parties ideologically and politically had clearly become impotent, the entrance into the political arena of intellectuals (*fi'a muthaqqafa*) belonging originally to the middle class led to the formation of parties whose radical (in some cases quasi-fascistic) ideologies were directed primarily at the middle strata. Among the new parties were the Muslim Brotherhood (1928), Misr al-Fatat (1932), the Syrian National party (1932), and the Ba'th party (1940). These parties propagated their ideologies through widespread distribution of political journalism (especially in Egypt and Syria), which contributed to the political mobilization of large sectors of the populace. The parties of the middle class and the left entered into a direct confrontation with the traditional parties in a vicious competition for power.

Therefore, one of the primary characteristics of the process of politicization and radicalization in the Arab East was the increasing polarization between the right and the left. The Cold War, American domination of the region, and the tendency of ruling groups to align with Western capitalist interests led to profound changes in the ideology and membership of the opposition parties just mentioned. The ruling groups now faced parties that enjoyed wide popular support, that presented alternatives to the "social question" (which by then had become the primary political issue), and that possessed effective ideological "weapons." The fact that these parties could also depend on the moral support of the Eastern European countries enhanced their appeal. Never before in modern history had the ruling groups in the Arab countries been more threatened. Thus, in an attempt to preserve the status quo, ruling groups found themselves pushed into a definitive and final alliance with imperialist forces (e.g., Nuri al-Sa'id, the minority parties after the Wafd left the cabinet on February 4, 1942, and the religious minorities of Syria and Lebanon after independence). They were also forced to escalate the use of violence and repression. In 1949, for example, three political leaders representing the political spectrum from the extreme right to the extreme left were either assassinated or executed. These leaders were Hasan al-Banna in Egypt, Antoine Saʿada in Lebanon, and Comrade Fahd (Yusif Salman Yusif) in Iraq.

The opposition met the violence of the ruling groups with counterviolence. Incidents of individual and group violence increased noticeably, making violence and terror prominent theoretical currents in middle-class parties and organizations and a primary element of their political practice. When the military seized power in the 1950s, violence would be institutionalized in the state in the form of military rule.

The ruling groups' alliance with Western capitalist interests, their general movement toward the political right, and the exchange of violence with the nationalist forces led to a rupture between the old ruling groups and the nationalist forces. After the humiliating defeat of the Arab armies in the 1948 Palestine war, and the incidents and popular turmoil that accompanied it, the lines of imminent confrontation became even more clearly drawn.

The political polarization between the ruling groups of the ancien régime and the opposition parties was the necessary extension of socioeconomic confrontation. Besides benefiting from the concentration of agricultural property and the social wealth mentioned earlier, the ruling groups used the state to increase their wealth at the expense of the poverty-stricken masses. For example, in Egypt during the early 1950s, 0.5 percent of the populace owned 34.2 percent of total agricultural land.[26] In Iraq, according to 1958 statistics, 3 percent of the population owned 66 percent of the agricultural land.[27] In Syria, according to Doreen Warriner, one family alone owned thirty-six villages in Dayr al-Zawr.[28]

As mentioned, the large landowners and merchants managed to control the legislative branch of the state, and their alliance with professional politicians (e.g., the Sharifian officers) gave them social and economic dominance. The "National" party (representing interests of the landowners and merchants of Damascus) and the "People's" party (which represented the same social classes in northern Syria, especially Aleppo) are two classic examples of how this class used the state to protect its property and increase its wealth. ʿAbd al-Muʿti adds that the large landowners in Egypt also dominated the most important ministries of the state between 1914 and 1952.[29] Hanna Batatu presents us with a telling example of the alliance between the concentration of wealth in Iraq and the use of the state to increase and maintain these private interests. He analyzed the class composition of the Constitutional Union, the administrative body of Nuri al-Saʿid's party, which dominated the political life of the country from 1946 (following the resumption of party activity) until the military seizure of power in 1958. The correlation between the concentration of ownership and party membership is clear.[30]

The Era of Military Dominance

The political polarization that dominated the Arab East after World War II did not lead to a preponderance of one element over another, as al-Ansari assumed. Rather, it led to a stalemate; the old ruling groups failed to weaken and destroy the opposition. Their failure to prevent the main radical currents from spreading among the masses (and this is the crux of the matter) was the result of many years of continuous politicization and radicalization. However, the ruling groups used all means available to weaken the opposition: Rightist parties were created that were provided with exceptional privileges; attempts were made to co-opt the nationalist elements and to create a rift among the main opposition parties; martial law was temporarily declared; and finally political oppression and physical violence occurred.

The major opposition parties (the Wafd in Egypt, the National and the People's parties in Syria, the Independence and the National Democratic parties in Iraq) failed to articulate a realistic platform that would strengthen their position. They also failed to develop and become sufficiently radical to absorb their militant members and new supporters who were highly politicized after years of popular turmoil and ideological propaganda. Luis ʿAwad expressed the general fear of the opposition parties that they could not contain the radical current when he said, "The only hope . . . for the Wafd was to develop itself into a socialist or a radical party, even with modest expectations (ʿala ʾaqal taqdir), the same way that the democratic parties in the West . . . developed from liberal to radical, and even moderate socialist."[31]

Although it has been over forty years since the beginning of the collapse of civilian governments in 1949, empirical research on the direct causes of this collapse is still lacking. However, it is clear that the task of controlling the radical current and solving the problem of sociopolitical polarization was falling on a "third actor." This "third actor" had no direct stakes in the economic and political process except its own institutional-professional interests, and therefore, it acted more decisively, more brutally, and more cohesively.

Only the military (al-ʿaskar) possessed these qualifications. Thus, in less than fifteen years after what is referred to as the year of the al-nakba (i.e., the "disaster"—the defeat of the Arabs in the 1948 Palestine war), more than two-thirds of the Arab countries fell under military or semimilitary rule: Syria in 1949 and again in 1961 after the end of the union with Egypt; Egypt in 1952; Iraq in 1958; Sudan in 1958; Yemen in 1962; Algeria in 1965 (with the military coup d'état against Ben Bella); and finally Libya in 1969. Thereafter, an increased number of coups d'état occurred in Arab states, totaling thirty-eight between 1960 and 1970. Of these attempts to seize power, twenty succeeded while the other eighteen failed.

Any attempt to explain this phenomenon in its regional or international context (i.e., as a link in the phenomena of militarism that swept the world after World War II under the auspices of American security) must consider the following questions:

• Prior to the military's seizure of power, in whose favor was the balance of power likely to tip: in favor of the "nationalist forces" (al-quwa al-wataniya) or the ruling rightist group?
• If the coups d'état had not occurred, what would have happened?

Would the nationalist forces have been able to seize power and establish democracy?

• Were these coups necessary or inevitable, to prevent the nationalist forces from obtaining control of the state? Were they necessary to save these countries from the calamity of civil war, economic disaster, or the dilemma of the development process?[32]

• Were the military juntas representative of class interests or factions within class groups to which they belonged, such as the "new middle class"? Or was the military working for the interests of some other class?

• Was the military conscious of its historic role and of its role in the struggle of the nationalist forces against the interests represented by the rightist ruling groups? Was the military conscious of its role in repealing the democratic and constitutional gains won by the general population?

• What is the relationship between military regimes and the industrialized capitalist countries? What is the role of military regimes in the international struggle and the phenomena of militarism? Were they the founders of states, or were they mere pawns in an international game?

A full consideration of these questions requires research beyond the scope of this study. Here we can only address the sociohistorical background of the military coup d'état and the regimes it produced applying the method suggested earlier. I will also attempt to clarify the general features of the status quo brought about by these coups d'état and their sources of legitimacy. Therefore, it is first necessary to situate the phenomenon of the military coup that occurred after World War II, or more precisely, after 1949, in an appropriate historical perspective.

Unfortunately it has become common among Western thinkers and analysts to assume that violence, and particularly military violence, is a "natural" or historically acceptable method for settling social and political conflicts in the Third World. In order to support this contention, Arab societies under Ottoman and Mamluk rule are often cited as concrete examples of an order in which the military is the real and effective social force in the larger political system. The question remains: Why was violence an inherent characteristic of this kind of regime? Western "experts" answer that these political regimes lacked the institutional mechanisms for the normal and peaceful transfer of power from one ruler to another, or one group to another. Therefore, the various actors in political conflicts in these societies continuously attempt to resolve the conflict in their favor through the use of violence, or any other available means (conspiracy, assassination, rebellion, invasion, and civil war). Thus the rise of the military to power via coups d'état is nothing unexpected or new in these societies. For the Western Orientalist "expert," the modern phenomenon of military takeovers in the 1940s and 1950s was nothing more than an unchanging "anthropological"-historical extension of a long-standing tradition.[33]

This explanation is in fact based on an ahistorical understanding of sociopolitical processes, and, to a great extent, neglects the structural discontinuities in the persistence (*istimrariya*) of civilizations. Indeed, political violence is a widespread phenomenon with social psychological and historical dimensions in all human societies, including the West.[34] However, there are qualitative differences between military violence during ancient times and the violence represented in the contemporary military coup d'état. First, changes have occurred in the nature of the state, especially in its functions. The task of suppression, and the administration of coercion, is a *function* of the ruling regime and is no longer a sufficient basis for legitimizing the ruling order.

Second, coercion and political violence have become more comprehensive, despotic, and arbitrary as well as more pernicious, given the dangers posed by modern weapons. In the past, if an act of violence had a specific political goal, in most cases it usually ended with the achievement of that goal. Today violence does not necessarily end with the attainment of a specific goal. In some cases it becomes an end in itself.

Third, if armed political violence in previous eras aimed at imposing a certain regime, in the age of contemporary imperialism it aims at total, covert enslavement (*isti'bad*) of the economy, politics, and culture to the states of the imperialist centers. This process of enslavement does not require the direct use of armed violence. Conversely, it cannot be fought by armed violence alone.

Finally, the increase in military coups in the Arab East coincided with the decline of colonialism (i.e., following World War II). As mentioned, this was a period of transition for the Arab countries from Ottoman and British hegemony to a new era of American domination of the Middle East. It should be abundantly clear that armed violence in the current era of Pax Americana is no longer a choice to be made by the Arab or other Third World peoples. Rather, it has been imposed upon them as their fate. This is the "puppet theater" whose strings are controlled by the imperialist centers. The cycle is vicious: Armed violence brings the military to power, which leads to the expansion of the military apparatus, which in turn drains the money needed for development. Having come to power through violence, the military is forced to employ violence to stay in power.[35]

Military coups contributed to, if not indirectly caused, the establishment of armed violence as a norm in Arab societies. Major armed conflicts that occurred in Arab countries between 1945 and 1957 could be divided into three categories: (1) those with a foreign element, usually directed against the industrialized capitalist countries, (2) regional conflicts among the Arab countries, and (3) internal armed conflicts or civil wars.

The thirty conflicts that occurred between 1945 and 1957, constitute an average of one conflict per year. It is important to note that after 1961, armed conflicts, which until then had been directed primarily against the advanced industrialized countries (type 1 conflicts), suddenly became conflicts among the Arab states and their own populations (types 2 and 3). Also note that military regimes were able to stabilize their rule around 1961. It is no secret that most civil wars during this period were financed or supported by foreign sources intent on preoccupying the Arabs and exhausting their resources. The Arab wars against Israel were no exception. Indeed, this was their basic raison d'être.

Another temporal factor helps explain the timing of the first coups. Dankwart A. Rustow claims that "There is a remarkable parallel in the timing of the initial military coups in Iraq, Syria and Egypt. Iraq was released from mandate status in 1932; in 1936, Major General Bakr Sidqi performed his military coup. In Syria, the French withdrew in mid-1945; in 1949, there were three suc-

cessive military coups under Colonels Za⁼im, Hinnawi and Shishakli. In 1947, the British discontinued their wartime occupation of
Egypt proper, concentrating their remaining troops in the Canal
Zone . . . in 1952, the Free Officers (*al-dubbat al-ahrar*) seized
power under General Najib and Colonel Nasir."[36] Four or five
years separated the end of colonial rule and the military's seizure
of power. It is difficult to determine if there were any underlying
trends or movements behind this sequence of events; nonetheless,
it is a very interesting phenomenon.

The declared objective of most of the "military elections"
(*al-intikhabat al-⁼askariya*) was the achievement of "security and
stability." Such slogans recurred in most of the initial declarations
that immediately followed the seizure of power by military regimes. They intended to establish a new status quo whose legitimacy was, in the first instance, derived from naked force, armed
violence, and organized terror. We can clearly see that ideological
loyalties did not play a significant role in the initial coups that followed World War II. They did, however, play an important role
at a later stage.

The military used its calls for security and stability not only to
justify its rule, but also to destroy constitutional and democratic
institutions in Arab countries. The military did not come to power
with the popular support of the opposition—neither the underground nor the public (except in the case of the 1958 Iraqi revolution where it had coordinated efforts with the National Front
parties). However, it is also true that these military coups were
met with a widespread collective sigh of relief since the populace
at large hoped that the prevailing cycle of polarization and stagnation would cease. It was also hoped that violence would be cur-
tailed through increased security and that the cycle of chronic
cabinet shuffles would end, leading to greater stability. Once that
had been accomplished, the situation would normalize and the
military would return to its barracks with thanks for having
achieved what the country badly needed. These popular expectations were to prove all too naive.

According to the military's rationale, the problem was not in the
ruling group's falsification of popular demands for democratic

freedoms (e.g., freedom of opinion, expression, elections, and majority rule) and constitutional guarantees (e.g., specifying rights
and duties, separation of powers, and equality under the law).
Rather the military saw the problem as existing in these demands
themselves. The connection made between instability and violence,
on the one hand, and democracy and constitutionalism, on the
other, invented the myth that "partyism" (*al-hizbiya*) and democracy were the source of all evils. This myth, propagated by the
state-controlled media, prevailed through two generations that
became politically conscious during the 1950s and 1960s.[37] It is
strange, and rather sad, that a substantial number of thinkers and
intellectuals continue to believe in, refine, and embellish this myth.
It is said, for instance, that democratic freedoms are contrary to
Islam, or that capitalism represents a corrupt order that is inap-
propriate for Arab societies. As for the apologists of military rule,
they argue that for democracy to be acceptable, it has to be
"social," "popular," and "centralized" to safeguard it from personalities guided by selfish interests and from the "ignorance of
the people."

During the late 1950s and early 1960s, when the military began
to lay new foundations for socioeconomic and political reorgani-
zation, it gradually became clear to the general public that the
military regime was not a temporary phenomenon. The military
was planning to retain control of the state and needed new sources
of legitimacy to remain in power beyond sheer force and armed
violence.

Military apologists justified the lack of civilian rule either by the
military's "extraordinary concern" in the "higher interests" of the
nation and its lack of faith in traditional nationalist politicians, who
were the "heirs of partyism" and "the allies of the colonialists," or
the "exceptionally critical" stage through which the Arab nation
was passing and the internal "conspiracy" and the external threat
to which it was exposed. It is clear that the military needed an
immediate and formidable accomplishment to enhance its continued political legitimacy.

Independence (in the case of Egypt between 1952 and 1954 and
in Iraq, 1958), and the preservation of independence via the Arab

Union (in the case of Syria, 1958), provided a powerful momentum for the military and gave it a cardinal source of legitimacy. The military was able to achieve what had eluded civilian governments throughout thirty years of continuous struggle, turmoil, and popular support. Given this context, accomplishing independence was enough to make national heroes of the military overnight.

With the period of colonial retreat having already begun, and as the superpowers had divided the world among themselves, political independence was a relatively attainable goal. In the aftermath of World War II, there were no "colonized and dependent" countries in the British or French colonialist sense of the word; rather, there were "dependent nation-states" in accordance with the American conception. To appreciate the difference between the two concepts, it is not enough simply to recognize the difference between colonialism and imperialism (as they are two interconnected and consecutive stages). Instead we have to understand the qualitative differences between British and French imperialism, on the one hand, and American imperialism (which is based on the hegemony of monopoly capital), on the other.[38] Indeed, American imperialism has, since the end of World War I, used the issue of political independence for colonized countries (the principles of President Woodrow Wilson) as a means to supplant British hegemony.[39]

Did the military realize, or anticipate, this situation before the civilian politicians and the intellectuals? Did it understand that political independence was not going to be at the expense of American security, but part of its plans and goals? Whatever the answers to these question might be, a crucial point remains: The Egyptian Free Officers achieved in four years (1952–1956) what the Wafd party, with its broad popular support, had been unable to achieve in over thirty years—the evacuation of foreign troops and independence. As for Iraq in 1958, the abrogation of the Baghdad Pact and the evacuation of the British bases was resolved almost in a "friendly" manner. In Syria, the first coup d'état occurred in 1949–1950, after the gaining of independence. Clearly it was an attempt to stop the widespread process of radicalization, politicization, and the movement toward the left. Several years later the

goals became clearer, drawing the "lines of confrontation." As Patrick Seale states, "the Syrian elections of September 1954, held
seven months after Shishakli's downfall, drew up the internal bat-
tle order for the next four years."[40] When the process of radicalization and the movement toward the left reached its peak, the
officers of the Syrian army surrendered to Nasir in January 1958,
begging "Do with us as you wish but save us from the politicians
and ourselves." As a result of the new relations with Egypt, the
Syrian officers returned from Cairo as national heroes, having
achieved the goal of Arab unity that eluded two earlier generations of nationalists. Thus, for the Arabs, 1958 ended with the military appearing as national heroes—those who brought about the
evacuation of foreign troops, achieved independence, and took
the first step toward Arab unity, "from the Atlantic Ocean to the
Arab Gulf."

The military continued to search for an organizational framework (*sigha*) that could substitute for the banned political parties.
This would allow it to rule without having to resort to brute force
and armed violence except as a last resort. This period of experimentation lasted from 1952 until 1961 in Egypt, from 1950 to 1954
in Syria, and from 1958 to 1965 in Iraq. It included many stages
and various temporary alliances. In Egypt this entailed cooperation with the Muslim Brotherhood and the formation of the Liberation Rally (*hay'at al-tahrir*), the National Union (*al-ittihad
al-qawmi*), and the Arab Socialist Union (*al-ittihad al-ishtirakiya
al-ʿarabi*). In Iraq and Syria the assumption of military rule coincided with the explosive split in the Arab left, between the new
radical nationalists (*al-qawmiyun al-ʿaqaʾidiyun*), and the communists in 1959. In later years this split would play an important role
in the destruction of the radical leftist current in Arab politics.[41]

For the military, the most ideal arrangement was an alliance
with the radical nationalists and the apolitical technocrats, thereby
producing a new ruling group. However, there were qualitative
differences between the Egyptian formula and the Syrian-Iraqi
formula. The Egyptian formula failed miserably when applied to
Syria during the short-lived United Arab Republic (1958–1961).[42]
In this model, the military was predominantly aligned with the
technocrats, while in the Syrian and Iraqi cases, the military aligned

itself primarily with the radical nationalists. In the latter model, the centrists' conception of the vanguard party (*al-hizb al-qa'id*) materialized after 1963. This was a conciliatory, authoritarian formula that Tariq ᶜAziz, Iraq's foreign minister, explains succinctly: "The party by itself is still incapable of bringing about social change; therefore, it is necessary that the army is infiltrated and transformed from an agent of coups to that of revolution, and from preoccupation with politics to concern with ideology (ᶜ*aqida*). The army should not be left to its purely military functions."[43]

The alliances among these three groups—the military, the radical nationalists, and the technocrats—were not difficult ones; rather they were formed quite naturally and logically (so long as the distribution of authority was acceptable to all). The three groups were all drawn from a common class background, namely, the two divisions of the middle class: white-collar workers, such as clerks and employees, and the self-employed. According to the works of Hanna Batatu and Shahrough Akhavi, six out of the twenty Free Officers in Egypt, and twenty out of the twenty-four Free Officers in Iraq were members of the middle class. In Syria three of the eight leaders were drawn from the middle class and another three were from the lower class.

It is clear from available evidence that most of the Free Officers, the political leadership, and the radical nationalists who came to power belonged to the middle class and, particularly, the two groups of minor employees (bureaucrats) and small landowners (*sighar al-mullak*). In terms of the geographic and ethnic distribution of these class affiliations, most Free Officers in Egypt, Syria, and Iraq came from small cities and rural areas, not from urban centers like Cairo, Alexandria, Damascus, Aleppo, Baghdad, or Basra. In Egypt, most of the Free Officers came from poor marginal sectors of the urban and rural middle classes. In Syria many military officers after 1965 were ethnic minorities (the Kurds) and then religious minorities: first the Druze and then the ᶜAlawites. Years of army purges resulting from a succession of coups led to a decrease in Sunni representation within the officer corps.

In this chapter, I have avoided using terms such as "the bourgeoisie," "the proletariat," and similar jargon, as each has a historical specificity associated with the development of European capitalism that lacks an equivalence in the Arab world. How then can we describe the alliance among the military, the radical nationalists, and the technocrats? These ruling alliances that came to power via military coups do not, by virtue of imitating the life-styles and consumerist habits of the European bourgeoisie, qualify themselves for the historical role of a ruling bourgeois class as in Europe. Furthermore, as Akhavi states with regard to Egypt, "Corporate class interests are missing; and not only this, but the essential ingredients of class: industry, commerce, the use of money, credit, markets—these have not proliferated in a manner that would be required for the capitalist mode of production and a full-fledged bourgeois class. Thus, unless we change our definitions, would it not be more appropriate to talk of the neo-patrimonial, rather than the bourgeois elite of Egypt?"[44]

Some writers would state that this class is a bourgeoisie of a new kind, a salaried bureaucratic bourgeoisie that has assumed the functions of the European bourgeoisie or something similar to it. Others claim that this class is the "new middle class" led by the military (as those engaged in state formation), new in its constitution because it is comprised of technocrats, scientists, managers, and entrepreneurs who are not found in traditional Arab societies. Still others claim that this alliance does not represent a social class at all but merely constitutes the elite fractions of classes, the ruling elite (the military), and the "strategic" elite (the technocrats) whose immediate interests have brought them together. In any event, I do not intend to take sides in the chronic arguments that have been voiced repeatedly in sociology (and among Middle East specialists) about the legitimacy of employing the concept of social class in Third World societies. However, I do want, in principle, to settle a matter in order to understand the relation of the phenomena to the sequence of events that I have been describing.

Without a doubt, the military-radical nationalist-technocrat alliance springs from the core of the consuming classes that occupy the middle range of the Arab social stratification system. Although these class groups are not united ideologically or politically, they are aware of their social positions and of their material and politi-

cal interests and are united in their antagonism toward the old ruling groups composed of the large landowners and large merchant
classes. This hostility greatly assisted the military in breaking up
the old ruling classes and in limiting their threat to its rule. Therefore, when I state that the military-radical nationalist-technocrat
alliance represents the middle class, I am not claiming that it seized
power in the name of the middle class or that it is working in the
interests of the middle class (which is socially diverse, geograph-
ically dispersed, and lacking in class consciousness). Rather, what
I mean is that the alliance represents the middle class because it is
derived from it. The new leaders emerged from its ranks to
monopolize authority and power in society, excluding the repre-
sentatives of other classes. Nevertheless, how was an alliance of
middle-class factions transformed from groups that seized political power by force into an authoritarian, socioeconomically and
culturally hegemonic "class"?

One of the most important characteristics of ruling regimes
under the dominance of the military is what can be referred to as
"the effective monopoly of power" in society. What I mean by this
is the monopoly of the sources of authority and social power, not
just key positions within the state. The seizure of the state by brute
force and armed violence by groups that have no role in the process of production or in the political process cannot lead to endur-
ing dominance and hegemony. As already indicated, the ruling
alliance found its source of legitimacy in achieving independence
and in the adoption of a nationalist ideology. The next goal was to
realize the effective monopoly of power.

There are usually three sources of power in society: quantitative
superiority (numerical power), qualitatively superior social organization (organized power), and power derived from the ownership of social resources (property, wealth). The state, for example,
represents what I mean by organized power: a network composed
of social institutions such as the government, the parliament, and
the instruments of coercion.[45] Unions and syndicates derive their
power from their numerical strength. As for the old ruling groups,
which were alliances between large landowners and large merchants,

they derived their power from their disproportionate ownership of social resources (agricultural land, real estate, and various
forms of capital). When the military came to power with their
middle-class allies, they possessed only the organizational source
of power—those assets derived from their professional role of
monopolizing the instruments of repression and violence.

The military sought to seize control of the entire state immediately after it overthrew Arab governments. It proceeded to dis-
solve the parliament and elected councils, appointing officers to all
levels of government from the cabinet to local government. The
realization of this step required that the military seize the state,
not as an organization of the Free Officers, but rather as a corporate apparatus in which the Free Officers (later, the Revolution
Command Council [*majlis qiyadat al-thawra*]) was to be the center of gravity.

The second step was the destruction of all other forms of organized power, such as parties and political organizations, in order
that the military could control the entire political system. The implementation of this goal required the suspension of constitutions
and the abrogation of constitutional guarantees. It also necessitated
the reordering of the legal system with the continued use of emergency laws and martial decrees. In this manner, the military in
Egypt, for example, gave the Revolution Command Council legislative and executive functions as well as supervision over the judiciary. In short, the military assumed unlimited political and social
authority. Moreover, once the political arena was devoid of organized social forces, some in the military attempted to develop organizations of their own, such as the *hizb al-qa'id* (vanguard party),
which included the Arab Socialist Union in Egypt and, later, the
National Front in Syria and Iraq.

The third step sought to extend the military's power among the
masses—that is, control over labor and other professional organizations—in order to contain their potential "disruptiveness." The
importance of these unions and organizations as instruments of
control and manipulation should not be underestimated. The control the military exercised over the entire media network and a
substantial portion of the intelligentsia gave it tremendous power

and almost unlimited authority.[46] Furthermore, there was a significant expansion of the intelligence apparatus and the use of "national security" as a pretext for instituting armed violence, organized terror, and maintaining a monopoly over the state. Consequently, the military attempted to co-opt the process of politicization and radicalization in ways that served its own interests. In this manner, it becomes clear how the military was able to exclude from political participation the general populace, its forces and organizations, and to limit its role to support, especially hoopla in the form of pro-government demonstrations.

The fourth, and final, step in the realization of the effective monopolization of power was directed at the only domain outside the military's immediate control—namely, the social power derived from the ownership of land, capital, and wealth in general (in short, material power). The laws of land reform represented only a precursor of the military's extension of control over the entire economic system. This control was completed with the "socialist" measures (in 1961 in Egypt, and after 1965 in Syria and Iraq) that the military employed to nationalize banks, industrial companies, commercial establishments, and the main service enterprises through decrees of confiscation and sequestration. Some of these measures were serious reforms that led to changes in the distribution of material wealth and the realization of some social justice. However, these procedures shattered the illusion of a transitional military government; through them the military effectively monopolized power. More important, these procedures led to the total destruction of the old proprietary class by depriving it of its traditional sources of power. Remnants of this class tried to adapt to the marginal mobility that it retained under the maximum agricultural property allowed and through loopholes in existing laws. The military presented many (sometimes reasonable) justifications for its confiscations. Nevertheless, these justifications do not challenge the validity of my conclusions regarding its effective monopolization of political power.

In this manner, the military was able to achieve the effective monopolization of the sources of power and authority in Arab society that ultimately led to the emergence of a new proprietary class, a class that owned the state. By June of 1967, most of the countries of the Arab East would be, in one form or another, under the control of these contemporary authoritarian states.

NOTES

1. I would like to thank Charles Moscows, Fu'ad Zakariya, Shakir Mustafa, Mutaᶜ Safadi, ᶜAbd al-Rahman Husayn, and particularly Dr. George Tuᶜma for reading and commenting on parts of this manuscript in its draft form. However, I alone take responsibility for any shortcomings of the final product.

2. In Arab political literature, no one seems to have analyzed the development of these terms in their historical context. However, in his latest book al-Jabiri analyzes their meanings from a *maᶜrifiya* (epistemological) standpoint. Muhammed ᶜAbid al-Jabiri, *al-kitab al-ᶜarabi al-muᶜasir; dirasa naqdiya tahliliya* [*Contemporary Arabic Writing; An Analytical and Critical Study*] (Beirut: Dar al-Taliᶜa, 1982).

3. See Amir Shakib Arslan, *limadha taᶜakhar al-muslimun wa limadha taqadama ghayruhum* [*Why Are the Muslims Underdeveloped While Others Have Progressed?*], 3d ed. (Cairo: ᶜIsa al-Babi al-Halabi, 1939). In 1859, Butrus al-Bustani had already anticipated Arslan's question. Although representing a different intellectual current, al-Afghani raised the same question at about the same time. Quoted in al-Jabiri, *Contemporary Arabic Writing*, 23.

4. Regarding the contradictions in modern Arab thought, see al-Jabiri, *Contemporary Arabic Writing*, 133.

5. Muhammad Jabir al-Ansari, *tahawwulat al-fikr wa-l-siyasa fi-l-mashriq al-ᶜarabi, 1930–1970* [*Intellectual and Political Transformations in the Arab East, 1930–1970*] (Kuwait: ᶜAlam al-Maᶜrifa, 1980), 91.

6. For clarification of the meaning of the tendency for *al-talfiqiya* (reconciliation-hypocrisy), see Tayib al-Tayzini's *min al-turath ila al-thawra* [*From Heritage to Revolution*], vol. 1 (Beirut: Dar Ibn Khaldun, 1976), 136–39. However, the two best studies of the epistemology (*al-nahiya al-maᶜrifiya*) and ideology of *al-talfiqiya* in modern Arabic thought are those of al-Jabiri, *Contemporary Arabic Writing*, and al-Ansari, *Intellectual and Political Transformations*.

7. ᶜAbd al-Karim Rafiq, *al-ᶜarab wa-l-ᶜuthmaniyun, 1516–1916* [*The Arabs and the Ottomans, 1516–1916*] (Damascus: Maktabat al-Atlas, 1974), 330, 384.

8. It is possible to consider the legislation of 1865 (especially the law of *Tabu*), the ᶜUrabi movement of 1882, and the first Arab Conference in 1913 as major turning points.

9. For an eyewitness account by a contemporary of that period, see Salama Musa, *tarbiyat salama musa* [*The Education of Salama Musa*] (Cairo: Dar al-Kitab al-Misri, 1948), esp. 142–44 and 155–57. See also George Antonius,

al-yaqdha al-ʿarabiya [The Arab Awakening], 6th ed. (Beirut: Dar al-ʿIlm li-l-Malayin, 1980), esp. chap. 9, "Great Britain's Pledge: 1915."

10. Amin Saʿid, al-thawra al-ʿarabiya al-kubra [The Great Arab Revolt], vol. 2, chap. 7 (Cairo: al-Salafiya Press, 1935), 50–51.

11. ʿAbd al-Razzaq al-Hasani, al-thawra al-ʿiraqiya al-kubra [The Great Iraqi Revolution], 4th ed. (Beirut: Dar al-Kutub, 1978), esp. 110–11. See also Amin al-Rihani, muluk al-ʿarab [The Arab Kings], 2 vols., 4th ed. (1924; Beirut: Dar al-Rihani, 1960).

12. See Luis ʿAwad, tarikh al-fikr al-misri al-hadith: min ʿasr ismaʿil ila thawrat 1919 [History of Modern Egyptian Thought: From the Age of Ismaʿil to the 1919 Revolution] (Cairo: al-Hayʾa al-Misriya al-ʿAma li-l-Kitab, 1980); Rifʿat al-Saʿid, al-asas al-ijtimaʿi li-thawrat ʿurabi [The Social Basis of the ʿUrabi Revolution] (Cairo: Maktabat al-Madbuli, 1966); and ʿAbd al-ʿAziz Nawwar, tarikh al-ʿarab al-muʿasir: misr wa-l-ʿiraq [Contemporary Arab History: Egypt and Iraq] (Beirut: Dar al-Nahda al-ʿArabiya, 1973), esp. 189–212.

13. On Iraq, see Hanna Batatu, The Old Social Classes and the Revolutionary Movements of Iraq, bk. 1, pt. 2 (Princeton, NJ: Princeton University Press, 1978); David Pool, "From Elite to Class: The Transformation of Iraqi Political Leadership," in Abbas Kelidar, ed., The Integration of Modern Iraq (New York: St. Martin's Press, 1979), 63–87; and al-Hasani, The Great Iraqi Revolution, chap. 10. On Syria, see C.E. Dawn, "The Rise of Arabism in Syria," The Middle East Journal 16 (Autumn 1962): 145–68, and Saʿid, The Great Arab Revolt, pt. 1, 35–46. See also al-Hasani, The Great Iraqi Revolution, 65–83, and tarikh al-wizarat al-ʿiraqiya [The History of Iraqi Cabinets], 10 vols., 6th ed., pt. 1 (Beirut: Maktabat al-Yaqdha al-ʿArabiya, 1982), 115–25.

14. Concerning the development of the notables and the ʿulama, see Ira M. Lapidus, ed., Middle Eastern Cities: A Symposium on Ancient, Islamic and Contemporary Middle Eastern Urbanism (Berkeley: University of California Press, 1966), and William Polk and Richard Chambers, eds., Beginnings of Modernization in the Middle East: The Nineteenth Century (Chicago: University of Chicago Press, 1968). On the compradors, see Khaldoun al-Naqeeb, Preliminary Studies In Social Stratification in Arab Countries, vol. 1, monograph 5, (Kuwait: Annals of the College of Arts, Kuwait University, 1980), 47–49.

15. Concerning Muhammad ʿAbduh, see al-Ansari, Intellectual and Political Transformations, 55–78, 161–68.

16. J.C.B. Richmond, Egypt, 1798–1952: Her Advance Towards A Modern Identity (London: Methuen, 1977), 192.

17. For more details on this subject, see al-Hasani, The Great Iraqi Revolution, and Yunan Labib Rizq, al-ahzab al-misriya qabla thawrat 1952 [Egyptian Political Parties before the 1952 Revolution] (Cairo: Center for Political and Strategic Studies, al-Ahram, 1977). See also Muhammad A. Tarbush, The Role of the Military in Politics (London: Kegan Paul International, 1982), 44–54, and Batatu, Old Social Classes and Revolutionary Movements, bk. 1, chap. 10.

18. See Marius Deeb, *Party Politics in Egypt: The Wafd and Its Rivals, 1919–1939* (London: Ithaca Press, 1979), 349. See also Gabriel Baer, *Population and Society in the Arab East* (New York: Praeger, 1966), 208 and passim.

ʿAsim al-Disuqi provides us with estimates of the holdings of large landowners in the Egyptian parliament for the period between 1936 and 1952. See his *kibar mullak al-aradi al-ziraʿiya wa dawruhum fi-l-mujtamaʿ al-misri, 1914–1952 [Large Landowners and Their Role in Egyptian Society, 1914–1952]* (Cairo: Dar al-Thaqafa al-Jadida, 1975), 212.

19. See R. B. Winder, "Syrian Deputies and Cabinet Ministers, 1919–1959," pt. 1, *Middle East Journal* 16, no. 4 (1962): 409–19.

20. ʿAbd al-ʿAzim Ramadan, *al-jaysh al-misri fi-l-siyasa, 1882–1936 [The Egyptian Army in Politics, 1882–1936]* (Cairo: al-Hayʾa al-Misriya al-ʿAmma li-l-Kittab, 1977), chap. 7, 276. See also P. J. Vatikiotis, *The Egyptian Army in Politics* (Bloomington: Indiana University Press, 1961), 48.

21. S. H. Longrigg, *Syria and Lebanon under the Mandate* (Beirut: Librarie du Liban, 1968), 341.

22. See ʿAbd al-Ghani al-Mallah, *tarikh al-haraka al-dimuqratiya fi misr [The History of the Democratic Movement in Egypt]* (Beirut: al-Muʾassasa al-ʿArabiya li-l-Dirasat wa-l-Nashr, 1980), 109–60; ʿAbd al-Razzaq al-Hasani, *al-asrar al-khafiya fi harakat sanat 1940 [The Hidden Secrets of the 1940 Movement]*, 3d ed. (Sidon: al-ʿIrfan Press, 1971); and Tarbush, *Role of the Military*, chap. 7.

23. Patrick Seale, *The Struggle for Syria* (Arabic trans., Beirut: Dar al-Kalima, 1980), 19–32. Also, Rashid al-Badawi, *mashruʿ suriya al-kubra: ʿard, wa tahlil wa naqd [The Greater Syria Project: Exposition, Analysis and Criticism]* (Cairo: Maktabat al-Nahda al-Misriya, 1947).

24. Seale, 341.

25. For a preliminary evaluation of the role of Bank Misr and its companies, see Mahmud Mitwalli, *al-usul al-tarikhiya li-l-raʾsmaliya al-misriya wa tatawwur-uha [The Historical Roots and Development of Capitalism in Egypt]* (Cairo: al-Hayʾa al-Misriya li-l-Kittab, 1974). See also P. J. Vatikiotis, *The History of Egypt from Muhammad Ali to Sadat*, 2d ed., chap. 15 (London: Weidenfeld and Nicolson, 1980); and Patrick Clawson, "The Development of Capitalism in Egypt," *Khamsin* 9 (1981): 116.

26. Anwar ʿAbd al-Malik, *Egypt: Military Society* (Arabic trans., Beirut: Dar al-Taliʿa, 1974), 84. For a general discussion of this subject, see Ibrahim ʿAmir, *al-ard wa-l-fallah [The Land and the Peasant]* (Cairo: al-Dar al-Misriya li-l-Tibaʿa wa-l-Nashr, 1958); and Mahmud Husayn, *Class Struggle in Egypt, 1945–1970* (Arabic trans., Beirut: Dar al-Taliʿa, 1971), 32–78.

27. See M. S. Hasan, "The Economic Development of Iraq, 1864–1964: A Study in the Growth of a Dependent Economy," in M. A. Cook, ed., *Studies in the Economic History of the Middle East* (London: Oxford University Press, 1970), 363, and Batatu, *Old Social Classes and Revolutionary Movements*, 129–32.

28. Doreen Warriner, "Land Tenure in the Fertile Crescent," in Charles Issawi,

ed., *The Economic History of the Middle East* (Chicago: Chicago University Press, 1966), 77.

29. See ʿAbd al-Basit ʿAbd al-Muʿti, *"al-tharwa wa-l-sulta fi misr"* ["Wealth and Authority in Egypt"], *Majallat al-ʿUlum al-Ijtimaʿiya* [*Journal of the Social Sciences*] 10 (3 September 1982): 1975.

30. Batatu, *Old Social Classes and Revolutionary Movements*, 357.

31. ʿAwad, quoted in al-Ansari, *Intellectual and Political Transformations*, 209.

32. al-Ansari, *Intellectual and Political Transformations*, 218, n. 39, alludes to the debate in Arab political thought that military coups d'état were aimed at aborting popular revolutions rather than expressing the popular will following the failure of traditional parties as the military claimed. See also Husayn, *Class Struggle in Egypt*, 104; and Muhsin Husayn al-Habib, *haqaʾiq ʿan thawrat 14 tammuz fi-l-ʿiraq* [*The Facts of the July 14 Iraqi Revolution*] (Beirut: Dar al-Andalus, 1981), 27–48.

33. This assertion was made by John C. Campbell, a high-ranking expert in the Department of State, in "The Role of the Military in the Middle East," in S. N. Fisher, ed., *The Military in the Middle East: Problems in Society and Government* (Columbus: Ohio State University Press, 1963), 105.

34. The current stable cultural and political life of Western Europe belies the role of violence in its political development. To stress that political violence is a peculiar characteristic of the Third World amounts to a form of racism. For more on this point, see the studies in Wolfgang J. Mommsen and Gerhard Hirschfeld, eds., *Social Protest: Violence and Terror in Nineteenth and Twentieth Century Europe* (London: Macmillan, 1982).

35. Paul A. Baran, *The Political Economy of Growth* (New York: Monthly Review Press, 1968), 256–61.

36. Dankwart A. Rustow, "The Military in Middle East Politics," in Fisher, *Military in the Middle East*, 10.

37. I am indebted to Dr. Fuʾad Zakaria for clarifying this point.

38. A popular study in explaining the differences between European and American imperialism is Harry Magdoff's *The Age of Imperialism: The Economics of U.S. Foreign Policy* (New York: Monthly Review Press, 1969), esp. 27–66. I am also indebted to Michel Aglieta's study, "World Capitalism in the Eighties," *New Left Review* 136 (1982): 5–41, and his *Theory of Capitalist Regulation* (London: New Left Books, 1979).

39. See David Thomson, *Europe since Napoleon*, 2d ed. (London: Longman, 1983), 804–27.

40. Seale, 218–19.

41. See the following books "of the hour": Clovis Maksoud, *azmat al-yasar al-ʿarabi* [*The Crisis of the Arab Left*] (Beirut: n.p., 1960); and al-Hakam Darwazih, *al-shuyuʿiya al-mahalliya fi maʿrakat al-ʿarab al-qawmiya* [*Regional Communism in the Nationalist Arab Struggle*] (Beirut: n.p., 1961).

42. The Egyptian formula also failed miserably when al-ʿArif (1963–68) tried

to implement it in Iraq. See Batatu, *Old Social Classes and Revolutionary Movements*, 1027–72.

43. Tariq Aziz, "*al-jaysh wa makanuhu fi-l-thawra al-ᶜarabiya*" ["The Army and Its Role in the Arab Revolution"], *al-Maᶜrifa* 101 (July 1970), quoted in al-Ansari, *Intellectual and Political Transformations*, 219.

44. Sharough Akhavi, "Egypt: Neo-Patrimonial Elite," in *Political Elites and Political Development in the Middle East*, ed. S. Akhavi (New York: John Wiley, 1975), 78.

45. It is crucial to remember that the state is not restricted to the institutions of government. See Ralph Miliband, *The State in Capitalist Society* (New York: Basic Books, 1969), 49–55.

46. See Nazih Nasif al-Ayubi, "The Development of the Political and Administrative Organizations in Egypt, 1952–77," in Saᶜd al-Din Ibrahim, ed., *misr fi rubᶜ qarn, 1952–77* [*Egypt during a Quarter of a Century*] (Beirut: Maᶜhad al-Inma' al-ᶜArabi, 1981), 106–19.

3. Legitimacy, Identity, and the Writing of History in Libya

Lisa Anderson

All governments use historical symbols and historical writing to inspire loyalty and to convey an official interpretation of the meaning and purpose of political life. The relationship between historical studies and civics training or between scholarship and ideology is therefore inevitably complex. Official symbols—holidays, monuments, the illustrations in primary school textbooks—certainly describe and commemorate genuine historical incidents. These incidents are not selected at random from the great variety of events and personalities in history, however, but so as to establish and reiterate the official view of the political system and society. Patterns of official permission, encouragement, and support for historical research thus reveal much about the contours and contradictions in the self-image of the regime and populace.

For countries newly independent or recently "reborn" in national or social revolutions, such as Libya, reinterpretation of the historical record provides one of the most powerfully resonant vehicles by which to convey new images of society and to discard old or unpalatable ones. Indeed, as David C. Gordon has observed, in the Third World, the "concern, if not obsession, with the past of one's own people takes many shapes, sometimes contradictory, usually passionate: it ranges from the feeling that history is a nightmare from which one must awake, a history that must be exorcised, to the feeling that an illustrious past that the colonist has disparaged must be resurrected."[1] In some cases, including that of Libya, this very disparagement—the Italian imperialists' denial of a Libyan identity and history—is among the most nightmarish qualities of the past. Thus, as we shall see, among the purposes of the writing of history in Libya is the simple demonstration of its existence.

As important, however, is the way history is used to convey a definition of the "Libyan," or to use the phrase more commonly employed in Libyan writing during the Qadhdhafi era, the "Libyan Arab" national identity, while simultaneously strengthening the regime's claims to loyalty. These two purposes are not necessarily consistent, in part because, as in much of the Middle East, the state bears an ambiguous—not to say contradictory—relationship to the nation. The individual states of the Arab world are not congruent with, and cannot wholly appropriate, the powerful nationalism of Arab identity, yet they are equally unable to fully transcend or replace it by cultivating purely local loyalties. Thus the political elites of the region have vacillated between attempts to portray themselves as the vanguard of Arab unity and to rely on provincial identities and loyalties to engender political support.

Precisely because history is amenable to symbolic manipulation and can serve the various purposes of regime legitimacy, state formation, and nation-building, reconciliation of the imperatives of state legitimacy and national identity is often accomplished symbolically, through historical texts, holidays, and monuments.[2] What cannot be accomplished politically may be achieved symbolically. For example, within a year of Mu'ammar al-Qadhdhafi's accession to power in 1969, Libya had four new holidays. One celebrated the coup d'état that inaugurated the revolution of which Qadhdhafi was the leader, and the other three commemorated the evacuation of British and American military bases and the expulsion of Italian residents in the year after the regime came to power. In simple but evocative public festivities, Libyans celebrated the expulsion of foreigners from their territory. In doing so, they both defined themselves by contrast and asserted their claim to international respect. Simultaneously, the celebrations credited the regime with having accomplished this long overdue exercise of state sovereignty. The purposes of regime legitimacy, state loyalty, and national identity were all served economically and efficiently.

The symbolic reconciliation of the imperatives of regime legi-

timacy, state loyalty, and national identity through historical references is universal in politics and civics, but it is not necessarily
conducive to the production of scholarly history that meets international standards of intellectual rigor. Insofar as celebrations such
as the commemoration of the centennial of the American Statue
of Liberty, for example, kindle interest in the history of the population of the United States, they may contribute to history-writing.
As historical interpretation itself, however, the self-congratulatory
portrayal of the United States that accompanies such celebrations
is naturally distorted and partial. Political imperatives can provide
a powerful impetus to historical investigation; they cannot dictate
historical facts. The extent to which professional historians contribute to creation and maintenance of the "official version" of a
country's past, and the extent to which they can retain their professional independence from the wishes of the rulers, varies mark-
edly not only from country to country but from era to era within
a single country.

In the course of the twentieth century, Libya has known three
quite distinct periods of political historiography: the Italian preoccupation with the Roman legacy during their occupation of the
country (1911–1943); the monarchy's attention to the development
of the religious brotherhood, the Sanusiya, which produced the
king who ruled between independence in 1951 and 1969; and the
Qadhdhafi regime's emphasis on the popular resistance to Italian
imperialism. Although the historiography during each of these
periods was largely unrelated to that of its predecessor, the standards of historical scholarship rose with each phase. History as a
professional pursuit became increasingly standardized and routin-
ized as its practitioners were more often Libyan and their education more often specialized.

The potential for conflict between regime ideologies and professional historians was always inherent in these circumstances, but
it was probably most acute in Qadhdhafi's Libya. The availability
of substantial oil revenues permitted active government encouragement, direction, and control of historical research and investigation. This was a matter of degree, of course, because at no time

in the twentieth century did Libyans bear the major part of financing the government of the region: The Italian colony ran staggering annual deficits; the operating budget of the monarchy was subsidized by the United States and Great Britain; and, of course, the revolutionary regime supports its ambitions with oil revenues. These governments were always better equipped to support historical research than were any other institutions in the society. Nonetheless, government financing and control of historical research was particularly great under the revolutionary regime, both because the enormity of the oil revenues tipped the state-society balance so decisively in favor of the "public sector" and because the regime's revolutionary ideology was intentionally less laissez-faire than its predecessors, in culture as well as economics.

Yet the disproportionately important role of cultural production within the Libyan work force as a result both of the oil-based economy—virtually all agricultural or industrial labor in Libya was performed by foreign nationals—and of the regime's initial interest in new interpretations of the nation's place in the world meant that the political power of professional or service sector workers was unusually great.[3] Certainly in the early days of the revolutionary regime, the government was eager for new interpretations of the past better suited to its new visions of the present and future, and the relationship between the professional "producers" of Libyan historical scholarship and the "consumers" in the Libyan state was not simply an economic exchange: The producers were not entirely at the mercy of their market. Just as professional historians relied on state financing, the regime was dependent on the cooperation of professional historians to provide critical elements of the vocabulary of regime legitimacy and national identity.

The historians' ability to sustain this position ultimately rested, however, on the strength of the demand for their product. As the revolutionary regime aged into a "status quo power," at least domestically, and as it became increasingly dogmatic, the critical perspective afforded by professional historical studies was no longer the useful and important tool it had been in establishing the legitimacy of a new regime and new policy. Rather it became annoying and potentially dangerous. At this point the dilemma in officially sanctioned historiography became apparent; the historians whose power to convey new ideas and programs had been recognized in the early days of the regime could not be considered inconsequential later.

To trace the development of historical studies in Libya and their intimate ties to the vagaries of politics, this chapter reviews the nation's political status during the twentieth century and then turns to a closer examination of the trends in historical research.

Libya in the Twentieth Century

Libya entered the twentieth century as the last Ottoman territory in North Africa. Having benefited from the reform efforts of the imperial government during the nineteenth century, the three provinces that made up the Ottoman holdings were shaken by the Young Turk Revolution of 1908. The provincial elite was consumed with the ensuing internal political upheavals when in 1911 the Italians—whose ambitions in North Africa had long been well known— declared war on the Ottomans and invaded the territory they would call Libya. Although the Europeans were to acknowledge Italian sovereignty in Libya, neither the Ottoman empire nor most local Libyan leaders conceded the legitimacy of Italian control. The Italo-Turkish war lasted only a year, but Ottoman political and military influence in Libya did not end until the close of World War I, by which time the battles for control of the province among the Italians, Ottomans, and provincial leaders had severely undermined the local administration and economy.

The aftermath of World War I saw a number of local efforts to create independent states in the territory, including the short-lived Tripoli Republic and the Sanusi government. The latter, organized around a nineteenth-century religious order or brotherhood, the Sanusiya, was instrumental in organizing early battles against the Italians. With the outbreak of World War I, the order's leader, Ahmad al-Sharif, was persuaded by his Ottoman allies to attack British positions in Egypt as an adjunct to the Ottoman war effort. The attack proved a costly mistake. In its wake, Ahmad al-Sharif turned over leadership of the order to his cousin, Idris, and left the country. The British found in Idris a compliant political figure and he soon found in the British an important protector, as they lent their good offices to negotiations between the Italians and the Sanusiya after the war. The Tripoli Republic, by contrast, though it was easily as uncompromising in its opposition to Italian imperialism, benefited from no such European patronage, and it failed to win international recognition.[4]

By 1922 the new fascist government in Rome had decided to forgo negotiation with any of the local parties, and it began the military conquest of the territory. In one of the most brutal colonial wars of the twentieth century, the Italians captured control of their North African territory mile by mile, facing fierce resistance for well over a decade. In the course of the fighting, large portions of the Libyan population were interned in detention camps to prevent civilian cooperation with the resistance fighters. Wells were poisoned, civilian settlements bombed, and captured resistance fighters hanged on the spot.

By the mid-1930s, when Italian control of the colony was finally secure, famine, war casualties, and emigration had halved the Libyan population. Particularly significant was the loss of much of the educated elite and middle class, as coastal agriculture and domestic trade had been severely disrupted. Even with that, however, the Italian victory was to prove short-lived; after a long series of difficult and destructive battles, the North African campaigns of World War II left Libya in British and French hands.

During the war the British in Egypt promised Idris, then in exile in Cairo, that eastern Libya—Cyrenaica—would not be returned to Italian control if he agreed to provide troops from among his followers to fight with the Allies. After the war this promise proved decisive in the debates over Libya's future. The newly established United Nations was unable to agree on a suitable alternative mandatory power, and the three provinces—Tripolitania, Cyrenaica, and Fazzan—were granted independence in 1951 as a united kingdom under Idris.

At the time of independence, Libya was the poorest country in the world. The per-capita income of the approximately one million inhabitants was under $50 a year. The country's major export was scrap metal from the debris of the North African military campaigns of World War II, and the literacy rate was under 20 percent among adult men—approximately what it had been at the turn of the century. For all intents and purposes, the country was a ward of the United States and Britain, which subsidized the operating budget of the monarchy and provided foreign exchange in rents for military bases on Libyan territory.

As if the upheavals of the previous half-century had not been enough, oil was struck in 1959. Within a decade per-capita income rose to more than $1,500 a year. Despite efforts to revamp and strengthen the administration, the bureaucracy's procedures were too fragile to withstand the pressures of new wealth. It proved impossible to separate the public administration from the private patrimonies of the king and his court, and development planning and even everyday administration soon faltered in the face of system-wide corruption, as the king's court and entourage failed to distinguish the public treasury from the privy purse. The military coup that brought Mu'ammar al-Qadhdhafi to power on September 1, 1969 therefore came as little surprise. The king, who was out of the country, abdicated.

At each stage of this complex and tortuous experience of the twentieth century, the ruling elites in Libya undertook to justify their rule. Not only did they argue that theirs was the best government, but they also drew on history and historical interpretation to bolster their claims to international respect and domestic acquiescence. The emphases and contours of the histories elaborated by each regime reveal much about their self-images and aspirations.

Libyan History under the Italians

The Italian justification for colonial rule in Libya was twofold: The colony was to provide an outlet for the home country's burgeoning population and to preserve its precarious Great Power status. As a consequence, from the outset it was a much-heralded settler colony. Bearing burdens of colonial rule was justified with the twin arguments that the colony was virtually devoid of population and what inhabitants there were had no right to the land in any event. As Claudio G. Segre has shown, the Italian poet Giovanni Pascoli very early summarized the arguments that would become the bywords of the fascist period: The nomadic Libyans were "creatures who sequester for themselves and leave uncultivated land that is necessary to all mankind," and, moreover, the Italians had special prerogatives in the region: "We were there already, we left signs that not even the Berbers, the Bedouins, and the Turks could erase; signs of our humanity and civilization . . . We are returning."[5] The notion that the local populations were illegitimate interlopers in a continuous history stretching from the glories of the Roman empire to the triumphs of the twentieth-century Italian empire even gave the country its contemporary name: Part of the region was known in antiquity by the term the Italians adopted for it—"Libya"—although the local inhabitants and their Ottoman rulers had called the territory "Tarablus al-Gharb," or "Western Tripoli." This perspective also informed virtually all Italian scholarship on the province between 1911 and 1943.

Much of what Italian scholarly interest there was in Libya was devoted to archaeology. As the magnificently excavated ruins at the Roman sites of Sabratha and Leptis Magna in Tripolitania and the Greek Cyrene in Cyrenaica attest, the Italians spent lavishly in attempting to demonstrate the priority of their claims to the region. The corollary of this interest in antiquity was a distinct lack of interest in more recent history. Most of the work done by Italians on the indigenous population of Libya was ethnography: identification and tracing of races, ethnic groups, tribes and tribal territories, and collection of photographs and specimens of native costumes, proverbs, customs, and folklore of various kinds.[6]

The history of the local inhabitants was usually treated superficially when it was treated at all. The attitude of the Berber-speaking population of the Western Mountains toward the Italians—generally less hostile than the Arabic and Turkish speakers in the province—was attributed to their greater appetite for civilization, for example, an appetite said to have been first exhibited and cultivated during Roman times when the Italians forebears supposedly enjoyed cordial relations with the indigenous North Africans.[7] The Ottoman period—indeed the entire Islamic era—in Libya was portrayed as one of virtually unremitting decline and stagnation. This meant not only that it was unworthy of sustained examination, but more important that the Italians believed that the local population would welcome liberation from "the Turkish yoke" and introduction to the benefits of Western civilization. Indeed, in this instance, Italian ignorance of Libyan history proved very costly in quite practical terms, as it contributed to the repeated failures to predict the strength of local resistance.

Since the indigenous inhabitants were not a major constituency or even concern of the Italian state in Libya, however, mistakes in estimating their preferences did not prompt renewed efforts to understand local history or society. The Italian colonial officials complained of having to deal at all with the local population, while the Italian scholarly community did not develop the tradition of Orientalism in the service of imperialism at which the British and French excelled. Apart from the work of a few exceptional scholars who were not in any event schooled in the country's colonial experience, Italian scholarship on Islam and the Arab world is as remarkable for its paucity as for its intellectual poverty. This may reflect the fact that, for all the importance attributed to the colony as an outlet for population and an attribute of a Great Power, the empire was an expensive and short-lived luxury for Italy that (apart from classical studies) neither merited nor financed scholarly careers.

In any event, the Italian preference for ethnography and anthropology over history as the favored discipline by which to investigate local life was one that would be reflected in Libyan studies well after the Italians no longer ruled. In part because relatively few Libyans were prepared to undertake historical studies, in part because historical fashion gave preference to the exploits of kings and statesmen and it was hard to conceive of a largely illiterate population bearing a respectable history—traditions perhaps, but not "real" history—the European view of what was interesting in the country and how to best approach it continued to prevail well beyond independence. There were political elements in this as well, however, for it was not without its advantages to the monarchy.

Libyan History during the Monarchy

The British administered Tripolitania and Cyrenaica between 1943, when they won the provinces from the Italians in the North Africa campaigns of World War II, and 1951, when the country became independent.[8] Although the British scholars who doubled as colonial officers and military administrators during and after the war employed themselves principally with continuing the ethnography and anthropology begun by the Italians, they did not neglect history quite so dramatically. Indeed, they had no reason to ignore recent events—after all, they had liberated the country from the still bitterly resented fascist regime—and considerable reason to hope that recent history would be portrayed in a light favorable to their local allies. Their success in fostering such a portrayal was to ensure not only that they maintained their political influence in the country after its independence, but that they also played a role in shaping Libyan historiography under the monarchy.

King Idris's government was not only closely associated with Western—particularly British and American—interests, but it cultivated a regional hegemony within Libya that reflected its own origins in the Sanusi brotherhood. From its beginnings in the nineteenth century, the Sanusi order had been an important institution in Cyrenaica but relatively weak in the rest of the country. Its failure to take hold outside Cyrenaica was rooted in many causes—including the greater urbanization and educational facilities elsewhere in the country when the order was founded—but one of its principal consequences was a deep distrust on the part of the order's leaders of the urban, settled, and populous regions of Tripolitania to the west and, to a lesser extent, the Fazzan in the south. After independence this regional distrust translated into, among other things, divisive political favoritism and competition for historical preeminence. Virtually all the literature on twentieth-century Libyan history written before 1969 emphasized the role of the Sanusiya in the struggle against Italian rule in Cyrenaica to the virtual exclusion of the other groups who had opposed Italian imperialism elsewhere in Libya. The Sanusiya had a powerful ally in this effort to dominate the country's history: the British, who had found in the order a useful ally in their World War II campaigns in North Africa and who subsequently supported the Sanusi claims to power in Libya after the war.

This support—and its influence on the writing of history—is illustrated by E.E. Evans-Pritchard's *The Sanusi of Cyrenaica*, an illuminating example of scholarship in the service of imperialism.[9] This book is probably still the best-known treatment of the Libyan resistance to Italian rule, and it has been widely influential not only in anthropology, where its author was a highly respected authority and where the book quickly became a classic text, but in Libyan studies and modern Arab and Islamic history as well. As we have seen, British interests in Libya grew out of World War I when, in order to secure Egypt's western frontier, the British entered into discussions with Idris, the head of the Sanusi order. Partly to annoy the Italians, partly to shore up their flagging reputation for good faith in dealings with "native Arab chieftains," the British then began the process of transforming Idris into a genuinely important political figure. As Evans-Pritchard himself observed, "from this time, the British authorities favored his pretensions to the leadership of Cyrenaica."[10]

That there were other aspirants to nationalist leadership in Libya, including the founders of the Tripoli Republic of 1918 to 1922, is hard to ascertain from *The Sanusi of Cyrenaica*; the book is not about those who failed to win British support. Indeed, the few references to the order's competitors cast them as usurpers: Idris's cousin "just failed to bring the whole country under the Sanusiya flag . . . chiefly because of the ancient feud between the bedouin . . . and the urban and coastal party represented by Ramadan al-Shtaiwi, self-made lord of Misurata."[11] In fact, during World War I the Ottomans, recognized Ramadan al-Shitaywi al-Suwayhli, who was a founder of the Tripoli Republic, as governor of the Misurata region. The "urban and coastal party" of Tripolitania had for the British none of the romance of the Arabs of the desert of Cyrenaica, however, and more important, it was less amenable to British direction.

The British were the arbiters of Libya's future after World War II, and it was they who sponsored Idris as the king of independent Libya. Most of the historical chapters of *The Sanusi of Cyrenaica* are based on the British Military Administration's *Handbook on Cyrenaica: History*, written by Sir Duncan Cumming, then the chief British official in Cyrenaica, who also gave Evans-Pritchard his unpublished notes.[12] The purpose of the *Handbook* coincided with the larger purpose of the administration: to ensure the smooth transition from Italian rule to independence under pro-British Idris. While *The Sanusi of Cyrenaica* may not have been intended as an apologia for British policy, it reflects its sources. In its emphasis on the order's organization and independence, it exaggerates the Sanusiya's vitality and coherence, neglects the role of Ottoman and later British support, and distorts the equally valiant struggles of Libyan nationalists who fought both Italian rule and British influence and who acquiesced in the British-sponsored kingdom under Idris only when it became clear they had no other choice.

The Sanusi of Cyrenaica was published in 1949, before the country became independent, but it was to serve as virtually the only historical text for the next twenty years. In part this reflected the fact that there were few educated Libyans at independence—estimates of the number who held college degrees at the time range from seven to fourteen—and their skills were sorely needed in less academic pursuits. The national university was established in 1955, with largely foreign staff, and it was not until quite late in the following decade that adequate financing and candidates were available to begin sending substantial numbers of Libyan students abroad for advanced study in history and the social sciences. It would be the revolutionary regime that would harvest much of the fruit of this earlier investment, and in the meantime, the "British-Sanusi" interpretation continued to dominate Libyan historical studies.

The continued influence of *The Sanusi of Cyrenaica* also reflected the interests of the monarchy in a portrayal of Libyan society as "traditional" and politically unsophisticated, satisfied to be tutored in "modern" ways by a benevolent king who was himself intimately acquainted with the country's traditions. The banning of political parties soon after independence and the continued failure of the regime to accommodate demands for genuinely popular participation in government seemed justified by the ostensible backwardness of the people. Whatever merit this portrait of Libyan society may have had on the eve of independence—and it was at best a very partial picture even then—by the late 1960s it was a very serious distortion. This was evident not only in growing political unrest but even in stirrings on the academic scene.

In 1968 the Faculty of Arts of the University of Libya sponsored its first conference, producing a volume of proceedings called *Libya in History*.[13] The contents of this volume demonstrate a continued preoccupation with classical history and antiquities—a legacy of the Italian period—and an avoidance of topics more recent than World War I, which was the subject of a contribution by Sir Duncan Cumming. Of the thirty-eight papers, twenty-seven treated prehistory and classical Libya, and the dean of the faculty of arts, himself a geographer, felt constrained to remark: "We know that pre-history, the Greek and Roman periods have been the subjects of intensive detailed study. However, I feel that the period between the eleventh and nineteenth centuries deserves more detailed research work. The history of this period is almost entirely blank. This phenomenon has led some writers to describe Libya as a country without a written history."[14]

By the end of the 1960s, the male literacy rate in Libya approached 50 percent; three thousand students were enrolled at the national university and many more were studying abroad. For the first time significant numbers of Libyans had been trained in history. Simultaneously, the study of history was changing in Europe and the United States. The new emphasis on social or popular history fit well the needs of a country without a long tradition of political independence and state achievement. The political climate would soon be conducive to the rediscovery of Libyan history.

Libyan History in the Era of the Masses

The regime inaugurated with the coup of September 1, 1969, had
ambitions for Libya that far outstripped those of the king's government. The monarchy's humility and passivity, its willingness to
be "backward," dependent on Western powers, and outside the
mainstream of Arab politics, were unacceptable to the new government. The Qadhdhafi regime was to launch what it would call
a popular revolution, exhorting the masses to participate in their
own government so as to serve as a model and beacon of social
equity and moral righteousness for the whole world. This emphasis on equality and participation at home and on a more active
role in world affairs was echoed in novel approaches to history: If
Libya was to take a more important international role, its right to
that role had to be demonstrated, and one of the ways it would be
asserted was symbolically, through demonstration that Libya enjoyed a history which deserved the respect and admiration of
friend and foe alike.

The change in atmosphere with the coming of the new regime
almost immediately permitted the publication or distribution of
works whose focus had not coincided with the interests of the old
regime. These included Ahmad Sidqi al-Dajani's *libya qubayl
al-ihtilal al-itali* [*Libya on the Eve of the Italian Invasion*], which
describes the Ottoman influence in the nineteenth and early twentieth centuries as somewhat more dynamic than an emphasis on
the Sanusiya's position in Cyrenaica alone would have suggested.
al-Dajani, a Palestinian, taught at the University of Libya and
worked with one of the country's premier archivists to bring out a
collection of Ottoman documents several years later. More dramatic, however, was the publication in both Beirut and Tripoli in
1970 of *jihad al-abtal* [*The Holy War of the Heroes*]. This description by one of the participants in the resistance to the Italians in
Tripolitania is not particularly flattering to the Sanusiya but praises
the actions of Ramadan al-Suwayhli and the Tripoli Republic leadership. Qadhdhafi appointed its author, Tahir Ahmad al-Zawi,
Grand Mufti of Tripoli that year.[15]

Indeed, the resistance to the Italians soon became a central preoccupation of the scholarly community in Libya, after decades of relative neglect. The Qadhdhafi regime was to spend considerable money and effort to support rewriting that history to include not only the Sanusi and Cyrenaica but the other populations and regions of the country as well. Students were sent overseas for advanced training in history in even greater numbers, vast educational programs were established at the universities in Libya, and several research units founded. Among the best organized and funded of these was Tripoli's *markaz dirasat jihad al-libiyyin dhud al-ghazw al-italyani* (Center for the Study of the *Jihad* of the Libyans Against the Italian Occupation), known in English as the Libyan Studies Centre, which opened its doors in 1978. All of these efforts contributed to the researching, writing, and dissemination of a new interpretation of Libyan history.

By and large, the new writing has exhibited a more serious concern with the conventions and fashions of international historical studies. While retaining earlier interests and approaches, the Libyans expanded their purview and experimented with popular media. Scholarship on the prehistoric and classical eras was not abandoned, which meant that next to Egypt, Libya's antiquities and ancient societies were among the best studied in North Africa. Indeed, even the Sanusiya was given its due, and although information on the dark side of the family that led the order became now more easily available, the role of the order's shaykhs in the resistance to the Italians was also well documented. The government-funded and widely distributed film *Omar al-Mukhtar* or, as it is known in the United States, *Lion of the Desert*, which starred Anthony Quinn in the title role, was a case in point: It is quite faithful to the historical record of Sanusi shaykh 'Umar al-Mukhtar's guerilla war against the Italians in the late 1920s and early 1930s, including its pointedly unflattering portraits of several Sanusi family members. Equally important was new work on, for example, the roles of Ottoman officers from elsewhere in the Arab and Islamic world in aiding the resistance, of the Tripoli Republic in organizing and representing the interests of the Tripolitanians after World War I, and of the ordinary *mujahid* in providing the backbone of the resistance.

A glance at the early publications of the Libyan Studies Centre provides an indication of the content and style of the new scholarship. Not only had the Centre, whose name in Arabic underscored its focus on the resistance to Italian imperialism, sponsored translations of the memoirs of figures as disparate as Italian Prime Minister Giolitti and Ottoman Minister Enver Pasha—both of whom played important roles in the Italo-Turkish war—but it published biographies of important figures in the resistance, such as 'Umar al-Mukhtar, and accounts of significant battles. Indeed, the mandate of the Centre was interpreted broadly to extend to more general regional and local history, and the Centre published scholarly histories of, for example, the Fazzan and the oasis city of Ghadames and a multivolume popular account called *tarikhuna*, or *Our History.*[16]

In addition to books and monographs, the Libyan Studies Centre published the semiannual *Majallat al-Buhuth al-Tarikhiya* (*Historical Studies Review*). Here short monographs on, for example, the role of tribal social structure in the organization of the resistance in Cyrenaica, the nineteenth-century Ottoman administrative system in Libya, and the work of a late eighteenth-century historian of Libya appeared side by side with articles treating methodological questions. Indeed, the attention to methodology was quite striking in Libyan historiography of this period, as how best to assess and use sources as different as Western travelers' accounts, Ottoman documents, and oral narratives was discussed and debated in detail.[17] In part this attention to methodology reflected the fact that the usual constraint on historical research—financing— was not an issue for historians in Libya and thus the rigor of the discipline was, as it were, self-imposed. It also reflected avoidance of more substantive—and more controversial—historical questions.

Nonetheless, as Habib al-Hisnawi pointed out, history writing in Libya—both indigenous and imported—had conventionally emphasized the exploits of heroes to the neglect of social and economic forces. Moreover, reliance on written documentation, largely Western, but even that from Ottoman and local sources, can ordinarily be expected to provide only a partial picture of events when a great proportion of the society was illiterate. Thus in its efforts to portray the history of ordinary people, the Centre pioneered methods of oral history, recording interviews with surviving participants of the resistance to the Italians; between 1978 and 1982 alone, four thousand hours of interviews were registered. This project made Libyan historians aware of the partiality of oral history—many of those interviewed, for example, molded their personal memories of people and events into the stylized format of the oral tribal or family history—and it contributed to making them particularly sensitive to the advantages and pitfalls of various methods of collecting data.[18]

All of this work reflected and contributed to an interpretation of Libyan history as that of a cohesive, nationalist, anti-imperialist society, loyal to its Arab and Muslim culture, opposed to Western political and cultural domination, and actively participating in world history. The emphasis on social and economic history fit nicely not only with contemporary fashions in history and the social sciences worldwide but also with the regime's abhorrence of the theory and practice of conventional statesmanship and its preference for "popular" or "mass" movements. Moreover, it also coincided with the regime's interest in simultaneously establishing the country's national identity and revolutionary credentials. Since Libya did not defeat the Italians and did not win independence in its resistance, and because it was very nearly divided into several separate countries, the answers to questions of identity and legitimacy are not necessarily self-evident. Thus, for example, the emphasis in the historiography of the late Italian period and World War II on the enormous devastation of the Libyan population— painstakingly documented in collections of photographs as well as other records—which accompanied the government's demands for reparations from the Western powers served to explain and justify, both historically and ideologically, the inability of the Libyans to rid themselves of the imperial powers until the coming of oil wealth.[19]

In other respects as well, the new approaches to Libyan history have served the purposes of the regime. The emphasis on conventional, chronological history rather than "tradition" demonstrated that Libya participated in the developments of world history, that it had not been the timeless and unchanging backwater the Europeans said it had been. Hence the appeal of history superseded the earlier preference for anthropology and ethnography. Popular culture was incorporated in the new approaches, however, and the regime's inauguration of the "era of the masses" and its insistence on popular participation in the revolution were well served by the emphasis in social and oral history on the importance of ordinary people.

Finally, the great merit of emphasis on the *jihad* from the point of view of the revolutionary regime in Libya was that it symbolically reconciled the government's aspirations to the special identity of a unique nation and its loyalties to the common identities of Islam and the Arab world. The *jihad* was both a specifically Libyan struggle—Libya was the only Arab land occupied by Italy— and a common cause of the Muslim and Arab worlds. Indeed, Mustafa Kemal, later better known as the leader of republican Turkey, Ataturk, and ʿAbd al-Rahman ʿAzzam, eventually the first head of the Arab League, were among the volunteers from throughout the Middle East who fought side by side with anonymous Libyan *mujahidin*. Thus Libya's struggle maintains its uniqueness while simultaneously symbolizing the struggles of anti-imperialist forces throughout the Muslim and Arab worlds, and this was precisely the role the Qadhdhafi regime saw for its country.

Among the problems with so close a fit between the interests of the regime and the historical research it finances is the possibility of politically subservient history. The interests of the producers and consumers of the historical research diverge. In circumstances where the political context of historical interpretation can and has changed suddenly and dramatically, the position of the professional historian is precarious. Within a decade of its publication in Libya, Zawi's *jihad al-abtal* had joined *The Sanusi of Cyrenaica* in the restricted access rooms of the libraries of that country as the religious elite of which Zawi was a member fell afoul of the regime. By the mid-1980s it was apparent that the period of intellectual freedom enjoyed by academics during the early days of the Qadhdhafi era was drawing to a close. It is no surprise, there-

fore, that Habib al-Hisnawi, in his discussion of the work of the
Libyan Studies Centre before a largely Tunisian audience in Tunis
in 1984, warned of the dangers of "official history" that serves
ideological and political ends. He referred specifically to the Libyan experience during the monarchy, but it was clear that the
American-trained Libyan historian felt compelled to guard his
own professional reputation in international circles. By that time
the regime's ideological framework was solidly in place, and independent professional historians had outlived their usefulness. As
historians of a variety of political persuasions and personal backgrounds came to figure on the lists of political prisoners, those still
practicing the craft risked the appearance, if not the reality, of
political sycophancy.

The impact of the substantial oil revenues Libya enjoyed since
the early 1960s on the reexamination of the country's historical
record and the professionalization and later repoliticization of the
historian's vocation has been ambiguous. Obviously the existence
of those revenues allowed the government to subsidize the education and training of many more historians much more quickly than
would have been possible otherwise. This in turn contributed to
the quite large body of research and writing that supported a new
interpretation of Libyan history. Sufficient numbers of people were
engaged in history to engender the intellectual excitement and
corporate sentiment that marks the appearance of professional
identity. It seems fair to say that this happened more quickly than
would have been the case had Libya remained as poor as it was at
independence.

Moreover, the availability of the oil revenues seems not to have
allowed the government to distort seriously the findings of the historians or to suborn, as it were, the testimony of the historians
themselves. Obviously both the monarchy and the revolutionary
regime gathered apologists—some paid, some ideologically committed, some merely hopeful—as do all governments. Equally
obviously, the revolutionary regime did not exempt historians when
it began its campaigns against the ideologically impure; the political implications of various historical interpretations were lost on

neither the political elite nor the historians themselves. Nonetheless, as perhaps an unintended consequence of the professionalization of the practice of history in Libya, the reinterpretation of the historical record there has contributed to an important reevaluation of the history of the Middle East and North Africa as a whole that will outlive both the historians who wrote it and the regime that first tried to use and then to discard those historians.

NOTES

1. David C. Gordon, *Self-Determination and History in the Third World* (Princeton, NJ: Princeton University Press, 1971), 15. The utility of history is treated nicely in Eric J. Hobsbawm, "The Social Function of the Past," *Past and Present* 55 (1972); its malleability is suggested in Eric Hobsbawm and Terence Ranger, eds., *The Invention of Tradition* (Cambridge: Cambridge University Press, 1983).

2. Although he does not emphasize the symbolic uses of history and historiography in the Middle East, Rifaat Ali Abou El-Hajj's work is among the most thoughtful critical reading of contemporary Arab historical research. See "The Social Uses of the Past: Recent Arab Historiography of Ottoman Rule," *International Journal of Middle East Studies* 14, no. 2 (1982).

3. This argument is a variant on that made by Jacques Delacroix that "in the absence of surplus extraction, the relation between the elite and the remainder of the population is not a class relation." See "The Distributive State in the World System," *Studies in Comparative International Development* 15, no. 3 (1980): 10.

4. Lisa Anderson, "The Tripoli Republic, 1918–1922," in E. G. H. Joffe and K.S. MacLachlan, eds., *Social and Economic Development of Libya* (London: MENAS Press, 1982). This historical discussion draws on the more detailed treatment in Lisa Anderson, *The State and Social Transformation in Tunisia and Libya, 1830–1980* (Princeton, NJ: Princeton University Press, 1986).

5. Claudio G. Segre, *Fourth Shore: The Italian Colonization of Libya* (Chicago: University of Chicago Press, 1974), 22–23.

6. For a survey and bibliography of Italian anthropology and ethnography, see Ester Panetta, ed., *L'Italia in Africa: Studi Italiani de etnografia e di folklore della Libia* (Roma: Ministero degli Affari Esteri, 1963).

7. This argument was made, for example, by Francesco Beguinot in a well-known Italian study of Berbers and Berber life, "Roma e i Berberi," *Roma* (1939). Efforts to distinguish Arab and Berber populations and to win favor among the Berbers were not limited to the Italians; the French followed similar policies in, for example, Morocco. The Italians merely emphasized their alleged long-standing

ties with this "true" indigenous population. See Ernest Gellner and Charles Micaud, eds., *Arabs and Berbers* (London: Duckworth, 1973).

8. France administered Fazzan, and although the French argued somewhat halfheartedly for absorbing the province into their Algerian territories after the war, they did not make elaborate historical arguments to justify their position.

9. E. E. Evans-Pritchard, *The Sanusi of Cyrenaica* (Oxford: Clarendon Press, 1949).

10. Ibid., 126.

11. Ibid., 123.

12. D. D. Cumming, *Handbook on Cyrenaica: History* (Cairo: British Military Administration, 1947). In an interview in August 1980 in London, Sir Duncan told me that he had given Evans-Pritchard his notes.

13. Fawzi F. Gadallah, ed., *Libya in History* (Banghazi: University of Libya, 1968).

14. Ibid., xi.

15. Ahmad Sidqi al-Dajani, *libya qubayl al-ihtilal al-itali, 1882–1911* [*Libya before the Italian Occupation, 1882–1911*] (al-Matbaᶜat al-Fanniya al-Haditha, 1971); Ahmad Sidqi al-Dajani and ᶜAbd al-Salam Adham, eds., *watha'iq tarikh libya al-hadith: watha'iq al-ᶜuthmaniya* [*Documents of Modern Libyan History: Ottoman Documents*] (Banghazi: University Press, 1974); Tahir Ahmad al-Zawi, *jihad al-abtal fi tarablus al-gharb* [*The Hero's Struggle in Western Tripoli*] (Beirut: Dar al-Fatah, 1970). al-Zawi's account had been written in the 1950s and circulated in Libya privately.

16. See the list of publications of the Libyan Studies Centre, Tripoli, Libya.

17. These examples are taken from the first four annual volumes of the *Majallat al-Buhuth al-Tarikhiya*, 1979–82.

18. See Habib al-Hisnawi, *"al-riwayat al-shafawiya wa-l-tarikh li-harakat al-jihad al-libi: mulahazat manhajiya"* [*Oral Narrations and the History of the Libyan Liberation Movement: Methodological Notes*], *Actes du IIème séminaire sur l'histoire du mouvement national: Sources et methodes de l'histoire du mouvement national tunisien (1920–1954)* (Tunis: Imprimerie Officielle de la République Tunisienne, 1985); Muhammad Tahir al-Jarari, *"limadha markaz buhuth wa-dirasat al-jihad al-libi?"* ["Why the Center for the Study of the Libyan Struggle?"] *Majallat al-Buhuth al-Tarikhiya* 1, no. 1 (1979); and Muhammad Tahir al-Jarari, *"hawla tahrir al-tarikh min al-fikr al-istiᶜmari"* ["On Liberating History from the Colonial Mentality"], *Majallat al-Buhuth al-Tarikhiya* 1, no. 2 (1979). al-Jarari is the director and al-Hisnawi a senior research associate of the Libyan Studies Centre.

19. See the Libyan Studies Centre, *The White Book: Some Examples of the Damages Caused by the Belligerents of World War II to the People of the Jamahiriya* (Tripoli: author, 1981).

4. Social and Political Dimensions of the Historiography of the Arab Gulf

Assem Dessouki

Does the discovery and extraction of oil in a region influence the writing of its history? This question might sound somewhat strange, or even peculiar in terms of traditional understandings of history and historiography, in which material conditions, religion, the individual, and class struggle all play an important role. This issue of whether oil has had a similar impact deserves attention because it is a new dimension that has not yet been subject to historical scrutiny.

The question of the impact of oil wealth on the writing of Arab history did not arise until oil production led to an increase in prices during the early 1970s and until the societies of the Arabian Peninsula began to enjoy economic prosperity. This question also did not arise until oil wealth began to influence the creation of new modes of thought (*mafahim*) and social values and until religion came to be employed to prevent a just distribution of oil wealth. The prosperity derived from oil has had both a conservative and a progressive influence on such modes of thought and social values. Most peculiar of all is that oil wealth has injected a new vocabulary into popular discourse. In Arabic, the word "*al-khaliji*"—one who resides in the Gulf—has recently appeared. Internationally, terms such as "petrowealth," "oil era," and "the oil interpretation of history" are commonly used to express the unique character of the evolution of Gulf societies and to refer to the power structure that dominates these oil-rich countries.

In the Arab world, the countries most significantly influenced by oil wealth are those confined to the Arabian Peninsula, Iraq, Libya, and Algeria. No doubt oil wealth has played a similar role

in other oil-producing countries of the Third World. The same influence is not as noticeable in those countries of Western and Eastern Europe and North America that also produce oil.

Why is this the case? Part of the answer can be obtained by ex-
amining the Industrial Revolution that has dominated the West
and, since the second half of the nineteenth century, has resulted
in the process of substituting machinery for human labor. In the
West, numerous energy sources exist: coal, electricity, hydropower,
and oil. At the time of its discovery, oil provided a new method of
powering machinery as well as a new source of wealth. Oil still
maintains its importance in the production process despite the discovery of new alternative sources of energy, such as solar and nuclear energy.

In Arab oil-producing countries oil has served more as a source
of wealth than as a means of powering industrial machinery. For a
long time and for reasons that are beyond the scope of this study,
oil was sold as a raw material to the industrialized countries. This
is the difference between the role of oil as a source of energy in
the industrialized countries and its role as a source of wealth in
Arab oil-producing countries. As a source of energy, oil led to a
revolution in industrial production in the West; as a source of
wealth, it has led to superficial changes in the Arab world, such as
the consumption of expensive and high-quality consumer goods.
It also strengthened the power of ruling groups in Arab oil-producing countries.

In the Arab Gulf states the role of oil has been limited to providing a source of wealth that enabled ruling tribes to transform
themselves into a state apparatus and to develop a balance of
power among competing tribes. The state has "purchased" the
loyalty of these tribes by providing tribesmen with generous social services in the form of health care and education. Consequently, tribesmen have acquired a sense of belonging to the
nation-state rather than to the tribe. This has resulted in the establishment of a network of patron-client relations under the auspices
of a dominant tribe.

Another significant issue in dealing with historiography in Arab
oil-producing countries is that of social class. As revolutions have
occurred in Arab societies, attempts have been made to rewrite

the history of these societies, whether they were previously dominated by a large landowning class (*tabaqa iqta°iya*) or a capitalist
bourgeoisie or by both, or whether they were under colonial rule.
The pretext for this effort is that the ancien régime was purported
to have manufactured history to conceal its own machinations and
to distort the sociopolitical consciousness of the people, thereby
preventing them from participating in the making of their own
history. As a result, new attempts have been made to criticize the
past, particularly to belittle the ruling bourgeoisie by labeling it as
treasonous, oppressive, and unjust. Concomitantly, an effort has
been made to portray the masses as constituting the social force
behind every progressive development in society. In this manner,
history is being structured in such a way as to tie the masses to the
new political order.

Oil Regimes with a Revolutionary Tradition

In those Arab oil-producing countries that have undergone revolutions, oil wealth has played an important role in the rewriting of
history. The former ruling classes have been portrayed as neglecting the interests of the masses by allowing foreigners to plunder
the nation's wealth through the sale of oil while distributing very
little to the masses. In an attempt to "rewrite history," the new regimes have established a large number of research centers and allocated resources to be spent on studies, publications, conferences,
and seminars. These resources are meant to encourage writing and
translations that will support the regime's social and political
perspectives.

Perhaps the clearest examples of this model are to be found in
Libya, Algeria, and Iraq. Regional circumstances have helped to
shape the particular form that the rewriting of history has assumed
in each of these countries. In Iraq, for example, a central role is
given to the Ba°th party and its understanding of politics and national development. Great emphasis is placed upon criticizing the
era of the Hashimite monarchy and the extent to which it was
dominated by the British. In Libya the focus is upon criticizing

Sanusi rule, the Italian occupation, and on propagating the ideas of Mu'ammar al-Qadhdhafi's *Green Book* as a "third path" to development. Algeria emphasizes the historic role of the National Liberation Front and its violent confrontation with the French occupation force. Liberal politics, and those Algerians who cooperated and benefited from it, are considered a bankrupt legacy of the French occupation. None of the states just mentioned has limited itself merely to reevaluating the past. Indeed, each has gone further, attempting to spread its revolutionary ideology and experiences beyond its borders. These developments allow us safely to conclude that oil wealth has played a vital role in supporting the rewriting of history and the dominant ideology in each of these countries. Without the existence of oil, ruling groups would not have been able to dominate the state to the extent that they do.

Oil Regimes Lacking a Revolutionary Tradition

In those oil-producing countries that did not experience revolutions against colonial powers or the ruling class, such as those in the Arab Gulf, power was transferred peacefully to local tribes whose rule was based on a hereditary form of government. In reality, however, the dominant tribal families of the Arab Gulf continued to be controlled by European neo-colonialism under the guise of treaties based on asymmetrical power relationships. It is notable that in these societies there was no effort to "rewrite" history in the directed sense as in the aforementioned model. The reason for this is clear; it stems from the continuity in rule of the ruling tribal group both before and after political independence. The only real change that occurred was that this class consolidated its power in domestic politics due to the decline of foreign influence in that area.

In contrast to the first model, no noteworthy writings were produced by local authors during the pre-oil period that served the interests of the ruling class. Therefore, there were no works that had to be "rewritten." The only exceptions were memoirs and manuscripts, and historical chronologies. Since the tribal ruling class considered itself part of the past, there was no need to re-examine it. The best examples of this second model are the states of the Arab Gulf that stretch from Kuwait through Saudi Arabia to ʿUman in the south.

In summary, where revolutions occurred, there were attempts to rewrite history within a populist framework. No such rewriting occurred in those countries in which no revolution took place. There oil wealth was used to consolidate the power of existing regimes and to exclude any external influences, such as Nasirism, that might undermine the established rule. While oil wealth was employed in the first model to support revolutions of national liberation and to strive toward a program of comprehensive development, in the second model it was used to combat such revolutions and to safeguard reactionary social and ideological values. By limiting its redistribution to citizens who were tribally organized, oil wealth was also used to prevent any change that might lead to social disturbances even in the distant future. The concern with national security assumed a strategic dimension to the extent that Arab Gulf regimes aligned themselves with conservative forces in the West against those of the left in the Arab world.

Oil Wealth and *al-Hawla*

Nevertheless, in the countries of the second model that prevailed in the Arab Gulf, historiography assumed a specific character in the hands of a generation that was able to obtain secondary and university education and enter the higher levels of the civil service as a result of oil wealth. This generation, the majority of whose members came to be known as *al-howla* or *al-hawla*, embarked on writing the history of the economic, social, and political development of their respective countries during the past two centuries.[1] Their writings resulted in criticism of both British and tribal influence. Conscious of tribal privileges and frustrated at their exclusion from participation in political decision making, the *hawla* historians called for social and political justice.

Both historiographical models that I have outlined share a number of characteristics, such as the concern with economic and social development. The first model stresses the legitimacy of revolutionary change as a means of helping oppressed classes, while the second emphasizes the use of oil wealth to expand the role of underprivileged groups that are outside the dominant tribal system in the process of social and political development. For the most part, *hawla* historians, among others, belong to this underprivileged stratum. In their view, unless underprivileged groups are integrated into the social and political system, the existing regimes, as well as political and social justice and even revolutionary change, cannot be considered legitimate.

The Gulf as an Object of Study

Most early writings about the countries of the Arab Gulf were dominated by Westerners, first Europeans and later Americans who were primarily travelers and diplomats. They spanned a significant period of time beginning with the circumnavigation of Africa and European efforts to explore the non-Western world. These writings reflected the concerns of Western European interests during various historical periods. The authors' personal interests, ranging from commercial to strategic to economic, were also reflected in these writings.

Naturally, Western writing on the Arab Gulf changed over time, reflecting changing interests in the area. Western interests in the region were limited in scope during the period of commercial capitalism (before the nineteenth century); much broader interests developed during the period of industrial capitalism, especially as oil began to be used in Western industries and as a means of transportation, and communication improved during the early twentieth century. Understandably, Western economic, political, and strategic interests in the Arab Gulf increased with the beginning of oil extraction during the 1930s. As is well known, the October 1973 Arab-Israeli war and the subsequent Arab oil embargo played a critical role in increasing interest in the Gulf as a vital source of energy for Western industry.

Paralleling the Gulf's increased economic and political significance, Western interest in the region spread to academic and cultural fields as well. The proliferation of conferences, seminars, and masters' theses and doctoral dissertations concerned with the history of the Gulf constituted an important dimension of increased understanding of the contemporary period. A survey of Western writings according to year of publication indicates the changing foci of outsiders' interests in the Gulf. For example, writings that appeared in 1691, 1819, 1865, and 1866 were concerned primarily with travel and descriptive history. Subsequent writings focused on more specific themes: the slave trade (1873), the Persian question (1892), the Portuguese role in India (1894), Britain and the Persian Gulf and the passage to India (1905, 1915), the tribes and countries of the Gulf (1919), and the British route to India (1928). Following World War II, topics became even more sharply defined, as publications focusing on specific countries, such as Kuwait (1956) and the Arab Amirates (1962, 1964, 1967, 1968, 1970), indicate.[2]

The heightened interest in Arab nationalism and increased concern with history of the Gulf by Arab historians, indigenous and nonindigenous alike, was stimulated by the creation of the Arab League in 1945. Writings of Arab historians who were not natives of the Gulf region began to appear only at the end of the 1950s and the beginning of the 1960s. One of the causes was the Egyptian Revolution of 1952, which resulted in the spread of Arab nationalism. Intended to unify the Arab Middle East from the Atlantic Ocean to the Arab Gulf, Arab nationalism stimulated nonindigenous Arab historians to write about the Gulf. Another factor was the spirit or ethos of the era, which was represented in the popular slogan "Arab oil belongs to the Arabs." Arab interests in the Gulf region began to be reflected in master's theses and dissertations produced by students in Arab universities. These works were not based on primary sources or original data from the Gulf; rather they were based on secondary Western European sources and historical documents. Perhaps what is most noteworthy about these writings is that not only did they convey information about the Arab Gulf that was derived from Western sources, but they also conveyed Western point of views as well. Indeed, in some instances these writings appeared to be merely Arab translations of Western studies of the region.

Thus the writings of Westerners and nonindigenous Gulf Arabs on the region during the 1950s and 1960s was not based on local source materials. Western writers may have neglected these sources due to ignorance of the local Arabic dialect, which contains many Persian, Urdu, and European words. Arab writers, on the other hand, suffered from not having lived among the people about whom they were writing. A comprehensive explanation of the overall impact of Westerners and nonindigenous Arabs on the writing of Gulf history is beyond the scope of this study. Suffice it to say that, traditionally, Arab historians were accustomed to writing histories of specific regions without firsthand knowledge of these regions or their inhabitants. The writings so produced provided a superficial representation of the history and customs of the Gulf.

Gulf Historiography after Independence

The process of achieving independence from British rule that had begun with Kuwait in 1961 was completed in the Arab Gulf states during the early 1970s. At that time a new generation of Gulf Arabs who had studied in Egyptian universities, the American University of Beirut, or European and American universities began to return to their countries. This generation differed from the previous generation of intellectuals in its culture and education, because it had been exposed to a much greater variety of ideologies and methodologies. Some of its members became university professors while others entered influential occupations that helped formulate public opinion, such as journalism, radio, and television.

The rise of this new generation of intellectuals coincided with two significant and interrelated developments in the Arab Gulf: the termination of British occupation and the consolidation of new Arab regimes under the domination of tribes with deep historical roots in the area. As a consequence, these tribes developed a form of rule that more closely resembled that of an oligarchy with all the rights and obligations such a form of government entails. Although direct British political control of the region disappeared with independence, Western interests still maintained their domination of the region through control of economic resources.

Another important change was the rise of local regional powers: Iran, Saudi Arabia, and Iraq. Each of these countries sought to inherit the mantle of British influence and to fill the vacuum left by the withdrawal of the colonial powers. The same motives influenced the United States when it attempted to become involved in the region in accordance with the Eisenhower Doctrine, which was based on the notion of the need to fill a "political vacuum." Due to the geographical location of the Arab Gulf, a number of complex cultural and ethnic identities intersect to shape its character. The Gulf is located at the Arab world's easternmost flank and constitutes the heartland of the Muslim world. A third important geographical dimension is its proximity to Persian and Indian cultures.

These geographical and cultural aspects played an important role in motivating the quest of the new generation of intellectuals for self-identity as well as their reexamination of history to represent the character of the Gulf from the point of view of its inhabitants rather than that of the West. The writings of this generation are significantly different from those of Western Europeans or non-indigenous Arabs. It is perhaps ironic that the new generation of Gulf intellectuals benefited from the scientific research methods they learned in the West and used them to help their own countries solve problems of development. Breaking with the traditional educational pattern, they chose not to follow in their professors' footsteps. Rather, they were similar to the Arabs of the French colonies of North Africa who had been educated in France. French authorities attempted to create an educated elite that eventually would support French colonial policies. Instead, Arab students returned to North Africa well versed in the ways of national liberation movements and opposition to colonialism. Some students, for example, had joined the ranks of the French left wing movement and learned new methods of struggle.

Clear differences distinguish the writings of the new generation of Gulf intellectuals from those who preceded them. While the historiography of Westerners and non-Gulf Arabs was concerned with documenting the political, economic and social history of the region during its various eras,[3] indigenous Gulf historiography sought to place this documentation in a broader theoretical framework in order to understand the sociopolitical structure and international relations of the region. Consequently, the new generation of indigenous Gulf historians undertook an in-depth study of the economic foundations of the region in order to comprehend its social structure and the nature of its Arab character. Their writings also criticized American and British policies, viewing them as the cause of the region's underdevelopment. Finally, their writings included demands for social and political rights for the nontribal groups from which most of them came.

It is important to recognize that Gulf historians do not all share the same theoretical orientation. Among them one finds traditionalists, progressives, and even liberals to the extent allowed by the regimes in power. This chapter focuses on the progressives, who represent a new approach to the reading of history that appeared only after oil wealth. This new approach involves a comprehensive and forthright analysis of social structural differentiation and political problems. It differs from the approach of progressive historians who followed a liberal or traditionalist orientation prior to the educational and political impact of oil.[4]

A striking and highly significant characteristic of the new generation of progressive historians is that the overwhelming majority of them are descendants of the *hawla*. The experience of the *hawla* has had a significant impact on their analysis of the Gulf and represents a key element in understanding its character. *Hawla* intellectuals believe that their origins can be traced to the Arab tribes that migrated from ʿUman and the eastern coast of the Arabian Peninsula to the Iranian side of the Gulf. This migration occurred as a result of Ottoman pressure during the Wahhabi wars or during the seventeenth and eighteenth centuries, a period of Arab political expansion under the Qawasimi state that left a distinct imprint on those portions of the Iranian coast that it ruled. When groups of *hawla* returned to the Arab region of the Gulf following the discovery of oil early in the century, they faced a problem of social integration. Inhabitants of the area of Iranian descent considered the *hawla* to be foreigners due to their Arab origins and their sunni confession. The Arab tribes, on the other hand, considered themselves superior to the *hawla* for two reasons. First, these tribes saw the *hawla* as having abandoned their Beduin tribal way of life in favor of seafaring or agricultural pursuits along the Iranian coast. Second, they looked down on them for having adopted certain aspects of Iranian culture.

Consequently, the *hawla* were alienated from Arab Gulf society during the first half of the twentieth century. In their desire for self-assertion and social recognition, first-generation *hawla* entered numerous professions, excelling in trade, culture, and public service. The second generation assumed positions of leadership in the higher echelons of the state bureaucracy and in shaping public opinion. The end result was that the *hawla* came to represent an important segment among the region's intelligentsia.

Contrary to what some writers and tribal Arabs maintain, the *hawla* intellectuals do not consider themselves part of the Iranian migration to the Arab coast of the Gulf. Rather the *hawla* assert that they should be considered a progressive, reformist, and urbanized Arab element that represents an integral part of the sociopolitical structure of Arab Gulf society, especially Kuwait, Bahrain, Qatar, and the eastern shore of the Arabian Peninsula.

Hawla intellectuals have initiated an intellectual renaissance in contemporary Arab Gulf society. It might be thought that the prosperity enjoyed by intellectuals in the Arab Gulf would have had an impact on historical writing, the main burden of which is born by the *hawla*. Heretofore intellectuals wrote only that which conformed to the views of the dominant regimes and accepted social values; they strove to avoid angering authorities when analyzing the social bases of the ruling tribes, prevailing relations between the public institutions of civil society (e.g., the educational system, government cooperatives, sports clubs, and professional syndicates) and the populace, and other delicate and sensitive matters. However, just the opposite is true among the *hawla*. Prosperity seems, in fact, to have encouraged independent thought and opinion, even to the point of the use, in some instances, of different variants of Marxist analysis for a critical scrutiny of the historical origins of the class structure of Arab Gulf societies.

While some intellectuals have opted to support the views of the ruling class, most of these seem to be drawn not from the *hawla* but rather were seconded to the Gulf from other Arab countries.[5] The position of such intellectuals in the Arab Gulf countries is a highly sensitive one. In order to maintain their resident status, they make every effort to ensure that their views do not anger anyone. This attitude is reinforced by their ignorance of the social structure of the region and their belief that all the inhabitants of the Gulf belong to one social class and that the *hawla* are only migrants like themselves. By way of contrast, the *hawla* intellectuals focus in their writings on socioeconomic factors, especially power relations in Gulf society. This dimension was ignored by Gulf historiographers who wrote prior to the emergence of *hawla* intellectuals and continues to be ignored by most non-Gulf Arabs. Indeed, it is not an exaggeration to say that, in the Arab Gulf states, the word "intellectual" and the word "*hawli*" (pl. *hawla*) are synonymous.

The new generation of regional historians drawn from the *hawla* has attempted to study the origins and development of the class structure of Gulf societies both prior to the discovery of oil as well as after the onset of oil production. The ultimate purpose is to demonstrate the legitimacy of demands for greater social and political justice. Social justice entailed an end to the social differentiation that distinguished the *hawla* from the dominant tribal groups —a differentiation often not noticeable to foreign observers. Political justice meant an expansion of the right of participation in legislative and executive decision-making processes.

Let us now examine some of the more serious efforts of these historians.[6] From the socioeconomic analysis contained in *hawla* writings, Gulf society appears highly stratified. Though not entirely ignoring material wealth, *hawla* analysis relies largely on the concept of tribal solidarity. In this model, tribes occupy the apex of the social hierarchy followed by merchants of Arab and immigrant origins; the lower classes that represent the labor force are situated at the bottom.

The Ruling Tribes in *Hawla* Historiography

The Arab tribal groups that dominate the social structure were able to maintain their position as ruling groups during the eighteenth and nineteenth centuries. In all the countries of the Arab Gulf, ruling tribal groups concluded alliances similar to those that occurred during the al-Jahaliya period and the rise of Islam. Revenues and social rank were assigned according to the tribe's social standing, its genealogy, and its role in raiding and conquering new territory. For example, the al-Sabahs, the ruling family in Kuwait, and the Khalifa family, the rulers of Bahrain, together with their client tribes, represent a unified Arab alliance in the Gulf. In the late seventeenth century when the Khalifa family migrated from Kuwait and settled in "al-Zabara" in the northern tip of the Qatar Peninsula, it became the leader of a new alliance comprised of a group of Arab tribes residing there that included the al-Nuᶜaym, al-Jalahima, al-Bin ᶜAli, al-Dawasir, and al-Muᶜawida. This alliance was known as the al-ᶜUtub, and members later settled in Bahrain. When the al-Thani family left the alliance and established its own rule in Qatar, it began a process of forming a new alliance under its own leadership.

Wherever tribes settled, the ruling family formed tribal alliances that incorporated the merchants. *Hawla* historians believe this process explains the broad influence that merchants currently enjoy in the Arab Gulf. Merchants comprise most members in consultative and "supervisory" councils, benefit from important business concessions, and exert great influence in public affairs, despite the fact that they constitute a small numerical minority compared to the middle, lower middle, and working classes (workers, artisans, professionals, intellectuals, and public servants).

The upper levels of the social hierarchy of the Gulf have thus been dominated by two sectors during the past two hundred years:

one tribal and the other merchant. Members of both sectors have a common denominator; they are all clients of a common patron, the ruling shaykh. The Arab tribal sector holds political power. The merchant sector has been and continues to be comprised of the Arab *hawla* and shi°a notables. Historically, both *hawla* and shi°a merchants were able to enter the commercial realm by virtue of wealth gained in agriculture or the social position they held. In addition, the merchant group includes a number of Iranians and Indians who, having originally migrated to the Gulf as laborers and artisans, rose rapidly into the ranks of the merchant elite. This particular characteristic of Gulf social structure was influenced by British colonial rule, which restricted migration of Arabs to the Gulf while encouraging the migration of non-Arab groups such as Iranians, Indians, and Baluchis.

The Working Classes in *Hawla* Historiography

During the past two centuries, the working class in Arab Gulf society has been comprised of seamen employed in pearl diving, fishing, and shipbuilding as well as agricultural laborers. The first three decades of this century witnessed the birth of an urban Arab "proletariat" that engaged in a number of uprisings (*intifadat*) against the pearl merchants (*tawashi*) and other exploitative sectors of the merchant class. However, the British worked consistently to suppress these uprisings in order to benefit the small group of merchants who assumed roles as agents for their growing economic interests in the Gulf, especially after the collapse of pearling at the end of the 1920s. British authorities undermined the power of the proletariat when they began to employ Iranian, Indian, and Baluchi seamen instead of Arabs on large European commercial vessels. When Arab divers and seamen met to talk in "*al-dur*" (literally "the houses"), which were places where sea songs were performed and worker affairs discussed, they were arrested. The British destroyed the *dur* and made the construction of new ones illegal. After the discovery of oil, seamen went to work for foreign oil companies as day laborers at low wages. Their situation

improved very little because they still faced exploitative working conditions.

Due to the limited amount of arable land in the Gulf, the agricultural working class drawn from the Arab shiʿa was small. These
workers were employed on the estates of landowners in Bahrain,
al-Qatif, and ʿUman. Working conditions and rules governing the
relationship between landlord and worker were similar to the
patron-client relationships that prevailed between the pearl divers
and the merchants. Agricultural land was owned by urban merchants and tribal leaders as well as rural landowners. These three
sectors formed a class which exploited agricultural labor in the
villages and seamen and other craftsmen in urban areas.

The Middle Class in *Hawla* Historiography

Prior to the discovery of oil, the middle class and petite bourgeoisie in the Arab Gulf comprised part of the base of the social stratification system. This class was comprised of artisans (*ʿarab al-mihan*)
and traditional craftsmen. Its base expanded appreciably with the
discovery of oil as agricultural workers and fishermen were transformed into various types of artisans and craftsmen. After acquiring modern forms of education, the second generation of this class
was able to secure employment in the state bureaucracy and in
managerial positions in private corporations. Local historians view
this class as the social agent entrusted with the burden of future
social, economic, political, and cultural change in the region.

While there has been a serious attempt at class analysis of Gulf
society, scientific methodology has been employed somewhat arbitrarily. This is perhaps most evident in the attempt to find a
well-defined middle class and proletariat in the Western sense in a
society that possesses only to a limited degree the objective conditions that would allow for the existence of these classes. Nevertheless, regardless of the terminology used by Gulf historians, studies
document the existence of a social structural differentiation based
upon wealth and influence.

Following the transformation of the old economy into one based on oil, the regional social structure also underwent a transformation. Local historians argue that the social structure did not retain its distinctive features and became more difficult to analyze as scientifically as had been possible prior to the discovery of oil. There were many reasons for this difficulty. For one thing, the differences in oil wealth among the Gulf countries led to the creation of serious contradictions among the same social strata in different countries. For another, oil wealth suddenly transformed those elements that had followed "primitive" ways of life (peasants, beduin, seamen, and craftsmen) into a commercial class with great wealth; thus they entered the modern era without undergoing a more prolonged and natural evolutionary process. One result was that these social groups suffered an identity crisis because they neither retained their historical roots nor did they acquire the norms, knowledge, and discipline of modern life. All they understand of modern life is the "cadillac," which is treated like a camel, and the villa, which is treated like a tent.

What makes analysis difficult for the *hawla* historian is the low population density in most areas of the Arab Gulf. Social fragmentation resulting from tribal organization laid the basis for the creation of separate political entities that impeded interaction among Gulf societies and the integration of social classes in such a manner that would have led to positive social development. Local historians note that this fragmentation did not exist under British rule where the entire Gulf was treated as an integrated region. Thus tribal rule is implicitly criticized for having fostered the fragmentation of the Gulf after the area achieved independence from direct colonial rule.

The *Hawla* as Reformists

As Gulf historians, the *hawla* express chagrin that oil wealth has not been used to abolish exploitation of the poor by the rich. Instead, the *hawla* maintain that socioeconomic contradictions have increased as wealth has been squandered on foreign consumer goods. In their view, the failure to use oil wealth productively exposes the entire Gulf to collapse if there is a precipitous decline in oil prices. Thus in analyzing the Gulf, the indigenous *hawla* historian has assumed the role of a social reformer who proposes social change fearing the collapse of the existing order. However, these proposed reforms are unacceptable to both the dominant classes and the subordinate groups. The wealthy are unwilling to accept limitations on their profits and capital accumulation, while the poor and the middle classes reject reformist methods, opting to retain their access to material goods under the existing social system.

Given his position in the social order, the indigenous historian or intellectual who is drawn from the *hawla* comprehends the reality of the social contradictions afflicting the countries of the Arab Gulf. The solutions he presents, in turn, are governed by his conceptualization of Gulf society. Thus he sees that the basic socioeconomic and political contradiction facing Gulf society pits the wealthy merchant class, on one hand, against the petite bourgeoisie and working classes, on the other. The demands of the middle class are the traditional historical demands of this social stratum: constitutional rule, representative government rather than hereditary tribal rule, freedom to organize professional associations, guarantees of freedom of expression and the freedom of the press, and a wide range of cultural, ideological, and artistic freedoms. The middle classes also seek the establishment of a system of taxation, the enactment of legislation protecting the rights of workers and the poor, and the curtailment of the tremendous privileges enjoyed by the wealthy merchant class.

According to this analysis, *hawla* historians depend on the middle class to assume a dominant role in the struggle against the large merchant class. In other words, in their view, the middle class is historically destined to implement desired democratic reforms. Undoubtedly the French revolution of 1789 is the model in the mind of the indigenous historian, as this represents the classic model of a revolution of the bourgeoisie against feudal rule. Given this perspective, the *hawla* reject the Arab left's assertion that the working class and the poorer tribes are able to lead the nationalist

struggle in the Gulf, viewing it as an extremist and romantic perspective that cannot be supported by existing conditions. Indeed,
if *hawla* historians believe that labor might play an important role
in the future after the middle class has performed its historical
role, they do not express this view openly. In short, the emergence
of sociopolitical contradictions as a consequence of oil wealth and
the *hawla*'s sense of oppression have been responsible in large
measure for their sociological interpretation of the Gulf's history
and their demands for social and political justice.

The State in *Hawla* Historiography

In analyzing the political structure of contemporary Gulf society,
hawla historians observe that there is a fundamental contradiction
between existing political regimes that dominate the state in Arab
Gulf society and the rate of socioeconomic development after the
onset of oil production. Put differently, the political regimes that
came to power after independence are to be considered an extension of tribal rule in the guise of a modern state. In pre-oil society
(i.e., a society based on pearling), political authority was based on
tribal social structure. The legitimacy of tribal authority was derived from traditions based on kinship and the tribe's privileged
status and the power of its leader. These traditions were, in turn,
structured by the nature of production, whether agricultural, nomadic, or maritime.

Under British influence, political conditions remained stable for
a long period of time despite the social changes brought about by
the onset of oil production. The only change that occurred was
that the paramount tribal shaykh was transformed from a traditional leader to a ruler enjoying foreign support, through treaties
concluded between Great Britain and Arab rulers in the Gulf. Thus
the modern state came into being as a result of a forced and un-
natural birth in which the title "*shaykh*" was changed to "*amir*"
(prince) and "*mashyakha*" became "*imara*" (amirate). *Hawla* historians have defined the social reforms necessary to establish truly
democratic states. These proposed reforms stand in sharp contrast

to the prevailing social conditions in the Gulf, where social conditions are characterized by discrimination, oppression, political domination, and autocratic rule.

In the forefront of the social changes sought by the *hawla* is national unity, which can be achieved only through the elimination of traditional patterns of social differentiation such as confessionalism, tribalism, and kinship solidarity. The proposed reforms are themselves indicative of the social antagonisms that exist between the *hawla* and the dominant classes in the Gulf. Thus the call for an end to social discrimination is an indicator of the *hawla*'s antagonism toward the feelings of social superiority that tribesmen express toward them and other groups occupying lower positions in the social hierarchy, such as lesser or weaker lineages, and the rapaciousness of local and international forces that threaten the social order of the Gulf. These proposed reforms also symbolize a desire for an end to the disparities in income distribution in Gulf societies, despite a dramatic rise in per-capita income relative to other Arab societies. The reforms indicate a desire to use democratic processes to ensure political accountability of regimes and to broaden political participation, thereby reducing the alienation felt by the populace at large, and the desire to abolish tribal autocracy that relegates the educated and wealthy to the periphery of political life.

The *Hawla* View of the British

While the ruling classes in the Gulf still feel gratitude toward the British for support of their rule and privileges, *hawla* intellectuals direct overt criticism toward local British policies and consciously link them to world imperialism. In the view of *hawla* historians, the British entered the Gulf on the pretext of abolishing the slave trade in the nineteenth century. However, slavery continued until 1970 in the Sultanate of ʿUman in the sultan's palace under the very eyes of the British. Furthermore, British presence in the Gulf did not bring about any noticeable social or political development. Instead, Britain contributed to the isolation of the region by stipulating, through its treaties with shaykhs, that none of the Gulf countries could establish contacts with foreigners without its permission. Such contact was forbidden even for such basic purposes as opening a school or employing foreign teachers or doctors.

According to *hawla* historiography, the British are responsible for the region's underdevelopment. During the century and a half in which they dominated the Gulf, the British did not build a single road or open any elementary schools or infirmaries for basic health care. Indeed, the opposite was true: They prevented any such development. Britain began to concern itself with construction, health, and education projects only after the discovery of oil in order to facilitate the work of foreign petroleum companies.

Hawla historiography is quite specific in documenting the negative impact of British colonial rule. For example, the numerous difficulties experienced by the United Arab Amirates following independence can be traced to the lack of any sort of administrative or institutional infrastructure. The fault lies with the British, who prevented the establishment of such an infrastructure during their hegemony. Likewise, British imperialism destroyed Arab Gulf society by crushing local trade networks along the ʿUmani coast, thereby weakening ʿUman's ability to play its natural role as a Gulf power as it had done prior to the advent of colonialism. The British helped suppress the revolution during the 1970s in the province of Dhufar in southwest ʿUman. In the process, Great Britain earned millions of pounds that ʿUman paid from oil revenues to British mercenary officers, from compensation to British construction companies for machinery and maintenance, and from payments to the British-dominated air force that helped to contain the revolution. In reality, the *hawla* historians' criticism of British policies is also an exposé of the ruling tribes that chose to cooperate with the British in return for support in their domestic political struggles.

In criticizing the role of imperialism, the Gulf historian has not neglected criticism of American policy that has sought to dominate the Gulf through neo-colonialism rather than through the old form of direct colonial control. The founding of the Gulf Cooperation Council by six of the Arab Gulf states in 1981 is viewed as an American attempt at domination and is thus also criticized. In view of the council's charter, *hawla* historians conclude that its members have become economically dependent on the capitalist world. They believe this dependency has constrained independent decision making in the Gulf. The underdevelopment that afflicts Arab Gulf regimes serves the interests of the capitalist world and helps to solidify its domination over the Gulf and the Arabian Peninsula. As the Gulf Cooperation Council's defense policies are linked to those of American military strategy, they are, in the final analysis, a consequence of the relationship of dependency on the capitalist world. In the view of the *hawla*, the founding principles of the council conflict with the aspirations of the peoples of the Arab Gulf for unity, independence, and progress.

According to *hawla* historiography, the prevailing form of cooperation among the Gulf states suggests that the United States reinforces political fragmentation instead of promoting a larger political union that would facilitate greater social and economic development. True cooperation among the Arab Gulf states at this highest level would necessitate the coordination of policies under the aegis of existing regimes. The current state of affairs corresponds to colonialism's objective, which, in the *hawla* view, is to prevent the various Arab states from unifying within a larger political framework.

Conclusion

After the discovery of oil and the development of means for oil production in the Gulf, Arabs began to focus their attention on the Gulf and migrate there in order to benefit from its oil wealth. *Hawla* historians have tried to provide an understanding of social life in the Gulf in order to combat migrant Arabs' stereotype of Gulf inhabitants as "swimming" in a sea of oil wealth. *Hawla* historians have examined the past, beginning with the era of pearling and the discovery of oil. In the final analysis, the true Gulf intellectual continues to demand in his writing the right to personal and material security as well as to social justice and political participation. His motto remains: "This or the flood."

NOTES

1. The *hawla* are those Arabs who, for various reasons, emigrated from the Arab to the Iranian side of the Gulf, from Bandar ᶜAbbas to Bu-Shahr. After settling in this region for a lengthy period, they began to speak a mixture of Persian and Arabic. Among the Arabs and along the Iranian coast, this social stratum came to be known as *al-hawla*, or those Arabs who migrated to the Iranian side of the Gulf. The term seems to be of Arab origin (from a local Arabic dialect in which *hoolo* means *return*), as the Arabic letter *ha* has no equivalent in Persian. Members of this group returned to the Arab region of the Gulf with the appearance of oil wealth. "al-howla" is a Persian pronunciation of the term. [Translators' note: The classical rendering of the term *al-hawla* is used in this chapter.]

2. See, by way of example, the following limited survey on the basis of year of publication: John Chardin, *Travels in Persia and the East Indies* (reprint, London: Argonaut Press, 1961); William Huede, *A Voyage up the Persian Gulf and Journey Overland from India to England in 1817* (London: Longmans, 1819); A.G. Palgrave, *Narrative of a Year's Journey Overland from Central and Eastern Arabia 1862–1863*, 2 vols. (London: Macmillan, 1865); Robert Grant Watson, *History of Persia from the Beginning of the Nineteenth Century to 1856* (London: Smith, Elder, 1866); R.N. Colomb, *Slavery in the India Ocean: A Record of Naval Experience* (London: Longmans, 1873); George N. Curzon, *Persia and the Persian Question*, 2 vols. (1892; reprint, London: Cass, 1966); F.C. Danvers, *The Portuguese in India*, 2 vols. (London: Great Britain, India Office, 1892); D'Arville, *Le golfe persique, route de l'Inde et de la Chine, Extrait de la revue des questions diplomatiques et coloniales* (Paris, 1905); Montague Bell, "Britain and the Persian Gulf," *Journal of the United Empire*, 6 (April 1915); Samuel Miles, *The Countries and Tribes of the Persian Gulf*, 2 vols. (London: Harrison & Sons, 1919); Halford Hoskins, *British Routes to India* (London: Octagon Books, 1928); H.R.P. Dickson, *Kuwait and Her Neighbours* (London: Allen & Unwin, 1956); John Marlowe, *The Persian Gulf in the Twentieth Century* (London: Cresset Press, 1962); Major Clarence Mann, *Birth of an Oil Sheikhdom* (Beirut: Khayats, 1964); R.G. Landen, *Oman since 1856: Disruptive Modernization in a Traditional Arab Society* (Princeton, NJ: Princeton University Press, 1967); John Kelly, *Britain and the Persian Gulf, 1795–1880* (London: Oxford University Press, 1968); and Donald Hawley, *The Trucial States* (London: Allen & Unwin, 1970).

3. See, by the way of example: Ahmad Mahmud Subhi, *al-bahrayn wa daᶜwat iran* [*Bahrain and the Claims of Iran*] (Alexandria, 1962); Ahmad Mustafa Abu Hakima, *tarikh al-kuwayt* [*The History of Kuwait*] (Kuwait, 1967); Arnold Wilson, *The Arab Gulf and the Sultanate of Oman* (trans.); Amin al-Rihani, *muluk al-ᶜarab* [*Arab Kings*] (Beirut, 1960); Amin Saᶜid, *al-khalij al-ᶜarabi: dirasa li tarikhahu al-siyasi wa nahdatahu al-haditha* [*The Arab Gulf: A Study of Its Political History and Its Modern Renaissance*] (Beirut, n.d.); Jean Jacques Paribi, *The Arab Gulf* (trans., Beirut, 1959); J.J. Lorimar, *Guide to the Persian Gulf*, 14 vols. (al-Dawha, 1967); Jamal Zakariya Qasim, *al-khalij al-ᶜarabi: dirasa li tarikh al-imarat al-ᶜarabiya,*

1840–1914 [*The Arab Gulf: A Study of the History of the Arab Emirates, 1840–1914*], 2 vols. (Cairo, 1973); John Kelly, *Britain and the Gulf, 1795–1880* (trans., Oman, 1979); Hassan Ahmad Ibrahim, *al-matami* *al-urubiya fi-l-khalij al-ᶜarabi min mutlaq al-qarn al sadis ᶜashar hatta muntasaf al-qarn al-tasiᶜ ᶜashar: mu'tamar dirassat tarikh sharq al-jazira al-ᶜarabiya* [*European Designs on the Arab Gulf from the Beginning of the Sixteenth until the Mid-Nineteenth Century: A Conference on the Study of the History of the Eastern Arabian Peninsula*] (Qatar, 1976); Sayyid Nawfal, *al-awdaᶜ al-siyasiya fi imarat al-khalij wa junub al-jazira al-ᶜarabiya* [*Political Conditions in the Gulf Amirates and the Southern Arabian Peninsula*] (Cairo, 1960); Salih Awziran, *The Portuguese and the Ottoman Turks in the Arab Gulf* (trans., Basra, 1979); Salah al-ᶜAqqad, *al-tayarat al-siyasiya fi-l-khalij al-ᶜarabi* [*Political Trends in the Arab Gulf*] (Cairo, 1965); and Mahmud ᶜAli al-Da'ud, *al-khalij al-ᶜarabi wa-l-ᶜalaqat al-duwaliya, 1890–1914* [*The Arab Gulf and International Relations, 1890–1914*] (Cairo, 1963). See also note 2.

4. See, by the way of example: Ahmad Qasim al-Burini, *al-imarat al-sabᶜ ᶜala al-sahil al-akhdar* [*The Seven Amirates on the Green Coast*] (Beirut, 1957); Husayn Khalaf al-Shaykh Khazᶜal, *tarikh al-kuwayt al-siyasi* [*The Political History of Kuwait*], 5 vols. (Beirut, 1962, 1972); Rashid ᶜAbdallah al-Farhan, *mukhtasar tarikh al-kuwayt wa ᶜalaqatuhu bi-l-hukuma al-baritaniya wa-l-duwal al-ᶜarabiya* [*A Concise History of Kuwait and Its Relations with Britain and the Arab Countries*] (Cairo, 1960); Salim Bin Mahmud al-Siyabi, *idah al-maᶜalim fi tarikh al-qawasim* [*Explanation of the Characteristics of the History of the Qawasim*] (Damascus, 1976); Sirhan Bin Saᶜid al-Azkazi al-ᶜUmani, *tarikh ᶜuman* [*The History of Uman*] (n.p., n.d.); Sayf Marzuq Shamlan, *min tarikh al-kuwayt* [*On the History of Kuwait*] (Cairo, 1959); ᶜAbd al-Aziz al-Rashid, *tarikh al-kuwayt* [*The History of Kuwait*] (Beirut, 1962); ᶜAbd al-ᶜAziz Husayn, *muhadarat ᶜan al-mujtamaᶜ al-ᶜarabi fi-l-kuwayt* [*Lectures on Arab Society in Kuwait*] (Cairo, 1960); ᶜAbdallah al-Hatim, *min huna bada'at al-kuwayt* [*Here Kuwait Begins*] (Damascus, 1962); Muhammad Bin ᶜAbdallah al-Salami and Naji Asaf, *ᶜuman tarikhun yatakalam* (*Uman's History Speaks*) (Damascus, 1963); Muhammad Bin ᶜAbdallah ᶜAbd al-Qadir al-Ansari, *tuhfat al-mustafid bi-tarikh al-ahsa fi-l-qadim wa-l-jadid* [*The Gem of Those Who Benefit Is in the History of al-Hasa in the Past and Present*] (al-Riyad, 1960); Nur al-Din ᶜAbdallah al-Salami, *tuhfat al-aᶜyan bi sirat al-ᶜuman* [*The Gem of Notables is in the Biographies of the People of ᶜUman*] (Cairo, 1961); Yaᶜqub al-Rashid, *al-kuwayt fi mizan al-haqiqa wa-l-tarikh* [*Kuwait on the Scale of Truth and History*] (Kuwait, 1963); Yusif al-Falaki, *qadiyat al-bahrayn bayn al-madi wa-l-hadir* [*The Bahrain Issue between the Past and Present*] (Cairo, 1953); and Yusif al-Qanaᶜi, *safahat min tarikh al-kuwayt* [*Pages from the History of Kuwait*] (Kuwait, 1946).

5. Translators' note: especially Egyptians, Palestinians, Syrians, Lebanese, Jordanians, and Iraqis who were sent to the Gulf during the 1970s.

6. The following books, which constitute a selected sample of these efforts, represent a single historiographical approach in dealing with the Arab Gulf and

provide the basis for the analysis presented in this chapter: Muhammad Jabir al-Ansari, *lamahat min al-khalij al-ᶜarabi: dirasa fi tarikh al-khalij wa thaqafatuhu wa rijaluhu wa fulkluruhu al-shaᶜbi* [*Glimpses of the Arab Gulf: Studies in the History of the Gulf, Its Prominent Men, and Folklore*] (Bahrain, 1970); (Anonymous), *al-khalij iran al-ᶜarab: wujhat nathar khalijiya, al-khalfiya al-tarikhiya wa ihtimalat al-mustaqbal* [*Iran of the Arabs: A Gulf Perspective, the Historical Background, and the Future*] (Beirut, 1972); Muhammad Ghanim al-Rumayhi, *al-judhur al-ijtimaᶜiya li-l-dimuqratiya fi mujtamaᶜat al-khalij al-ᶜarabi al-muᶜasira* [*The Social Bases of Democracy in Modern Gulf Societies*] (Kuwait, 1977); Muhammad Ghanim al-Rumayhi, *al-khalij laysa naftan: dirasa fi ishkaliyat al-tanmiya wa-l-wihda* [*The Gulf Is Not Oil: A Study of the Problematic of Development and Unity*] (Kuwait, 1983); Muhammad Ghanim al-Rumayhi, *al-bahrayn: qadaya al taghayur al-siyasi wa-l-ijtimaᶜi, 1920–1980* [*Bahrain: The Issues of Political and Social Change, 1920–1980*] (Kuwait, 1976); ᶜAbd al-Malik Khalaf al-Tamimi, "*al-khalij al-ᶜarabi: dirasa fi-l-tarikh al-iqtisadi wa-l-ijtimaᶜi*" ["The Arab Gulf: A Study in Economic and Social History"], *Journal of Social Sciences* 9, no. 2 (Kuwait, June 1981); ᶜAbdallah Fahd al-Nafisi, *majlis al-taᶜawun al-khaliji: al-itar al-siyasi wa-l-istratiji* [*The Gulf Cooperation Council: The Political and Strategic Dimensions*] (London, 1982).

5. Statecraft, Historical Memory, and Popular Culture in Iraq and Kuwait

Eric Davis and Nicolas Gavrielides

One of the most important problems facing the state in less developed countries is its lack of political legitimacy. Having recently achieved independence from colonial rule and comprised of populaces characterized by ethnolinguistic and sectarian diversity, many Third World states have yet to forge a national consensus about their country's future. Most of these regimes have used force and coercion to enforce compliance with public policy. A subset of Third World states, those endowed with oil wealth and hence possessing resources unavailable to most less developed countries, have followed a broader approach in attempting to shape a national consensus.

In the Arab world, such states have used oil wealth to promote scholarly journals, museums, institutes of higher learning, centers for folkloric research, festivals, conferences, and a mass media whose purpose is to reinterpret the country's history, traditions, and folk culture. These efforts point to a highly significant phenomenon that has yet to be studied by Western social scientists. In this chapter we examine efforts made by Iraq and Kuwait, two oil-producing countries with different historical trajectories, regimes, and ideologies, to promote a historical memory that would provide the foundation for a nationalist ideology intended to reconcile traditional social antagonisms as well as strengthen the legitimacy and authority of the central state.

This chapter is structured around a number of questions. How have Arab states that have experienced a rapid infusion of oil wealth been able to use that wealth to strengthen their legitimacy and authority? More generally, why should the examination of the

past be considered important to an understanding of state formation? In what way is this issue part of the discourse of political
economy? What implications does it have for more general theories of the state?

Most work on state formation in Third World countries has focused upon institution building, the state's ability to assert its authority over a given territory, and its ability to extract surplus from
its citizenry. Little work, however, has been directed toward the
ideological bases of state formation. What type of statecraft is entailed in appropriating the past to promote the power of the state?
Four concerns structure the argument presented here. In the first
section we analyze current trends among Arab intellectuals who
are engaged in reexamining the past, particularly the concept of
Arab heritage (al-turath). In the second we examine the concept
of state formation. In the third section we focus on examples of the
efforts of the Iraqi and Kuwait states to promote an ideologically
mediated reexamination of history, tradition, and folklore. In the
fourth we raise a critical methodological question: How is knowledge of the past transformed into increased power for the state?
Finally, given the Iraqi invasion and annexation of Kuwait, what
are the repercussions for both the Baᶜthist regime in Baghdad and
the Kuwaiti regime in exile in neighboring Saudi Arabia? In what
ways will the past be recast in order to confront the new problems brought on by the crisis?

The Argument in Brief

Most oil-rich Arab states are recent creations in that they achieved
independence from colonial rule only during this century. Once a
colony of the Ottoman Empire, Iraq became nominally independent from colonial rule with the end of the British mandate in
1932. Yet full political independence from foreign domination was
not achieved until the ousting of a pro-Western monarchy and
political elite during the July 1958 revolution. Following the revolution, Iraq underwent a decade of political and social turmoil
essentially centered around a struggle between the Baᶜth (Renaissance) party and the Iraqi Communist party. Only in 1968 was a

wing of the Baᶜth under Ahmad Hasan al-Bakr and Saddam Husayn able to form a stable government. Nevertheless, the state, which continues to be dominated by tribal elements drawn from the sunni north, still faces opposition to its rule from the country's shiᶜi majority in the south and the Kurdish minority in the north. Organizationally, opposition has come from the Iraqi Communist party and its sympathizers on the left, various Islamic radical groups such as the al-Daᶜwa al-Islamiya, and Kurdish political and guerrilla organizations. Clearly the state needs to forge a nationally accepted ideology.

While the Kuwaiti state has been under the dominance of the ruling al-Sabah family since the early eighteenth century, Great Britain began its domination of the country in 1899 when it signed an agreement with the Sabahs giving it control over Kuwait's foreign policy. Only in 1961 did Kuwait become a fully independent state. Unlike the Baᶜth in Iraq, the Sabah family has no recourse to revolutionary legitimacy, as it cooperated with colonial rule rather than struggled against it. Still, it is able to trace its rule back several centuries. Furthermore, the Kuwaiti state is organized around the concept of a hereditary monarch. While there is an advisory parliament, ultimate legislative authority rests in the hands of the amir (ruler) of Kuwait. Furthermore, only 40 percent of the Kuwaiti populace are citizens, a considerable number of whom are recently settled Beduin tribesmen. Other segments of these tribesmen, although settled in Kuwait, are not citizens. Not all Kuwaiti citizens have equal political rights; Kuwaiti women and males who hold second-degree citizenship are not entitled to vote. Large numbers of expatriates have traditionally provided the bulk of Kuwait's working class and service sector, including the important financial sector. Given the tenuous loyalty of most of the populace to al-Sabah rule, the Kuwaiti state, like the Iraqi one, rests on a weak ideological foundation.

The question facing the Iraqi and Kuwaiti regimes, as well as those in other Arab oil-producing countries, is how to transform revolutionary or traditional legitimacy into institutionalized forms of power, or what Weber calls rational-legal authority. Revolutions do not ensure political longevity. The military officers surrounding ʿAbd al-Karim Qasim who carried out the July 1958 revolution, as well as over 3,000 Communists, found themselves swept away by the Baʿth party in a bloody coup d'état in 1963. The current regime of Saddam Husayn that came to power in 1968 has also faced a number of challenges to its authority, including a number of coup attempts during the late 1980s.[1] Although the regime refers to events in 1968 as a revolution, in reality what occurred was closer to a traditional military coup d'état. Given the turbulence of the decade between 1958 and 1968, it can be argued that an exhausted Iraqi society accepted Baʿth rule in 1968, albeit without any great enthusiasm. Certainly, in the initial stages of the regime, the support of the military ensured its power. Still facing strong opposition from other sectors of the Baʿth, and many Communists, as well as the ever present threat of a coup by the military, it is understandable why Saddam Husayn's regime was so concerned with mobilizing political consent among the populace at large.

The situation in Kuwait differed from that in Iraq. The al-Sabah family represented a tribal grouping with deep roots in the Gulf, extending back to the eighteenth century. However, it found itself in constant competition with other powerful tribes and tribal confederations such as the Shamar, Mutayr, Ajman, and ʿUtayba. Often tribal loyalties transcended the boundaries of the Kuwaiti state. For example, there were large numbers of Shamar tribesmen in southern Iraq and northern Saudi Arabia. The problem facing the Sabahs was how to ensure loyalty to the boundaries of Kuwait among these powerful tribal groupings. They also faced hostility from members of Kuwait's powerful merchant families, many of whom were shiʿis and thus did not share the Sabahs' sunni Islam confessionalism. The traditional indigenous Kuwaiti working class composed of pearl divers, seamen, and shipbuilders also maintained a traditional hostility to tribal groupings who were economically and culturally oriented to the desert rather than the sea. Their hostility only increased once they found their traditional occupations rendered redundant by an oil-based economy.

In Iraq, Baʿth party members, particularly those drawn from

Takriti tribal origins north of Baghdad, occupy a privileged position in terms of access to both political and economic power.
Clearly a new bourgeoisie composed of contractors and industrialists, primarily drawn from two northern sunni Arab provinces, has
developed as a result of access to state contracts and revenues.[2]

In Kuwait, members of the al-Sabah family and affiliated "noble"
(*asil*) tribal and merchant groups enjoy a disproportionate amount
of political and economic power. One of the severest criticisms of
the Sabahs to emerge since the Iraqi invasion comes from Kuwaitis
who have complained that members of the royal family have
treated the country's $100 billion invested abroad as their privy
purse.[3] Thus the benefits of oil wealth have been largely limited to
those (male) Kuwaitis who are considered first-degree citizens
based on their ability to trace the residence of their ancestors in
Kuwait to 1913 or before.

Recent events in another Arab oil-producing country, Algeria,
have made it clear that privileged access to the benefits produced
by oil wealth can lead to severe challenges to the state's authority.
This point is an especially valid one because, as continual efforts
by OPEC have made eminently clear, political elites cannot control the world price of oil. In Arab oil-producing countries, ruling
groups seek to institutionalize their power by promoting a specific
understanding of the state. It is in this sense that the past becomes
so relevant, since each ruling group is seeking to appropriate the
past to promote the institutionalization of its power and influence
in the form of a strong state. The main questions that emerge are
in what history and culture should the state attempt to ground itself and how can that grounding be translated into enhanced
power for the state?

Conceptualizing the Past

In attempting to conceptualize the relationship between state
formation and historical memory, the logical point of departure is
how the concept of history or "heritage" (*al-turath*) has been used
and how it has changed within Arab political discourse. As one

prominent Arab thinker has noted, Arabs have been in a continual process of reexamining the past.[4] However, there is nothing inherently unique about this process since all societies engage in it. To understand the political dimension of thinking about the past, it is necessary to ask under what conditions it becomes politically salient. When does it become part of a struggle for power? Arab intellectuals constantly assert that without a historical consciousness, the Arab world cannot hope to achieve any meaningful level of development. In what sense have those in power in Arab oil-producing states tried and been successful in appropriating current modes of Arab discourse concerning how the past should play a role in development?

In conceptualizing this issue, Foucault's notion of an "archaeology of knowledge" is a useful point of departure. In an effort to avoid the pitfalls of reductionism and teleology often inherent in linear thinking, Foucault suggests a "layered" or more anarchic approach to history.[5] Political and social processes begin in spurts and often fail to achieve the ends that their originators intended, leading instead to unintended consequences. Foucault's metaphor of the past as a sedimentary residue is an attempt to capture the multifaceted and variegated character of the historical process. Events in the past build upon one another much in the way that sediments do. However, while all these sediments together form a structure, the component parts are not necessarily causally linked. Further, it is often impossible to deduce the shape of future sediments from an understanding of their current form. Applied to the Arab context, this metaphor suggests that it is not valid to view successive efforts to examine the past as somehow causally linked in a linear fashion. While Arabs have constantly reexamined the past, these efforts have been a response to different events and assumed different meanings at various points in their history.

Our concern here with the reexamination of history is confined to the "modern" period, that is, the nineteenth and twentieth centuries. We have limited our study because the reexamination of the past assumed a specific character during these two centuries as a result of colonial penetration of the Arab world and its integration into the world market. Almost all Arab states were formed as a result of struggles with colonial powers or through the actions of colonial powers once they were forced to withdraw their occupation. However, while Arab concerns with reexamining the past were in general a response to colonial penetration and the expansion of capitalism, this response assumed different ideological forms and was articulated by different social groups at varying points throughout these two centuries.

The Arab world's intensified interest with Arab history and heritage that began during the nineteenth century and continued into this one was thus a response to the problems caused by colonial domination. While some Arabs attempted to reduce this penetration to a continuation of a struggle between Islam and Christendom that extended back to the rise of Islam and the Islamic conquest of Spain and parts of Europe, European colonial domination presented the Arab world with challenges that were without historical precedent. Thus, even though Arab efforts to reexamine and reinterpret the past are part of a continual process, current efforts are of a different magnitude, given the challenges presented by European imperial domination—including industrial, military, political, and cultural subjugation.

European colonial penetration during the early nineteenth century provoked resistance and resulted in the *al-nahda* (Renaissance) of the late nineteenth century. However, the very effort of subsequent intellectuals to conceptualize this movement under the rubric of *al-nahda* tends to obscure the relatively diverse nature of Arab responses to colonial domination. Some intellectuals, such as the Egyptian Rifaʿa al-Tahtawi, wanted to synthesize Islam and Western liberalism. Some, such as the Iranian or Afghani expatriate Jamal al-Din al-Afghani, wanted to develop a pan-Islamic movement that would unite the Ottoman Turks and Arabs against European colonialism. Others, such as the Egyptian Mufti, Shaykh Muhammad ʿAbduh, emphasized the need for *al-islah*, or Islamic reform. Yet others, such as Christian Arabs in the Levant, sought to promote a secular Arab nationalism that contained strong components of Western liberalism. While ideologically diverse and unified in their opposition to European colonialism, all Arab thinkers who participated in the *nahda* and who sought to revive Arab historical memory in order to oppose European colonialism did share certain social characteristics. Most obviously, all came from educated backgrounds and could be considered members of the upper or middle classes. In pointing to the class component of the *nahda*, our purpose is not to engage in sociological reductionism but rather to point to the limited role of the masses in responses to European domination during this period.

The Period between 1920 and 1967

The twentieth century produced a more vigorous and mass-based anticolonial movement that intensified after the end of both world wars. Again it is interesting to note that the content of the nationalist response to colonial domination changed from the earlier emphasis on political reform and spiritual renewal to calls for nationalization of foreign agricultural, financial, and industrial interests in the Arab world. In large measure, the deepening underdevelopment of the Arab world as the twentieth century progressed, perhaps most manifest in the decline of the agricultural economy and the massive migration of peasants to urban areas in countries such as Iraq and Egypt, added a more explicit class and ideological component to Arab resistance to colonialism. That is not to say that earlier Arab responses to colonialism did not have a class component, as thinkers were largely drawn from the liberal-minded upper and upper-middle classes. However, only during the twentieth century did the question of class itself become an explicit component of Arab reexaminations of the past.

Arab historiography and conceptualizations of the past reflected the changing social and ideological component of Arab nationalism. The spread of underdevelopment and the increasing politicization of the lower-middle classes and even segments of the small working class and peasantry were key elements in injecting an increased concern with socioeconomic issues into Arab political discourse. No longer was it sufficient to look at the past simply in terms of the glories of the "Golden Age" of Arab empires to "justify" independence from European colonial rule. People began to examine the past more for social movements that sought to bring social justice to less privileged sectors of society. Islam, for example, was interpreted not only from the perspective of its moral superiority to Western society but also for its emphasis on equality in the distribution of wealth and political power. Radical movements in Arabo-Islamic history, such as the Kharijites, the Zanj Revolt, and the Carmathians (*al-qaramita*), that challenged autocratic rule and championed social equality assumed new significance. In short, the past began to be reconstructed in ways intended to address new political realities.

In addition to the struggle against colonial rule, an equally significant development was the emergence of intensified competition among Arab groups over who would define the nature of Arab society during the postcolonial era. The rise of Arab communist parties during the 1920s and 1930s and the emergence of radical Islamic organizations such as the Muslim Brotherhood in Egypt modified the divisions to include not only secular liberal and radical Arab nationalists against the colonial Other but Arab against Arab as well. Competition intensified over the manner in which the past was to be appropriated.

Another factor that caused the stakes to rise among competing Arab nationalist movements was the increased politicization of the mass populace. The growth of urban areas throughout the Arab world, due to the massive influx of peasants and tribesmen from rural areas and the desert, presented potential benefits as well as potential threats to the leadership of anticolonial movements. On the one hand, the masses had demonstrated their hostility to colonial rulers and their potentially radical nature through violent actions directed against the British and other foreigners during a number of uprisings, such as the Egyptian and Iraqi revolutions of 1919 and 1920, the Arab revolt in Palestine from 1936 to 1939, and the Iraqi *wathba* (uprising) of 1948. On the other hand, mass-based political behavior frequently tended toward the anarchic and could be volatile. As Arab nationalist protest assumed an ever larger mass-based component, the need of political elites both to channel and to manipulate mass consciousness also increased. At this point Arab political discourse began to broaden to include popular culture (al-turath al-sha'bi), since it now became important to be able to reach illiterate sectors of the populace in a way that was not possible through written discourse.

The intensified competition among Arab political movements challenging colonial rule points to an important dimension of the relationship between historical memory and state formation. None of these movements possessed significant legitimacy. The Ba'th party called for the re-creation of "the Arab nation" in an effort to link itself to the Golden Age of the first two Arabo-Islamic empires, the Umayyad (A.D. 661–750) and the 'Abbassid (A.D. 750–1258). As the Ba'th included many Christian intellectuals and many of its members were European-educated, Islam was subordinated to Arabism. The Ba'th party was primarily limited to the Levant. This area did not have a strong history of Islamic radicalism, partially because it and northern Iraq represented the only Arab colonies over which the Ottoman Empire still retained control in the early twentieth century. Since the Ottomans had emphasized an Islamic ideology as a means to bridge the ethnic divide between themselves and their Arab subordinates, many sectors of these former colonies did not look favorably on Islamic-based ideologies.

In Egypt the Muslim Brotherhood also sought to appropriate symbols associated with the Umayyad and 'Abbassid empires but through a historical prism colored by Islam. Arab was defined as synonymous with Muslim, and Arabs were considered first among equals within the ultimate goal of a unified state encompassing all Muslims. Islam was responsible for the Arabs' rise to greatness, and only through strict adherence to Islamic norms of behavior would Arabs be able to reclaim their historical greatness. Although its main strength was in Egypt, the Brotherhood was able to extend its influence to elements of the Palestinian and Syrian populaces through its vigorous support of the Palestinian cause.

The communists likewise sought to appropriate symbols associated with Arabism and Islam. However, those Arabs and Muslims to whom communists looked were those who struggled for revolutionary change and social justice and not necessarily those who were defined as "great" by traditional Arabo-Islamic historiography. When they examined the past for clues as to how to confront the present and future, Arab communists looked upon the upper classes during any period of Arab history with suspicion. The communists' great strength lay in their ability to cope with ethnolinguistic and sectarian difference in a way in which the corporatist ideologies of the Baʿth and Muslim Brotherhood could not. National development lay in unified political action on the part of all sections of the working class, peasantry, and progressive forces, no matter what their ethnolinguistic and confessional background.

Nevertheless, as discussions with former communists have indicated, these cleavages often plagued the internal unity of Arab communist parties, and, despite their ideology, the parties were not always able to transcend them. Furthermore, both secular and religiously based nationalists were able to weaken the legitimacy of the communists by attacking their position on Palestine.[6] Educated Arabs saw the creation of Israel as yet another colonial intrusion into the Arab world and an effort to prevent Arab unity. Arab communist parties expressed ambivalence on the Palestinian question. While condemning Zionism, they considered the fact that Arab states were dominated by reactionary bourgeoisies to be of greater political significance. Indeed, many Arab communist parties, which invariably included a significant Arab Jewish membership, called for a cross-class alliance between Arab and Jewish workers.

If the contenders for control of the postcolonial state did not possess extensive legitimacy among the Arab populace at large, it is likewise important to note that these groups were also seeking to forge a political identity in both a collective and an individual sense. The members of the Baʿthist elite that currently dominates the Iraqi state, for example, began their struggle for power during the 1940s. It would be reductionistic to see their struggle purely in instrumentalist terms, namely the pursuit of power and material benefits. To see their engagement with the past as simply a process whereby historical symbols are chosen for predetermined political ends fails to take into account the social psychological process of identity formation that is involved in a reexamination of the past. In Geertzian terms, ideology here is as much mediating reality for those who are articulating it as it is for those who are its intended audience.[7] The fact that an ideologically mediated construction of the past cannot be viewed from a purely instrumental perspective points to another shortcoming of an approach that is only based upon class analysis or ideology understood in the narrow social sense. At the same time that elites in Arab oil-producing countries have been promoting a particular understanding of the past, they have been simultaneously constructing their own self-identity. The fact that these elites came to power only recently highlights their own need to situate themselves within the past as well as within the existing social and cultural hierarchy of their own societies.

The loss of Palestine in 1948 and the massive defeat of Arab armies by Israel in 1967 further stimulated an examination of the past. It was particularly searching because, aside from the communists, Arab nationalist discourse had placed the blame for the lack of Arab unity and economic development on the region's colonial occupation. Even before 1967, Arab intellectuals and politicians who had seen colonial rule as the cause of the area's underdevelopment found that political independence did not alleviate these problems. Indeed, radical nationalist parties, such as the Baʿth, that emphasized Arab unity found themselves engaged in a struggle with communist parties who argued that the class nature of the Arab world was as much responsible for its underdevelopment as colonialism.

Thus it can be seen that a wide variety of groups have sought to appropriate notions of the past, whether it is history or what Arabs more broadly define as "national heritage" (al-turath). Although the concept of social class is important in understanding this phenomenon, it must be recognized that geographical, confessional, and ethnic divisions also helped shape the manner in which Arabs have looked to their history for clues as to how to confront the problems facing their societies. It is also obvious that any discussion of state formation and historical memory must take identity formation into account. The elements entailed in the process of identity formation may not be compatible with state formation.

Political ideologies may involve a mediation of reality that closes that reality off from any form of objective analysis. Nasser's miscalculations of Egyptian military power in 1967 and Saddam Husayn's miscalculations of Iranian military strength in 1980 and the Western reponse to his invasion of Kuwait ten years later are good cases in point.

Social Class and Arab Historical Memory

Despite the central role that social class has played in Arab and Western analyses of Arab responses to colonial rule, by itself the concept is too narrow, as it cannot be historicized. Resorting to social class is invariably an attempt to avoid a subjectivist approach to understanding ideologically mediated reexaminations of the past. This is a valid methodological concern. However, if the concept of social class is to contribute to an understanding of Arab historical memory, the analysis must be broadened to include Samir Amin's view of the Arab world in terms of multiple modes of production under the umbrella of an historically transmitted culture that itself once reflected a world empire relatively unified both politically and economically.[8]

To argue that the concept of social class cannot be historicized means that, standing alone, class cannot be related to processes of social change in the same way as the concept of mode of production. The fact that Egypt has been dominated by a mode of production organized around surplus extraction from agriculture, while most other regions of the Arab world have been characterized by surplus extracted from trade, provides an important point of departure for explaining Egypt's more inner-directed culture and its weaker identification with Arabism, compared with the pan-Arab orientation of significant areas of the Mashriq (the Levant, Iraq, and the Arabian Peninsula). With a homogeneous population relatively free of residual tribal identities and ethnic conflict, Egypt more closely resembles a class-stratified society.

Iraq and Kuwait, on the other hand, are societies beset by sharp internal cleavages of a class, regional, ethnolinguistic, and confessional nature. In Iraq, for example, the sunni minority dominates the shi'i majority in the south and the Kurdish (non-Arab) minority in the north. Iraq is a class-based society with a bourgeoisie spawned by the state comprised of senior Ba'th party members, army officers drawn from prominent sunni tribes, public sector managers, contractors, and industrialists, who dominate the political and economic power structures of the country. However, the sunni bourgeoisie and its much smaller shi'i counterpart stand in a mutually antagonistic relationship. Here Amin's analysis is instructive. Iraq still does not represent an integrated capitalist mode of production. Sectarian groups in the form of the sunni and shi'i communities still linked to different sources of surplus extraction have not been able to transcend deep-seated historical antagonisms.

In summary, Arab oil-producing countries are unique among Third World countries in possessing large amounts of revenue unavailable to most other less developed countries. It would be erroneous to overemphasize the extent to which these resources have been channeled to strengthen the ideological foundations of the state. The bulk of the revenue has been applied in many traditional ways to state formation. Large amounts have been spent on military goods and the development of a security apparatus. Much wealth has also been spent on developing a state bureaucracy. In certain Arab oil-producing countries, oil revenues have been used to develop a mass-based political party. However, a military, bureaucracy, or political party is only as effective as the motivations and commitments of its members. For this reason, regimes in Arab oil-producing countries have attempted to use an ideologically mediated reexamination of the past to promote greater loyalty to the state. Before turning to the questions posed earlier, a few comments on the state formation are in order.

The Concept of State Formation

In Western political economy, the literature on state formation has been focused on the development of European states during and following the Industrial Revolution. In terms of methodology, this literature has been dominated by a Weberian perspective that emphasizes the territorial authority of the state. In a representative study such as Charles Tilly's *Formation of National States in Western Europe*, the central concern is the manner in which the state was able to consolidate its hold over a particular territory.[9] Such research usually emphasizes the establishment of a modern standing army, the creation of a modern bureaucracy, and the extraction of the surplus. All these factors, it is said, allowed for the reproduction of the state over time. Each also entails a critical and implicit ideological perspective that has been largely avoided in the literature on state formation.

Weber, as is well known, defined the state as that agency that possesses legitimate rights to the exclusive use of a monopoly of coercion over a specified territory. For Weber, the modern state can be characterized by a legal order that can be changed through legislation, a rationalized administration (i.e., one that operates according to standardized criteria), binding authority over all citizens, and a legitimate monopoly over the use of force. The problem with Weber's analysis, which provides the intellectual basis for much contemporary Western theorizing about the state, is its taxonomic rather than explanatory quality. It presents a number of problems: Who controls the state and for what ends? And what is the role of subjective or ideological factors in the formation of the state?

On who controls the state, Weber largely assumes that the state is ideologically neutral. While recognizing the existence and importance of social classes, he says little about the group or class component of the state.[10] Since we know that the state does not, in reality, act to promote the interests of all its citizenry equally, the question of why this is so needs to be answered rather than merely assumed. Second, we also know that historically the state has not been open to political participation by the citizenry at large. Most states have been dominated by what many would call a ruling elite and what others, particularly Marxists, would call a ruling class. In Weber's defense, it might be argued that his criteria are only meant to provide an ideal-typical example of what modern states aspire to. However, his criteria might also be seen as constituting a myth designed to create the illusion of an impartial state that, in reality, cloaks its class/elite composition and its class/elite interests.

Weber's criteria themselves imply an ideological and cultural component. A legal system implies agreement (in the ideal-typical but not necessarily empirical sense) over legal norms and standards for defining what constitutes crime and punishment. A rationalized administration necessitates prior agreement over the rules by which administrative agencies function and the purposes for which they were created. Terms such as "binding authority" and "legitimate use of force" also encompass notions of agreement over norms and ends. Indeed, Weber's notion of the increasing subordination of individual behavior to a bureaucratic imperative brought about by the ever increasing rationalization of society implies a telos for modern society, a criticism often leveled against Marx. Does this subordination of the individual to the "rationalization process" help explain why those who have been influenced by a Weberian approach tend to play down or neglect ideology when discussing state formation?

Leaving aside the thorny issue of the teleology implied in Weber's notions of the modern state and society, what is the derivation of the norms and goals that are implied in his criteria for the modern state? Antonio Gramsci would argue that such norms and goals are derived from historical myths, myths that constitute a selective reading of the past. What explains their selectivity? It is precisely that myths, no matter how irrational, are usually not intended to benefit all sectors of society but rather the interests of a selected segment of that society. While notions such as "manifest destiny," "white man's burden," and "Aryan race" presented the illusion of being in the national interest, in reality they cloaked the interests of specific groups that had the most to benefit from these myths. Put differently, myths have to be created, and usually are created, for a reason. They frequently reflect social class or other group interests. It is not at all self-evident that the norms and goals that provide the underpinnings of Weber's definition of the modern state are ideologically neutral. The liberal notion of legitimate authority stemming from a social contract, the Marxist notion of authority rooted in the dictatorship of the proletariat, or Weber's notion of rational-legal authority can all be seen as much as myth as an objective description of the modern state.

The focus on rationality implied in power elite, instrumentalist and structuralist Marxist, Weberian and rational choice theories of the state all fail to take adequate account of the role of myths in state formation. Myths imply that the state was not created in a historical vacuum, as assumed by Weberian and rational choice variants of liberal theory. In other words, the state must be seen as emerging from a historical process of struggle. Just as Gramsci highlighted the efforts of the northern industrial bourgeoisie to disseminate the myth of a unified Italian state and culture during the Risorgimento, so groups that have dominated the Iraqi and Kuwaiti states have been engaged in the same process. Again, the focus on myth still leaves the question of class somewhat fluid. Despite the dissemination of the myth of the Italian state by the industrial bourgeoisie, actual control of the state bureaucracy remained largely in the hands of rural landowners from the south. While myths underlying the formation of states have a class component, the class that formulates the myth may not be synonymous with the class or class alliance that actually controls the state apparatus.

Statecraft, Historical Memory, and Popular Culture in Iraq

How then has the state in Arab oil-producing countries attempted to appropriate the past, and what are the intended outcomes of such appropriation? In Iraq, the main concern of the state has been to erase confessional and tribal loyalties from political consciousness. Under the al-Sabahs, the main effort of the Kuwaiti state was not to eradicate tribal identities but rather to channel them in directions that it saw as serving its own interests in promoting a paternalistic modern welfare state.

Iraq is unique in that it is the only country of which we are aware in which the president heads a "Project for the Rewriting of History." The ostensible reason is a valid one.[11] Iraqi historians claim that Western Orientalists have attempted to reduce modern Iraqi history to a conflict between the sunni north and the shi'i south in an effort to perpetuate social and political divisiveness, thereby keeping Iraq weak and divided, especially given its oil reserves that are critical to the West's economy. Weak and divided, Iraq would never be able to promote national development or challenge the West. Iraqis argue that Western efforts to establish an independent state for the country's Kurdish minority are rooted not in sympathy for the Kurds but rather in the fact that the northern portion of the country that they occupy is rich in oil. These fears may be well grounded. One scenario that emerged after the August 1990 seizure of Kuwait was the possibility of not only the destruction of the Iraqi military and the toppling of Saddam Husayn by an American-led invasion force but also the subsequent division of Iraq through the creation of an independent Kurdish state and seizure of parts of its territory by Turkey, Syria and Iran.[12]

The Iraqi state's efforts to promote a particular historical memory are directed at reducing the religious consciousness of the populace at large or, more precisely, marginalizing those who would seek to impose an Islamic discourse on Iraqi political life. At first glance this might seem to represent merely an attempt to reduce the power of religiously based radical challenges to the state's authority such as the al-Da'wa al-Islamiya (the Islamic Call). Such an interpretation would be misleading. Historically, the shi'i south has been oriented both economically and culturally toward Iran. The fertile Tigris and Euphrates river basin, which has allowed for extensive agricultural cultivation in southern Iraq, has also tended to produce a somewhat inner-directed cultural orientation. Thus efforts to produce a secular understanding of Arab history constitute more than simply the attempt to undermine system-challenging movements. Rather they represent an attempt to reorient political and social consciousness away from both Iran and the Tigris-Euphrates river basin toward the Iraqi nation-state as a whole.

This nationalist dimension can be found in one of the great debates that has been a consistent fixture in Arab political discourse, namely the question of the relationship between written tradition (*al-turath*) and oral or folk tradition (*al-turath al-sha°bi*). This debate is linked to a concern of how to conceptualize the period prior to the Prophet Muhammad's Revelation in the early seventh century A.D. How are the Arabs who lived before the Islamic Revelation to be viewed? This question is important since the Arabs of the pre-Islamic Arabian Peninsula enjoyed a rich culture, the most prominent characteristic of which was poetry, especially the *al-mu°allaqat*. Most Islamic thinkers came to look at this period with disdain as reflected in the term by which it has come to be known, *al-jahiliya*, the period of "ignorance." For Muslim thinkers, particularly those linked to the Umayyad and °Abbassid states, to have glorified the pre-Islamic period would tacitly deny the argument that it was Islam that accounted for the political, military and cultural achievements of the early Arab empires.

One of the central arguments used against those who lived in the *al-jahiliya* period was that they did not possess a written tradition and hence were less civilized than Arabs who possessed God's revelation in the form of the written Qur'an. The text thus became an important symbol of "civilization" or development, especially because the language of that text, classical Arabic, was the language of revelation. Any "corruption" of that language in the use of colloquial oral folk traditions is seen as blasphemous and an affront to God. The written word constituted proof of a logical structure of mind as reflected in the codification of norms governing the behavior of individuals and the state. The Arabs of the *al-jahiliya* period may have offered aesthetic beauty in their *qasa'id* (poetic verse), but theirs was not an ordered civilization. A subtext of this discourse was that the tribes of pre-Islamic Arabia were both nomadic and in a state of constant conflict that contrasted sharply with their unification under the banner of Islam within prospering urban areas such as Mecca, al-Madina, Kufa, Basra, Damascus, and Baghdad. Yet another subtext is the implicit assertion of the superiority of urban over desert life.

Placed in a modern context, the grounding of Arab history in Islam entails an implicit marginalization of Arabs who are illiterate, nonurban, and tribesmen. This interpretation of Islam is still dominant in Saudi Arabia, which is the wealthiest of all Arab oil-producing states. In Iraq, however, the state has rejected this interpretation of the past. Baᶜthist historiography does not refer to Arabs of Arabia before the seventh century as part of *al-jahiliya* but rather as simply "the Arabs before Islam" (*al-ᶜarab qabla al-islam*).[13] This change in terminology has profound implications; it implicitly argues that Arabs during all historical periods exist on an equal cultural footing. Furthermore, many Iraqi scholars have refuted the assertion that, because of the lack of written tradition, Arabs of the pre-Islamic period were lacking a rational mind. Indeed, the argument is made that through their poetry, the Arabs of pre-Islamic Arabia offered a coherent and empirically valid accounting of their history, of their social relations, and of their relations to their physical environment. Poetry formed the "ideology" or social cement that gave this society its specific character.[14]

The favorable manner in which the pre-Islamic Arab period is viewed by officially sponsored Iraqi historiography is meant to highlight another element crucial to state formation. Pre-Islamic poetry was largely concerned with the ecology of the desert in which the Arabs of the Arabian Peninsula lived. From this emphasis, modern Iraqi intellectuals stress the connection to the land and hence the "nationalist" orientation of early Arab society.[15] In this manner, the positive light in which pre-Islamic society is viewed provides the intellectual underpinnings for emphasizing a modern notion of nationalism. It strikes another blow against Islamically based ideologies of state formation, because the question of land is one that both educated and illiterate Arabs can grasp more readily than the more amorphous concept of a Muslim community that includes peoples from distant, non-Arab societies.

Another example of the state's appropriation of the past is the central role played by the thinker Abu ᶜUthman ᶜUmar ibn Bahr al-Jahidh (A.D. 776–869), usually known simply as al-Jahidh. One of Iraq's most prominent publishing houses is named after him, and countless annotated volumes of his writings are readily available throughout the country. He is attractive to the Baᶜth because he lived during the ᶜAbbasid empire when Baghdad was the center of the Arabo-Islamic world and because he followed the Muᶜtazilite doctrine (*madhhab*) of Islam. As the Muᶜtazilites used rational thinking in Islamic jurisprudence and philosophy (*fiqh*), modern Iraqi historians and folklorists give al-Jahidh a prominent position in their works because a basic tenet of Ba°thist ideology is secularism which is equated with Mu°tazilite rationalism.

Another reason for the popularity of al-Jahidh among a wide variety of thinkers drawn from Islamic and Arab heritage is the fact that he expressed his views through what Arabs refer to as "popular" culture, or what might be called the folklore of the time. Tales, sayings, riddles, proverbs, and the general setting of his writings deal with the life of the poor and the daily affairs of the common people. His writings thus are highly symbolic in the context of everyday life. Ba°th party intellectuals prefer to inject al-Jahidh into contemporary social life because, by using him, they can appeal to the "common man" both in Iraq and in the Arab world at large.

The symbols used by al-Jahidh still retain meaning in contemporary Iraqi society since they are simple and familiar, relating to eating habits, social interaction (especially visiting relatives and neighbors), folk tales, and proverbs and riddles that still survive as part of contemporary Arab culture. In this manner, his writings are not only entertaining and anecdotal but also simple and richly laden with symbols that the state can manipulate for its own ends. His appeal to a common Arab heritage with which the common person can relate coincides with the Ba°th party's espousal of a pan-Arab nationalism. That al-Jahidh, who was from humble origins, lived through the patronage of the rulers of the °Abbasid Empire seems also to have influenced Ba°thist interest in him. Although he often satirized members of the ruling hierarchy, he never suggested in his writings that their authority be challenged. Thus he provides an appropriate role model for the contemporary Iraqi citizen, someone who is mobilized but not necessary privy to decision-making power.

al-Jahidh wrote more than ten books and over twenty-five essays, and it is instructive to examine those works that the Iraqi state has chosen to republish with annotations. Most of his work was commissioned by court officials of the Caliphate in Baghdad, and many are satirical in nature. Two works chosen for publication are *al-bukhala'* (*The Misers*)[16] and *al-bursan wa-l-ᶜurjan wa-l-ᶜumyan wa-l-hawlan* (*The Lepers, the Lame, the Blind and the Cross-eyed*).[17]

In *The Misers*, al-Jahidh uses a wide variety of anecdotes to describe the character, life-style, and even ethos of Baghdad's misers. Mentioning by name a number of contemporary people who were presumably well known in the community, he engages these people in lengthy debates where they attempt to exalt the virtues of miserliness against those of generosity. It would not escape the Iraqi reader that al-Jahidh is treating generosity, one of the core principles of the Arab value system. Further examination indicates that the misers and those who exalt the virtues of miserliness are non-Arabs (*ᶜajam*), mostly Persian. The few Arabs who are misers are depicted as corrupt and despicable while none of the *ᶜajam* possess the quality of virtue.

It is easy to see why the Iraqi state finds al-Jahidh politically attractive, given its continuing conflict with Iran, even after the truce of 1988. However, this factor alone would not explain why his writings became popular even before the Iran-Iraq war began in 1980. In broader terms, the state's emphasis on al-Jahidh is an attempt to utilize Arab heritage to promote an Arab and Iraqi identity that accords with the ideology of the ruling Baᶜth party. In choosing al-Jahidh and other prominent Arabs from the ᶜAbbasid period, such as al-Hariri and al-Wasiti, the Iraqi state seeks to play upon the theme that the greatness of the ᶜAbbasid empire in its early days stemmed from its purely Arab quality and that its decline began once it was "adulterated" by the influx of minorities, such as the Persians and the Turks. While manipulating al-Jahidh for Arab nationalist ends, the state is, at the same time, potentially promoting political divisiveness because it is implicitly arguing that Kurds and shiᶜis are not "real" Iraqis. The Kurds do not speak Arabic, while the shiᶜa share a confessionalism with Iraq's historical archenemy, Iran. In this instance, Baᶜthist ideology seeks to repress rather than confront the problems of social difference that face Iraqi society.[18] The statecraft being employed here may be effective in promoting state formation in the short term but may ultimately be divisive in the longer term.

The Iraqi state has given added legitimacy to secularism and the "respectability" of pre-Islamic Arab culture by promoting the works of al-Wasiti.[19] Yahya bin Mahmud al-Wasiti, who lived in the seventh century A.H., was an artist known for his decorations in miniatures of the margins of al-Hariri's book, *al-maqamat*, that contained essays dealing with the feats of vagabonds during the ᶜAbbasid period. In addition to focusing on the folkloric material that depicts the life of the common people of Baghdad, the Iraqi state also focuses upon three elements in al-Wasiti's works. First, the works provide a pictorial representation of the life of the common people of Baghdad in the past that bears a strong resemblance to the present. Second, the drawings are portrayed as representing an Arab school of drawing that existed prior to the Islamic era and that has continued until the present. Third, the fact that pictorial art existed during the ᶜAbbasid period demonstrates the strength of secularism in Arab culture, as sunni Islam forbids pictorial representation. The Iraqis also use the appearance of certain flowers in al-Wasiti's drawings as proof of the continuity of Iraqi culture from the Sumerian period because such flowers are found in Sumerian inscriptions.[20] The state commissioned the artist Ismaᶜil Fattah al-Turk to create a statue of al-Hariri. Inaugurated during the al-Wasiti Festival in 1972, the bronze sculpture was erected at the al-Zahra Park in Baghdad.[21]

The most forthright statement of the principles that govern the reexamination of history and popular culture are set forth in a study by Saddam Husayn entitled *hawla kitabat al-tarikh* (*On the Writing of History*), published by the Ministry of Culture and Arts in 1979.[22] Saddam's contribution consists of the texts of four short speeches; the remainder of the volume contains essays by twenty-three Iraqi scholars who elaborate upon the themes set forth by the Iraqi president.

In outlining his approach to history, Saddam offers eleven "theses." He begins by asking the central question: For whom is history written? (*li man yuktab al-tarikh?*), implying in this question that history should have a purpose and not be written in the abstract. Second, he asks how history is written. He answers that history should be written not to glorify individuals at the expense of society but rather to glorify individuals who, as martyrs, serve the cause of those living in the present. Saddam's third "thesis" is that the writing of history is a social phenomenon where the individual interacts with society under the paternalistic guidance of the leader of the state. Here he uses tribal imagery to convey the notion of "democratic leadership" because the tribal shaykh is always readily available to his fellow tribesmen. However, this tribal imagery also incorporates the autocratic paternalism of the tribal leader.

The arguments offered in *On the Writing of History* emphasize a view of history that is purely instrumental. Saddam is explicit in affirming that history should be written to serve the interests of Iraqi society as defined by Ba‛thist ideology. History should always be written with specific audiences in mind, and these audiences should be presented with "incontrovertible facts." Thus history becomes totally fluid and the historian's work highly politicized.

Perhaps most interesting from the perspective of state formation is Saddam's seventh "thesis," that history should serve the national and regional interests of Ba‛thist ideology. Here an attempt is made to overcome the contradiction between the Ba‛thist assertion of Iraq's Arab character and its large minority population. History should serve the ends of pan-Arab nationalism (*al-qawmiya al-‛arabiya*) while simultaneously countering the dangers of regionalism (*al-qutriya*). The historian should employ symbols that demonstrate that the "Iraqi region" is part of the Arab nation and that the part relates to the whole, but without invoking parochialism and separatism on the part of the non-Arab minorities such as the Kurds (many of whom have been engaged in armed rebellion against the government). Saddam states that one should say that "*al-qutr al-‛iraqi juz min al-watan al-‛arabi*" ("the Iraqi region is part of the Arab homeland") rather than, "*al-sha‛b al-‛iraqi juz min al-umma al-‛arabiya*" ("the people of Iraq are part of the Arab nation") because the latter formulation invokes the anger and resentment of the Kurds and other Iraqi but non-Arab citizens. By establishing that all Iraqis are citizens of Iraq and showing that Iraq is part of the Arab nation, the issue of social difference is supposedly transcended.

This approach to Iraq's minority problem, Saddam argues, should be synchronized with the state's policy of granting autonomy to the Kurds. While it is difficult to envision how the populace would accept Saddam's assertion that within the Iraqi region there are no Arabs or Kurds, only citizens of Iraq, the symbolic manner in which he proposes to overcome ethnic differences is noteworthy. For example, if Kurds are conducting a folk dance in their homeland in the north, they should wear their traditional headdress, *al-lafa*. If, on the other hand, Arabs are performing a dance in their own area, they should wear their headdress, *al-ʿiqal*. However, if both groups are dancing together in a national festival in the capital, then Iraqis should produce new folkloric symbols that are truly Iraqi in character. It would still be possible to refer to dances from Kurdish and Arab areas but without the use of overt symbols that evoke separatism. This is an example of how the Baʿth feel tradition should be invented to serve specific national needs.

Statecraft, Historical Memory, and Popular Culture in Kuwait

Efforts of the Kuwaiti state to appropriate history and popular culture differ from those used in Iraq. As noted, one reason for this was the lack of a strong nationalist movement in Kuwait during British colonial occupation. Whereas the Iraqi state seeks to mobilize large segments of the populace in support of Baʿthist ideology (by having large numbers of Kurdish students spend their summer vacations in the south and Arab students spend their vacations in the Kurdish region, for example), the Kuwaiti state attempts to manipulate historical memory more to demobilize potential political activism in order to preclude challenges to its authority.

Unlike Iraq, which possesses a rich historical and cultural heritage, Kuwait lacks a "Golden Age" in which the state can ground itself. As the al-Sabahs come from a nomadic tribal background, they cannot appropriate symbols drawn from Arab *turath* from the Umayyad and ʿAbbasid periods or from archaeological ruins, because the only excavated sites at present in Kuwait date from the ancient Greeks. Furthermore, the sedentary communities that existed in recent history in the gulf were controlled by rival tribal groups such as the Shammar who, in the form of the al-Rashid lineage, controlled eastern Arabia during the eighteenth century. The gulf's Islamic history has also been problematic for the Kuwaiti state. The most prominent Islamic movements in the Gulf were the Zanj, the Zot, and the Carmathians (al-qaramita). However, each of these movements was unacceptable in the al-Sabahs' efforts to craft a new Kuwaiti identity as the basis for a modern state. The Zanj movement constituted a black slave revolt. The Zot represented a nonindigenous population that originated in Southern India. The Carmathians were an extremely egalitarian Islamic sect that dismissed private property and decried social and gender inequality. Thus to turn to Islam would have meant basing the state either in radical authority-challenging movements or in non-Arab Muslims from outside the gulf. The gulf region does not feature prominently in Arab turath. Small city-states and trading centers have existed only for the last two centuries. These were composed of merchant communities that were engaged in trade, shipbuilding, and pearling and were controlled by rival tribal groups or even dominated by Persians.

As it lacks a past that can readily be appropriated, the Kuwaiti state instead has emphasized ethnohistory and the oral tradition. In this context, folklore assumed greater importance than written history per se. This difference helps explain why the Kuwaiti Ministry of Information has sponsored such a large number of studies on folklore as well as why the state has channeled large amounts of funds into the establishment of folklore museums, such as the Bayt Sadu and Kuwaiti National Museum. The focus on Kuwaiti folklore is linked, however, to a larger entity in both the cultural and political sense, namely the Arab Gulf. The assertion of the unitary nature of gulf folklore thus becomes a means for linking Kuwait and the other small gulf states, all of which are also ruled by related hereditary families drawn from tribal backgrounds. It also is used to legitimize the emerging political integration of the gulf that has already been institutionalized to a limited degree in the form of a regional defense organization, the Gulf Cooperation Council.

The main theme in state-sponsored studies, such as *madkhal fi dirasat al-fulklur al-kuwayti* (*Introduction to the Study of Kuwaiti Folklore*) by Safwat Kamal, director of the Kuwaiti Folk Museum,[23] *tarikh al-ghaws ʿala al-luʾluʾ fi-l-kuwayt wa-l-khalij al-ʿarabi* (*The History of Pearl Diving in Kuwait and the Arab Gulf*) by Sayf Marzuq al-Shamlan,[24] and *tarikh al-kuwayt* (*The History of Kuwait*) by ʿAbd al-ʿAziz al-Rashid,[25] is that both Kuwait and the gulf had a thriving economy prior to the discovery of oil. One of the most important symbols is that of the sea. Since economic activities centered around the sea—pearl diving, shipbuilding, fishing, and trading—produced a rich culture in the form of sea songs, poetry, and epic tales that developed in the coffeehouses (*al-maqahi al-shaʿbiya*)[26] along the gulf, Kuwait can claim to have contributed to a larger Arab culture and heritage. Furthermore, the argument that the al-Sabahs rule only by virtue of their control of the country's oil wealth is thereby undermined, as no one can say that the history of the modern Kuwaiti state began with the discovery of oil. Indeed, one searches in vain for any symbols relating to oil in official state iconography. The ultimate importance of these studies is the enhancement of the power of the Kuwaiti state and the legitimacy of al-Sabah rule. It is nevertheless ironic that, of the two types of folklore that have been emphasized by the state, British professionals have been the most important source of documenting Beduin life while Egyptian scholars have been the main source of folklore that relates to the sea.

If ethnohistory provides the broader framework whereby the Kuwaiti state seeks to appropriate historical memory in order to legitimize its rule in pan-Arab terms, the synchretism of tribal and "modern" symbols is used to help solidify the power of the state at the domestic level. This is evident in a study published by the Kuwaiti government in 1972 entitled *maʿ dhikrayatuna al-kuwaytiya* (*Our Memories of Kuwait*) by Ayub Husayn.[27] "Folkloric" in nature, it is purely descriptive, dealing with three topics that ostensibly would seem to have little relationship to state formation: the traditional Kuwaiti house, potable water, and disease.

In addition to discussing these topics, the author states that his intention is to preserve those aspects of Kuwaiti tradition and popular culture that are ignored by the mass media in favor of topics such as pearl diving, traditional dress, and wedding customs. Ayub argues for the need to document the past in written texts, by which he means the period prior to oil production, and to accept that the past contains both positive and negative elements.[28] Overall the volume represents a conscious effort of the state to create a "popular (folk) heritage" (al-turath al-sha'bi) to which the "masses" can relate by using symbols that are considered traditional and authentic (asil), that is, not Western in origin, and to stress that Kuwait had a history, albeit one not without problems, prior to oil production.

Why, however, does the author focus on the traditional Kuwaiti house, potable water, and disease? Prior to the onset of oil production, life in Kuwait is portrayed as harsh because the populace suffered from poor housing, an inadequate water supply, and numerous diseases and superstition. Through the use of oil wealth, the Kuwaiti state had been able to foster extensive development projects that provide Kuwaiti citizens with social services, such as housing, water and medical care, all at no cost. While the author never makes an overt comparison between the pre- and post-oil eras, the clear implication is that the Kuwaiti state is acting as paterfamilias to the populace. As such, there is a synchretism between the traditional role of the paramount shaykh as provider for the tribe and the modern role of the Kuwaiti state as personified in the amir as benefactor of the nation. Clearly, the intellectual's role is to once again "invent tradition."[29] However, Ayub's study, more than any other, goes furthest in symbolically integrating oil wealth, tribal values, and the functions of the modern state.

Knowledge and Power in Arab Oil-Producing Countries

One of the key questions that arises from this chapter is the extent to which the state's efforts to promote a particular historical memory and understanding of popular culture have been successful. In what ways have the extensive efforts of the state to appropriate history and popular culture actually enhanced its power? Since both Iraqis and Kuwaitis have rallied in the support of the state following the August 1990 invasion of Kuwait, at least some of that support, we argue, stems from state efforts to define the types of national identity that we have been analyzing. However, a precise answer is not possible at this time. Nevertheless, it should be noted that an "instrumentalist" perspective on this question has numerous shortcomings. In other words, the processes that have been examined here cannot be reduced to a material imperative. Intellectuals do not engage in the "rewriting of history" or the "invention of tradition" solely for monetary gain (although obviously there is no doubt that monetary gain is often a significant motivation). Nor do the masses accept the state's interpretation of their heritage, both written and oral, merely because of the benefits that have been bestowed upon them as the result of oil wealth.

In Iraq and Kuwait, as well as in other parts of the Arab world, there is an appetite among the educated classes for the type of writings discussed here. For example, the Iraqi journal *Majallat al-Turath al-Sha°bi* (*The Journal of Folk Culture*) quickly sells out when it appears in bookstores and sidewalk stands. Its readership is by no means limited to prosperous Iraqis. Books dealing with history and culture also have a wide readership. The appeal of these types of state-sponsored writings counteracts the corrosive influence many Arab societies feel results from the onslaught of Western culture in the form of television programs, movies, clothing, and technological innovations. Many Arabs blame these aspects of Western culture for promoting a consumer-oriented culture in which traditional Arab values of generosity, hospitality, familial solidarity, respect for authority, and sexual probity have been seriously undermined. The state's efforts to appropriate the past for its own ends fall on fertile grounds, given a populace that is unnerved by the rapid pace of social change. The fact that the populace at large seems so willing, at least at a superficial level, to accept state-sponsored interpretations of Arab history and culture seems to indicate that there is a tremendous desire to find

answers to the questions of who is an Arab and to define what sep-
arates Arab culture from an ever expanding global culture that is
being defined by the advanced industrialized countries of the West.

One aspect that has not received significant attention here is the
state's relationship to the illiterate sectors of Arab society. To pose
this question is to gain further insight into the success of the state's
efforts to transmit its definition of society to the populace at large.
The widespread popularity of television and radio programs in
Iraq and Kuwait that deal with "popular" (folk) poetry, songs, children's games, wedding patterns, traditional dress, proverbs, and
traditional crafts, as well as the numerous publications dealing with
such subjects,[30] points to the need to see the processes that have
been analyzed here as part of a larger totality. In other words, the
"invention of tradition" is not limited to the "high culture" of journal articles and books. Rather it surrounds the ordinary citizen's
daily life in the form of radio and television programs, movies,
newspaper articles, festivals, socialization in elementary and secondary education, and symbols propagated in officially sanctioned
posters and photographs of those who control the state, especially
as these officials interact with the populace.

Oil wealth provides a beginning for this analysis because, without the tremendous revenues derived from the sale of oil, neither
the Iraqi nor the Kuwaiti state would have been able to engage in
such a massive effort to promote an ideologically mediated reexamination of the past. In terms of a theory of political economy,
we are suggesting that a deeper understanding of the processes
that have been outlined seems to offer a method for grasping how
the state's control of the economic surplus is actually translated
into greater political power through achieving conformity to its
ideological vision of society. Is not, therefore, a political economy
that is devoid of a subjective component problematic? If this study
is any indication, a political economy of state formation seems to
require the expansion of existing paradigms to include not only
questions of surplus appropriation, class formation, and bureaucratic and military power but also those of ideology, culture, and
social identity.

NOTES

1. Efriam Karsh, "In Baghdad, Politics Can Be Lethal," *New York Times Magazine*, September 30, 1980, 100.

2. ʿIssam al-Khafaji, *al-dawla wa-l-tatawwur al-ra'smali fi-l-ʿiraq, 1967–1978* [*The State and Capitalist Development in Iraq, 1967–1978*] (Cairo: Dar al-Mustaqbal al-ʿArabi, 1983), esp. 65–85, 87–105.

3. *New York Times*, October, 1990.

4. Hasan Hanafi, "*limadha ghab mabhath al-tarikh fi turathina al-qadim?*" ["Why Has Historical Research Been Missing from Our Ancient Heritage?"], *al-Fikr al-ʿArabi* 27 (May–June, 1982): 97–98.

5. Michel Foucault, *The Archaeology of Knowledge* (New York: Harper & Row, 1972).

6. See, for example, the five-volume series edited by Samir ʿAbd al-Karim, *adwaʿ ʿala al-haraka al-shuyuʿiya fi-l-ʿiraq* [*Perspectives on the Communist Movement in Iraq*] (Beirut: Dar al-Mirsad, n.d.).

7. Clifford Geertz, "Ideology as a Cultural System," in *Ideology and Discontent*, ed. D. Apter (New York: The Free Press, 1964), 62–64.

8. Samir Amin, *The Arab Nation* (London: Zed Press, 1978), 10–23.

9. Charles Tilly (ed.), *The Formation of National States in Western Europe* (Princeton, NJ: Princeton University Press, 1975).

10. Max Weber, *Economy and Society*, vol. 2 (Berkeley and Los Angeles: University of California Press, 1978), 926–32, 953–54.

11. For an extensive critique of Western Orientalism from an Arab perspective, see the special series "Orientalism" published in *Afaq ʿArabiya* 1–3 (January 1987, February 1987, and 1989). Among the many excellent essays, see Muhsin Jasim al-Musawi, "*al-istishraq al-siyasi: fardiyatuhu wa istintajatuhu*" ["Political Orientalism: Its Hypotheses and Conclusions"], no. 3 (1989): 4–13; and Hasan Muhyi al-Din al-Alusi, "*sura naqdiya li-l-istishraq al-taqlidi wa-l-jadid*" ["A Critical Overview of Traditional and Neo-Orientalism"], no. 3 (1989): 32–76.

12. *New York Times*, October 21, 1990.

13. See, for example, Nuri Hamudi al-Qaysi, *al-shiʿr wa-l-tarikh* [*Poetry and History*] (Baghdad: Dar al-Hurriya li-l-Tibaʿa, 1980), esp. chap. 2, "*al-shiʿr al-ʿarabi qabla al-islam*" ["Arabic Poetry Before Islam"], 29–50.

14. Ibid., 29.

15. Ibid., 30.

16. Annotated by Taha al-Hajiri (Cairo: Dar al-Maʿarif, n.d.).

17. Edited and annotated by ʿAbd al-Salam Muhammad Harun, (Beirut: Dar al-Taliʿa li-l-Tibaʿa wa-l-Nashr, 1982), for the Iraqi Ministry of Culture and Information (Baghdad: al-Rashid Publishing House, 1982).

18. See also ʿAbd al-Sahib al-ʿAqabi, *al-mawruth al-shaʿbi fi athar al-jahidh* [*Folk Heritage in the Works of al-Jahidh*] (Baghdad: Ministry of Culture and In-

formation, Dar al-Hurriya Press, 1976). This volume was published on the occasion of the conference "Folklore in the Service of the Arab Struggle" in Baghdad in 1977.

19. See the special issue of *al-Riwaq*, no. 15, 1985 (published in Baghdad by the Iraqi Ministry of Culture and Information). This issue was published on the occasion of the annual al-Wasiti Festival, which is sponsored by the Iraqi Ministry of Culture and Information. It contains the following articles: Nuri al-Rawi, "*al-wasiti bayn al-ramz wa-l-haqiqa*" ["al-Wasiti Between Symbol and Reality"], 2–3; "*madrasat baghdad fi-l-taswir al-islami*" ["The Baghdadi School in Islamic Representational Art"], 4–19; ʿIsa Salman, "*al-madrasa al-ʿarabiya fi-l-taswir al-islami*" ["The Arab School in Islamic Representational Art"], 20–23; Shakir Hasan al-Saʿid, "*al-mawqif al-thaqafi li yahya bin mahmud al-wasiti*" ["The Cultural Perspective of Yahiya Bin Mahmud al-Wasiti"], 24–28; Muhammad Makkiya, "*turath al-rasm al-bagdadi*" ["The Heritage of Baghdadi Drawing"], 29–41; Nuri al-Rawi, "*malamih madrasat baghdad li taswir al-kitab*" ["The Characteristics of the Baghdadi School of Miniature Art"], 42–47; Dirar al-Qadu, "*madrasat al-musul li-l-taswir*" ["The Musul School of Representational Art"], 48–52; Ahmad ʿAbd al-Majid, "*qiraʾa fi jaridat al-wasiti*" ["A Reading of the Journal of al-Wasiti"], 53–55; Jamal Hashim ʿAli, "*al-wasiti fi mahrajanihi al-thalith*" ["al-Wasiti's Third Festival"], 56–59.

20. Nuri al-Rawi, 44.

21. *al-Riwaq*, inside cover.

22. (Baghdad: Dar al-Hurriya li-l-Tibaʿa, 1979). For Saddam's contributions, see pp. 7–9, 13–19, 23–26, 28–40. See also another pamphlet by Saddam Husayn, *al-turath wa-l-muʿasara* [*Heritage and Modernity*] (Baghdad: Dar al-Hurriya li-l-Tibaʿa, 1977).

23. (Kuwait: Ministry of Information, 1973).

24. (Kuwait: Government Press, 1975, 1978), vols. 1 and 2, respectively.

25. (Beirut: Dar Maktabat al-Hayat, 1971).

26. *al-maqahi al-shaʿbiya* (folk coffeehouses) differ from *al-diwaniya* (the guesthouse) in that the coffeehouses belong to the sea tradition and the pre-oil working class while the guesthouses belong to the urban merchant–tribal ruling class. Thus while the coffeehouses relate to the past by appealing to the sea tradition, they also reaffirm the social standing of the old working class today by contrasting them with those who belong to the guesthouse, the merchant–tribal ruling class. The folk coffeehouses are relegated to the position of "past relics" and folkloric representations of the past. Unlike the guesthouses that are fully functioning institutions in contemporary Kuwait, they are treated and perceived as "living museums" that bear little relationship to modern life.

27. (Kuwait: Government Press, n.d.)

28. Pages 9–11.

29. See Eric Hobsbawm and Terence Ranger (eds.), *The Invention of Tradition* (Cambridge: Cambridge University Press, 1987).

30. The following works are a representative sample of publications dealing with these topics: Sayf Marzuq al-Shamlan, *min tarikh al-kuwayt* [*From the History of Kuwait*] (Cairo: Maktba°at Nahdat Misr, 1959); Ya°qub °Abd al-°Aziz al-Rashid, *al-kuwayt fi mizan al-haqiqa wa-l-tarikh* [*Kuwait between Truth and History*] (Kuwait: n.p., 1963); Safwat Kamal, *madkhal li-dirasat al-fulklur al-kuwayti* [*An Introduction to the Study of Kuwaiti Folklore*], (Kuwait: Ministry of Information, 1973); Muhammad Ahmad al-Nishaymi, *al-zawaj qadiman fi-l-kuwayt* [*Marriage in Kuwait in the Past*], (Kuwait: Dar al-Tali°a, 1974); Safwat Kamal, *min °adat wa taqalid al-zawaj fi-l-kuwayt* [*Marriage in Ancient Times in Kuwait*] (Kuwait: Ministry of Information, Center for the Protection of Folk Arts, n.d.); Ayub Husayn al-Ayub, *mukhtarat min al-lahja al-kuwaytiya* [*Selections from the Kuwaiti Dialect*] (Kuwait: Maqhawi Press, 1982); °Abdallah al-Nuri, *al-'amthal al-darija fi-l-kuwayt* [*Common Proverbs in Kuwait*], 2 vols. (Beirut: Qalfat Press, 1976). See also a study in English dealing with Beduin culture (as opposed to the sea tradition) by Jennifer M. Scarce, *The Evolution of Culture in Kuwait* (Edinburgh: Her Majesty's Stationery Office, 1985). It is interesting to note that, compared to the plethora of books published on the sea tradition and on urban Kuwaiti folk culture in Arabic, the only work dealing with Beduins and the desert nomadic tradition was commissioned by the Kuwaiti government, written by a British subject, and published by a Scottish Museum.

6. Power and Representation: Social Change, Gender Relations, and the Education of Women in Kuwait

Noura al-Falah

The tremendous wealth produced by oil has generated dramatic and rapid social change in Kuwait. One of the most significant aspects of this change has been in the "traditional" education system for both men and women. This chapter focuses on the position of women in Kuwaiti society as it has been affected by modern education. Dramatic social change has taken place in the position of women. By shattering the barriers between the private and the public spheres, education has allowed women to escape the confines of the private domain, the household. They have been able to enter the educational system and then to use their education as a bridge to enter the job market. These changes, though, have not been matched by changes in the patriarchal ideology or in the system of social values.

The process of modern education for men and women was not caused by oil; in fact, it preceded the discovery of oil. Modern education began after Kuwait signed a formal treaty with Britain in 1899. As a result, Kuwait became a protectorate through its formal political incorporation into the British empire and through its economic incorporation into the world market. A Western system of formal education was introduced for men in 1912 and for women in 1938.[1] As in many other colonies of the British empire, the formal education was geared toward the production of a group of "educated" people who could meet the clerical demands of the colonial bureaucracy and the local merchants. Later in the twentieth century oil wealth accelerated an educational process that had already been set in motion earlier.

As one consequence of the introduction of Western education in

Kuwait, a degree of equality developed between men and women in the 1950s. This equality provided social mobility for both. Prior to this change, Kuwaiti society could be characterized as patriarchal, patrilineal, and patrilocal. For lack of a better term and at the risk of using Orientalist terminology, I shall call the ideology that characterized Kuwaiti society "Arab patriarchal," a term that will be more fully elaborated later. Such an ideology stood in opposition to the ideology of modernization. This chapter raises a series of questions that examine how the process of social change affected the position of women in Kuwaiti society. To what extent has the traditional Arab patriarchal ideology functioned to prohibit women from totally breaking away from the confines of segregation? Has the new ideology of modernization introduced through Western formal education and the creation of job opportunities outside the household created a significant change in traditional patriarchal attitudes, norms, and values? Can the two ideologies coexist, and, if so, what form of accommodation does this coexistence take? What is the effect of modernization through education on the traditional social structure of Kuwait? In cases of social mobility, how have the old elites resisted the encroachment of the new "middle class"? What role do women play in the new social structure that emerged after the onset of oil production?

The Arab Patriarchal System in Kuwait

In order to provide answers to these questions, it is necessary to understand Kuwaiti social structure prior to the onset of oil production, that is, during the late nineteenth and early twentieth centuries. This social structure was divided horizontally into two ecologically based sectors, one urban and one nomadic. And each of these sectors was divided vertically into two hierarchical social groups that might be called classlike. The urban sector was composed of a merchant ruling class and working class of pearl divers, seamen, and craftsmen. The nomadic beduin sector was composed of "noble" tribes and "vassal" tribes, with nobility being defined on the basis of patrilineal descent.

Women in Kuwait, as in any other society, do not form a homogenous social group because society is organized on the basis of class, tribal, and ethnic groups that are hierarchical and contain both sexes. To understand gender relations in Kuwait, one has to analyze specifically each class, tribal, and ethnic group. Women are not a class or a social group in themselves but rather part of classes or social groups. In turn, the structure of social groups in Kuwait needs to be analyzed as it relates to the political economy of the state, specifically the means of production. Within this relationship, gender relations can be understood from the perspective of the division of labor between the sexes.

Kuwaiti Social Structure Prior to the Onset of Oil Production

Prior to the onset of oil production, the Kuwaiti economy was linked to the world market through pearl diving, trade and seafaring. The colonial expansion of the West influenced the formation of the Kuwaiti state. Social change occurring after the onset of oil production can be viewed more appropriately as the continuation of incipient socioeconomic and political processes that began prior to oil's discovery. Oil revenues led to changes in the national educational system, which in turn affected gender relations, and were used to transform Kuwait into a modern welfare state. In order to understand how relations were affected, we must examine the socioeconomic background against which these changes took place, specifically the position of women in Kuwait prior to oil production.

The Urban Sector Prior to Oil Production

Prior to oil production the urban merchant ruling class and the seafaring–pearl diving–artisan class both adhered to traditional "Arab patriarchal" values. Dominant social values were patriarchal in the sense that authority was vested in older males, patrilineal in that descent was traced through males only, and patrilocal as residence after the formation of a nuclear family unit was with the husband's group. These values encouraged and even prescribed father's brother's daughter's marriage, or *bint ʿam* marriage.

Urban women were generally removed, through the practice of spatial and social segregation, from the tasks of primary production that were symbolically deemed important by society at large. The sexual division of labor reserved these tasks exclusively for men as "proper" male occupations. The important and exclusively male tasks consisted of serving coffee ceremonially at the guest house (*al-diwaniya*) and leaving the confines of the household to run errands and frequent the market (*al-suq*). Thus the values that determined the social division of labor made it taboo for urban women to leave the house. This social segregation restricted the number of males with whom women could interact. Only fathers, brothers, husbands, sons, the father's brother, the mother's brother, and grandfathers were permissible. Kinship relations formed the basis of urban Kuwaiti women's interaction with men. A woman would interact with such people as daughter, sister, wife, mother, father's brother's daughter (*bint ʿam*), father's sister's daughter (*bint ʿamma*), and son's wife (daughter-in-law). After puberty she was forbidden to interact with her father's brother's son (*ibn ʿam*) or any other of her male kin who were eligible to marry her. This segregation was further strengthened in that she was not even allowed to appear in front of such male kin without covering her face.

In traditional Kuwaiti society, the father's role involved traditionally defined rights and obligations of the "Arab patriarchal" system. This role was highlighted by specific processes of socialization and enculturation. These processes entailed discipline, parenting, upbringing (*tarbiya*), and counseling of his children. However, the father's relationship with his daughter entailed additional responsibilities. As women were regarded as totally incapable of being emancipated, they were placed under the complete control of their fathers. A woman had no right to make any decisions that affected her life, regardless of how trivial, without her father's consent. He even had the right to make decisions affecting his daughter without consulting her.

As a male, the son had the right to be the father's agent in dealing with the women of the household—even if the son was younger
than his sisters. If it happened that the family had no sons or if the
sons were underage, then the father's father (*al-jid*), the father's
brother (*al-ʿam*), or sometimes the mother's brother (*al-khal*)
could act on the father's behalf. Patriarchal responsibility was
transferred to the husband after marriage. In case of the absence
of the husband or his death, responsibility was transferred to his
sons in turn. The eldest son then became responsible for his mother
and sisters.

Spatial Dimensions of Gender Relations

One consequence of the discrimination between the sexes was
spacial segregation even inside the same household. Prior to oil
production, those Kuwaitis who were permitted to interact socially,
such as brother and sister or mother and son, were segregated
within the household. This reinforced female feelings of inferiority, based on a broader social value that pertained to social hierar-
chies. In Kuwaiti society, people of higher social rank did not interact socially with those of lower ranks and were thus segregated
from them. Social segregation between social groups was a way
to define through behavior the inferiority or superiority of one's
social position. As a result of segregation from their male kin, Kuwaiti women were made to feel socially inferior.

In pre-oil Kuwaiti society, people of lower rank did not interact
socially or even engage in conversation with those of higher rank.
This social segregation resulted in the development of distinct sub-
cultures for males and females, marked among other things by the
use of different vocabularies and dialects and the practice of distinct customs. One example of such distinct customs is the complete "control" of the supernatural world of spirits by women. In
this respect, women were recognized as having exclusive knowledge and expertise to deal in matters affecting health and psychological well-being through such rituals as the *zar*. Such different
cultural realms between males and females became institutional-

ized and, strangely enough, were in turn used as "proof" of the inferiority of women. Segregation was further employed in the structure of the Kuwaiti household, which customarily was comprised of three generations. The house was arranged to have a section for males and a section for females (al-harim). Members of each sex congregated in their respective section where even meals were consumed in the exclusive company of members of their own sex. Guests were also segregated on the basis of sex. Thus male guests were received in the male guest house (al-diwaniya). The segregation of women profoundly restricted their social and political awareness. Only men, because of their exclusive possession of the right to venture outside the household into the public domain, were socially and politically aware.

Women of the Merchant and Ruling Classes

Although both wealthy and working-class women were subject to the same patriarchal value system, women of the ruling class were further constrained by being forced to confine their activities to the privacy of the household. Their tasks included childbearing and child rearing. In wealthy households, servants and slaves were assigned manual tasks such as cooking, cleaning, and general housekeeping. Males performed the primary economic tasks outside the household, such as trade and governing. Servants and slaves of both sexes were considered to be members of the household. Female slaves performed household tasks, such as cooking and cleaning, and also helped with child rearing. Male slaves, on the other hand, performed tasks outside the household on behalf of their masters. These tasks included serving as bodyguards and collecting rents, fees, and the like from their master's clients.

Women in the Pearl Diving, Seafaring, and Crafts Sector

Unlike upper-class women, working-class women performed all the manual tasks within the household. Such tasks were not considered secondary and demeaning by the patriarchal value system as long as they were performed within the confines of the household. Working-class women also supplemented the income of their households by performing wage labor for upper-class households. Some women of poor families worked as nannies and servants in rich families. The preference, however, was for work that could be performed in the privacy of one's household, such as sewing, weaving, and dyeing. Women also raised livestock and chickens and earned money by selling these products outside the household. In selling these products, women went to the "women's market" (*suq al-harim*) where only women traders peddled their wares to buyers of both sexes. Usually a woman trader would try to conceal her identity by veiling in order not to appear to be breaking the taboo of leaving the confines of the household for the public sphere. Women whose husbands and sons were engaged in seafaring and pearl diving had an especially difficult time in conforming to the segregation taboo. Such women were forced by necessity to perform tasks in the public sphere prescribed only to men. By so doing, a woman would diminish the reputation of her family and lower the status of the household.

Beduin Women

Spatial segregation and the division of labor in beduin nomadic society differed from the urban setting. Beduin tribes in pre-oil Kuwaiti society were engaged in nomadic pastoralism, herding sheep, goats, and camels. In this sector women performed both domestic and economic tasks. In pastoralism, where the household is a production unit, most household tasks are linked directly to the primary means of production. Women were therefore full, active participants in the economic production process and directly contributed to the economic well-being of the household. In addition, they performed the traditional female tasks of childbearing, child rearing, and housekeeping, tasks disdained by men. Since they usually lived outdoors, beduin Kuwaiti women customarily wore the veil at all times. Living conditions made it difficult for them to have any real privacy from males. The veils used by beduin women were different from those used by their urban counterparts. Urban women used a transparent cloth as a veil over their faces, whereas beduin women used a mask that left the eyes uncovered. As they had to perform manual tasks, beduin women could not afford to obstruct their vision with a full veil.

Although beduin women were full participants in the household economy, their social position was the same as that of urban women: They were dominated by men. Urban upper-class women performed what was perceived as "purely" female tasks. Economically productive tasks performed by urban working-class or beduin women were perceived as secondary and to be resorted to only in times of dire need. Men who worked as carpenters, smiths, masons, and fishermen were perceived to be the main contributors to the household economy. Women were allowed to contribute only in cases of emergency. Men controlled and manufactured the implements and tools, such as axes, adzes, drills, and looms, used in all the crafts.

The work performed by beduin women was essential to the household economy. Men did not spin and weave tents or fetch water, or when they did, they saw themselves only as helping women. Male roles—warriors, protectors and providers—were seen as primary, all important, and superior to the roles performed by women.

Marriage in Kuwaiti Society

A look at the institution of marriage in Kuwaiti society will further illustrate the nature of the relationship between the sexes. Sex roles and patriarchal dominance in Kuwait have been socially enforced and reproduced through the institution of marriage. The patriarchal values that characterize the traditional Kuwaiti ideology are most evident in the practice of marriage prior to the discovery of oil.

Historically, it was desirable for both urban and beduin women to marry at an early age, soon after puberty. Traditionally, marriage to a father's brother's son (*ibn ʿam*) was preferred unless such a person was unavailable. Families of all ranks were careful that their daughters married men of equal or superior rank. In both the urban and beduin sectors, tribal affiliation determined such ranking. Social ranking assumed priority over all other marriage considerations, such as age, economic status, personal appearance, and the marital status of the prospective husband (whether he had one, two, or three wives; whether he was divorced or widowed; or whether he had dependent children from previous marriages). The father chose a man he deemed suitable as a husband for his daughter. A women followed her husband to live with his family. The husband assumed the same role as the father in being a provider with full authority over his wife. She was not allowed to make any decisions that concerned her without first consulting her husband. However, a wife did not have the right to be consulted by her husband in matters that concerned him—nor even those that concerned her. Furthermore, a wife did not have the same rights as a mother that the husband had as father. For example, the father could overturn any decision made by the mother concerning herself or her children. On the other hand, the father might make a decision that concerned his wife and children without ever consulting them. Even if the husband chose to consult his wife, he was not obliged to consider her opinion. A marriage was considered successful if the wife obeyed her husband and he in turn was able to keep her within the confines of patriarchal authority (al-taʿa).[3] Termination of marital life by pronunciation of a divorce formula was likewise controlled by the husband. Unlike the husband, the wife was forced to resort to the courts to obtain a divorce.

Laws of divorce and inheritance allowed women to own property in their own right. A woman's wealth could exceed that of her father if, for example, she was the widow of a man who had been wealthier than her father. A woman could also have been wealthier than her husband if her deceased father had belonged to a wealthy merchant family while her husband did not. Since the main consideration at the time of marriage was equivalence in social ranking rather than wealth, such instances occurred frequently. However, as traditionally women, especially those from wealthier families, were proscribed from working outside the house and were uninformed on political and social matters, they were forced to be dependent on closely related males to manage their wealth. Marriage rules in Kuwait have served to regulate the control of wealth and perpetuate patriarchal control over women.

Women and Education Prior to Oil Production

Prior to the 1920s, some Kuwaiti males allowed their daughters to join "learning circles" (*halaqat*). Basically, the circles were led by a woman called *al-mutawiʿa* who recited the Qur'an. At the end of the 1920s, a small number of new study circles with women instructors were established, enabling upper-class girls to learn reading and writing. The reasons why there were so few of these circles are not known. Perhaps there was a shortage of teachers; the lack of appreciation of the importance of female learning might have played a part, as surely did the strict adherence to the taboo that prohibited females from leaving the household. These factors may also help to explain why formal education for women was established later than for men. The first school for women opened during the academic year 1938–39; that for men had been established in 1912 shortly after Britain, through formal treaties, consolidated its dominance over the Gulf. The curriculum for females was different from that for men. This difference lasted until the end of the 1940s, when oil revenues began to trickle in.[4]

The Impact of Oil Wealth on Education and Gender

There seems to be a correlation between the sudden influx of oil revenues in Kuwait and the equally sudden change in the educational system. The urgency to modernize the state due to oil revenues seems to provide the most plausible explanation for this change of the educational system. After the discovery of oil, recognition grew that Kuwaiti women had as much of an absolute right to an education as did males. Men's and women's educational programs were merged into a unified curriculum beginning in the 1950s. This equality in education was the first kind of equality between the sexes in Kuwaiti society. All women were able to enjoy the right to education because providing free education for both sexes at all levels became one of the functions of the state. This provision is credited to Shaykh ʿAbdallah al-Salim al-Sabah, the ruler of Kuwait at the time. He initiated the process of modernization and was an ardent proponent of the establishment of the present-day paternalistic welfare state that resulted in the proliferation of schools throughout the country.[5]

Although not all families paid equal attention to educating their female and male members, a large number of women in the urban sector, especially the upper class, left the confines of their segregated households daily to attend government schools where they spent the bulk of the day with "strangers." As the number of educated women increased, starting in the 1960s many left Kuwait to pursue higher education in foreign countries. Women were able to choose freely regarding their field of specialization. The increased physical mobility for women provided by education outside the home thus resulted in the broadening of their knowledge and life experiences.

Education, Gender, and Modernization

Education was the first independent source of power at the disposal of Kuwaiti women. They gained power not only by obtaining education but also by using it as a resource to gain access to employment outside the confines of the household. This might explain why women were very enthusiastic about obtaining an education as soon as the opportunity became available. Accordingly, after oil production began, educated women sought employment in managerial, technical, and service-oriented enterprises to serve as bank cashiers, television announcers, social workers, and teachers.[6] However, their employment was outside the mainstream of enterprises from which their households drew their main source of wealth, namely those linked to trade. Very rarely did women work in a family business related to trade because of the sex-segregation taboo. Thus most women opted to work for the state.

Education created these new roles for women. Their work has been directly related to their acquired educational specialty and not to the enterprises characteristic of the merchant, working, and beduin sectors. In the urban merchant sector, men have remained in their specialized areas of trade without any competition from women of their own class, because these women have worked in areas unrelated to trade, mostly in state institutions. As the result of the redistribution of oil wealth and the establishment of the welfare state, the state has become the largest employer. Thus one might even say that women in Kuwait belong to a new managerial and service-oriented social group because, regardless of their class background, they all work in occupations unrelated to the traditional occupations of their respective classes and ecological sectors.

As a result of education in the social sciences and in the humanities, Kuwaiti women have become more knowledgeable regarding foreign cultures than Kuwaiti men. Education has promoted an understanding of other cultures that in turn resulted in a desire for modernization. Educated women have met women from other Arab societies who have come to work in Kuwait. Arab women, such as those from Egypt, Palestine, Syria, Iraq, and Lebanon, tend to be modern in their worldview. They use Western implements, dress in Western-style clothing, and drive automobiles. In fact, a great deal of the material culture of Kuwaiti society has changed as a result of the interaction of educated Kuwaiti women with their Arab counterparts.

The sudden influx of oil wealth against the background of a traditional mercantile and a nomadic pastoral (beduin) tribal social structure has had a unique impact upon Kuwaiti society. Modernization has occurred rapidly as oil wealth has made free education available at all levels and provided a high standard of living in society at large, allowing most groups rapid access to various means of cultural communication and exchange through the media, travel, and trade. In addition, migration by other Arab nationals, especially Egyptians and Palestinians, has played a significant role in the transmission of modernization to Kuwait.

Segregation and Social Change

Modernization has affected the segregation of the sexes in Kuwait. The shortage of native workers and the very small indigenous population have helped females obtain work outside the household. The sudden influx of oil wealth provided the means to undertake vast projects to modernize the state's bureaucracy. Given the severe limitations of the native labor force to undertake such projects, the state encouraged large-scale migration of expatriate labor. Many positions in the state bureaucracy have been created by the numerous projects in housing, transportation, health, and communications that developed as a result of labor migration. Within the new bureaucracy, positions were created that only women could occupy, such as positions in girls' schools.

However, Kuwaiti women's enthusiasm for work has not paralleled their enthusiasm for education. Not all educated women have sought employment. Often this stems from the fact that both women and men believe female employment is desirable only under conditions of dire financial need. Furthermore, female employment was and still is considered an embarrassment to the Kuwaiti male, who is seen as the family provider. Some working Kuwaiti women need to repeat constantly that they are employed out of boredom and not financial need so as not to embarrass themselves and their male providers. Nevertheless, the small number of women who have sought employment after graduation and continue to work have learned to appreciate the value of work for its own sake. In terms of the dominant value system, however, most government positions occupied by Kuwaiti citizens do not entail productive work. Since most Kuwaiti women work for the state and such work is not taken seriously, the kind of work they perform is not conducive to producing a change of attitude toward work that provides for a sense of self esteem and a feeling of accomplishment.

Among wealthy families, no matter how high a woman's wages in the state bureaucracy, it could never reach the level of income that a merchant derives from trade. Self-employed men can see the immediate results of their work in the form of accumulated wealth. As a result, Kuwaiti men have a different outlook toward work than women. In contrast, Kuwaiti women work mostly for the state in bureaucratic "make-believe" positions that are only created to place people on the payroll and do not fully utilize womens' potential. Women from the wealthy merchant sector employed by the state have not had any economic and social impact on their respective households and, as a result, their roles and positions in the family have not significantly changed. Despite the influx of women into state employment, men have retained their role in the family as principal providers.

Thus the modernization of the state infrastructure after oil production began has affected the roles of the two sexes only slightly. As shown earlier, whatever change that did occur resulted from the equality achieved between the sexes in education. Even if education on its own could not change the perception that one sex is superior to the other, especially as the content of school curriculum continues to affirm such a difference, education and expanded knowledge have made it more difficult for some Kuwaitis to accept gender inequality at face value. Education increases self-awareness and critical thinking, which, in turn, are used to challenge justifications of sex-role differentiation and patriarchal control. Those Kuwaiti men and women who have achieved a semblance of education inevitably conclude that change is inevitable. One can detect a subtle change, for example, when a Kuwaiti husband no longer avoids mentioning his wife when conversing with other males in matters that relate to the family. He also no longer apologizes to other males when he mentions a woman in the course of conversation. In the past, according to the Kuwaiti writer al-Qana°i, "If a person engaged in conversation with a companion and he had to mention a woman he would say: 'may God honor you.'"[7]

Modernization produces social change that entails the delegation of familial functions of socialization and enculturation to newly established specialized institutions, such as women's schools. These newly established institutions deliver knowledge to both sexes in some classes, training them to think critically and objectively. Consequently, the Kuwaiti male's right to think on behalf of women within the confines of the household has been challenged.

Gradually during the 1960s leaving the house no longer was taboo for women. Women of all social sectors and classes could leave it to perform social obligations such as visiting other women, to shop, and to attend school and work. Today women can also travel outside Kuwait in order to obtain education or for recreational purposes. Kuwaiti women have the right to offer their opinions on family affairs. They have assumed new duties, such as being available for their children to help with homework. The older children of both sexes depend on women for counseling. Women now are in charge of making decisions regarding the health of family members by deciding what preventive measures should be taken or which doctor to visit and when. Women also assume the husband's duties when he is absent. A man no longer has more than one wife in the same household. In most cases, he does not choose his daughter's husband before first consulting the mother and the daughter.[8] This latter change has had perhaps the most profound effect on gender relations in Kuwait since the 1960s.

Wealthy Kuwaiti Women and Domestic Division of Labor

Women in wealthy families still do not perform domestic work. Every household contains a number of servants who specialize in child rearing, cooking, cleaning, driving the family car, and taking care of the garden. Women thus find themselves performing a new role as managers of servants at home while also being employed outside the house. Non-Kuwaiti expatriate women who are employed also find themselves managing servants at home.

There is no doubt that education has caused changes in sex roles in Kuwaiti society. However, changing modes of consumption, characterized by rampant materialism, have affected all classes and sectors with the lower classes emulating the shifting standards set by the wealthy.[9] This situation has exerted pressure on most families with relatively modest resources to allow their women to work outside the household in order to supplement the family income. Expenses have doubled since 1973, and most families desire to raise their standard of living. A rise in wages, both in the state and private sectors, has encouraged this trend. Among the less wealthy, the number of female workers has increased in proportion to the increase in the number of graduates from the various educational institutions. While the work of Kuwaiti women has been largely confined to the public sector, a small number did join the private sector during the 1970s and 1980s. As a result, women are now employed in all sectors of the economy in technical and manage- rial positions. Despite the difficulty of having to perform house- hold duties and manage servants and despite the chronic absence of model day-care centers for children under the age of four, wealthy women have managed to maintain outside employment. This new multifaceted role of working inside and outside the house- hold has had its impact on both the males and females of affluent Kuwaiti families.

Males have felt the change that female roles have undergone indirectly. However, while education has created new roles for women of all sectors outside the household, it has not liberated them from patriarchal control and traditional domestic tasks. Now women in less wealthy families contribute to the financial support of the family through their work outside the household. Some edu- cated women have assumed administrative positions, thus assum- ing leadership over men. Such events threaten many Kuwaiti males who sense that, as education increases, the supply for such posi- tions will exceed the demand, thus creating the possibility of com- petition between the sexes for the same jobs. The employment of educated Kuwaiti women outside the household has also limited opportunities for foreigners who migrate to Kuwait seeking mana- gerial or technical employment.

Their new roles have also affected Kuwaiti women themselves, especially those who have been successful in their chosen occupa- tions. Such women have come to realize that the traditional role for women as defined by the prevailing patriarchal ideology is only one of many roles available. Women have learned from prac- tical experience that obtaining employment outside the household influences the family's upward or downward social mobility. Women have also realized that mobility is partially linked to education and that the position of the educated woman who is employed will tend to be economically equal to that of the man within the family. Women's employment outside the family as a result of education might thereby affect the social mobility of the family as a whole. Social mobility can have an impact on either sex. For example, a woman might obtain the most advanced degrees and distinguish herself in her area of specialty while a man might fail. The opposite could occur; a male might succeed and a female might fail. When they both succeed, their chances of upward mobility within their social group greatly increases. The same conditions prevail within society at large. The efforts of each of the sexes help to increase productivity. Educated women, though still relatively small in number, have been able to change the social perceptions of women's work from being merely for the purposes of enjoyment or relieving boredom or even wasting time—a perception held even by some women themselves—to a perception that work is something useful because it leads to economic independence. After the spread of education during the 1960s, most Kuwaiti women no longer feel embarrassed when seeking employment. Today some women are also no longer afraid of people making a connection between a female seeking employment and her family's financial need. Perhaps one of the most noticeable changes is that at times even questions are raised when an educated woman *does not* seek employment after graduation. In the past, questions were asked if a woman sought employment. Now the embarrassment of not working has replaced the embarrassment of being employed. In terms of social attitudes, this represents a truly significant change in gender relations in Kuwait.

Those who have acquired an education and those who have obtained specialized educations in fields such as medicine have positioned themselves to gain power and prestige within their respective social classes and ecological sectors. Since both sexes have had equal access to the same educational opportunities, the impact of change would seem to be the same for both sexes. However, the result has been more drastic for women than for men; it has altered their subordinate rank within the family, class, and

sector and offered the possibilities of achieving leadership positions and even wealth. Such changes have led to new patterns of
social mobility.

Education, Female Social Mobility, and Ideology

As demonstrated, social changes have occurred in Kuwaiti society
as a result of the impact of oil wealth. Educated males have
achieved considerable upward mobility.[10] Analysis of social change
shows that a considerable number of educated male Kuwaitis have
moved into the merchant class. The increase in the size of the
merchant class since the 1950s is partly a result of this upward
mobility of administrators and technocrats. A number of educated
Kuwaiti males also achieved leadership positions in state institutions and private firms. Others have joined the ranks of the three
branches of government: the executive, the legislature, and the judiciary. Females of similar educational backgrounds have not
achieved comparable changes in their social status. If we take into
account the discrepancy between ideology and behavior, the social process termed "modernization" by Western social scientists
has largely failed to alter the prevailing traditional ideology.

Traditionalists do not object to certain behavioral changes
brought about by modernization. For example, they do not object
to modern Western dress, food, architecture, furniture, rampant
materialism, and the use of automobiles. They do not object to
women leaving the home for visits and other activities reserved
for females, such as going to a beauty salon, shopping, and spending vacations in foreign countries. Nevertheless, traditionalists espousing the Arab patriarchal ideology have found themselves in
conflict with the process of modernization over the education of
females and their subsequent employment.

Despite the equality of education in Kuwait, some members of
both sexes still believe that there are areas of educational specialization that are not the "proper" domain for females. This is obvious
when one looks at the behavior of females when choosing an educational specialization. Females tend to choose fields in the liberal

arts over technical ones.[11] In addition, despite the fact that equality of educational opportunity exists at all levels, fewer women reach the highest levels.[12] This social reality exists despite an ideology professing equal opportunity, free public education for all, obligatory education in the primary grades, and the successful efforts at eliminating adult illiteracy that are actively promoted by the state. Despite all this, women still lag behind men in education.[13] While Kuwaiti society faces a serious labor shortage, the number of females in the labor force is less than those who are of working age and hold advanced degrees or have acquired at least some formal education.[14] Kuwaiti women also tend to drop out of the labor force as soon as they qualify for early retirement, usually after ten years of service.

Kuwaiti society has continued to be completely dependent on foreign labor long after the indigenous educational system produced male and female graduates for the labor force. This fact tends to give the impression, particularly with respect to women, that their labor contributions outside the household are not required to meet social needs but rather to satisfy their own desire to be employed. Kuwaiti women know that their labor is expendable and can be replaced cheaply by foreign labor. In addition, the welfare state that was created during the 1960s and 1970s makes it possible for women to play the traditional role of an urban housewife[15] and to be supported by the state if they choose not to work and have no male providers. Thus state policies enable Kuwaiti women, no matter what their social background, to maintain a comfortable standard of living.

Women, Public Employment, and Social Development

When employed, Kuwaiti females are largely confined to positions in the public sector. This limits the opportunity for women to discover and achieve their full potential by performing new roles.[16] The security and sizable wages in the state bureaucracy have helped Kuwaiti women achieve a certain degree of economic independence. However, there is a drawback to this achievement—

the limited opportunity for professional development and the lack of avenues for advancement. In addition, there is a common perception in Kuwait that a government salary is nothing more than a vehicle for the redistribution of oil wealth. Thus women employed in such positions tend to feel that their role outside the household is really of little significance to society.[17]

Despite the fact that Kuwaiti women have lagged behind men at the same educational level in taking advantage of employment opportunities, recently a very small group of women has begun to appreciate the importance of employment outside the household. They have chosen to pursue professional carriers without allowing themselves to be placed under any patriarchal control within the confines of traditional families and households. One example can be found among Kuwaiti women who are university professors. This same process occurred earlier in other Arab societies that preceded Kuwait in integrating women into the workplace. During the twentieth century Egyptian women, for example, have achieved the right to work and to develop their own identity without patriarchal control. This has led them to question the male-dominated sexual division of labor and to expect instead to replace it by their own free choice and by a system based on knowledge, ability, desire, and inclination. In Egypt women established the right to work and choose their occupational specializations without any restrictions, rights that have enabled society to benefit from the talents of all its members. As educated females contributed to social development, they had no doubt in themselves that they could succeed in roles both inside and outside the household. Thus Egyptian women continued to enter all areas of work, gaining rights that were previously confined to males alone. It was an inevitable consequence that these social changes were reflected in the patriarchal ideology and behavioral patterns in Egyptian society itself.

In Kuwait, similar changes in patriarchal ideology have not occurred. In fact, during the past ten years Kuwaiti society began taking steps directed toward strengthening the traditional patriarchal system of the division of labor. Women began to avoid employment in areas that do not conform to the segregation of the

sexes and to prefer whenever possible female employment in traditional roles, such as teaching. Possibly the same conditions that
convinced a number of women that their role outside the household is insignificant continue to influence these women, causing
them to accept ideas that call for the alteration of the direction of
change and to revert to traditional modes of education and segregation within the household. In the early stages of European industrial development, the proliferation of economic enterprises
and roles due to the increase in the specialization and division of
labor led to greatly increased labor needs. As a result of the persistence of qualitative and quantitative changes, early industrial
society could not avoid utilizing female labor. Women, in turn,
could not support themselves and their families if they did not
work. In contemporary Kuwait, the enormous amount of state revenues derived from oil wealth led to rapid economic change. Indeed, it is only the existence of oil wealth that has enabled the
state to provide social services that allow women to work.

Females who had graduated from secondary school or the university were not critical to the labor force—foreign labor was
available at relatively cheap wages. Kuwaiti society was not really
ready to accept female employment outside of the household, nor
were women expected to work. Patriarchal attitudes and rules
persisted that allowed women to choose not to work outside the
household and to continue to be supported by males. Under these
circumstances, women became the wards of their husbands or
male kin and in their absence became the wards of the state. In
other words, if women did not choose to work, their male kin
and/or the state were obliged to support them.[18] Thus despite
their educational achievements and class and social sector affiliations, educated Kuwaiti women desiring work have faced adverse
conditions. As a result, only a very small number of these women
have succeeded in their careers.

Kuwaiti women have faced additional barriers as well. Even if
the pervasive traditional patriarchal ideology did not completely
prevent female employment outside the household, it did not support it either.[19] Doubts continued to be raised as to whether
women should work at all because many Kuwaiti men and women

from all sectors of society preferred that women remain at home. Some people, convinced that women did not have the intrinsic ability to work, supported their employment being limited to areas "suitable" for women, such as teaching and social services. Kuwaitis holding such views included members of the state bureaucracy and technocrats who, despite their disagreement on a variety of issues, happened to agree upon this one. Patriarchal attitudes caused many members of both sexes to doubt the ability of females to contribute in deed and in thought to the process of social development. Since they have no political rights to this day—they cannot vote or hold public office—most Kuwaiti women still do not take their right to work seriously.

Many Kuwaiti women continue to justify their inability to play more than one role on the grounds of incompetence and the failure of the social structure to provide normative as well as material conditions for them to be active members of the public sphere. Kuwaiti society, for example, still lacks model day-care centers. Instead child care devolves to nannies, mostly Indian, who are a burden upon the mother and a danger to infants because they are usually neither trained or experienced nor can they speak Arabic. Instead of helping the Kuwaiti mother, they create new problems that increase her work and preoccupations. Since both sexes still adhere to the ideology of the sexual division of labor inside the household, wives do not accept the idea of husbands helping with household tasks. As a result, the working woman ends up performing more than one role and is burdened to such an extent that her roles in both the public and private spheres are negatively affected. Women thus face a double oppression—if they fail in their household duties, they are blamed for taking outside employment; if they fail in the public sphere, they are blamed for lacking the innate ability to perform such "male" tasks. This patriarchal ideology is no doubt one of the causes for the success of Kuwaiti males in maintaining their hold on authority in matters pertaining to the public sphere. In all cases, the male's chances of assuming leadership positions are better than those of the female. For example, the number of Kuwaiti women employed in the private sector is very small, and rarer still is it for women to occupy leadership positions there. Most women employed in this sector perform clerical and other routine tasks.

There is no doubt that the conditions in which employed Kuwaiti women find themselves contribute to their belief that they possess limited abilities. These conditions promote acceptance of the idea of the traditional Arab patriarchal sexual division of labor as well as acceptance of a gender-based educational specialization that confines women to specific roles without taking into consideration their inclination and abilities. To better understand this situation, it is useful to examine recent changes in female roles. As noted, educated women have recently begun to reevaluate their exclusion from roles outside the household. At first they began to feel dissatisfied with traditional roles based on patriarchal ideology. In the early 1970s women began to explore the possibility of new roles, such as entering politics. In 1971 women demanded the right to run for political office. However, during the 1980s a number of women also objected to calls for extending political rights to women and strongly opposed such moves.[20]

The Impact of Oil Production on the Sex Roles of Urban Working-Class Women from 1960 to 1988

In the past, in addition to performing household tasks, urban working-class women produced crafts by performing manual labor. Women were engaged in such tasks in order to secure basic necessities such as food, clothing, and shelter for their families. Some women were totally responsible for their families, because the kind of work that the man performed, such as seafaring and pearl diving, took them away from home and country for long periods of time. After pearl diving was no longer a viable occupation, nor were seafaring and the crafts that supported those activities, urban artisans, divers, and seamen came to be employed en masse by the state. Increased revenue from oil production and the concomitant expansion of social welfare programs enabled the state to afford to employ them in a variety of jobs. A small number worked in the oil sector. Women who had formerly worked in the craft sector abandoned their roles of supporting themselves and their families to be financially supported by males whose income had increased. The state also provided financial assistance to those families whose income fell below minimum levels, as determined by newly created social welfare agencies. Those females who had no male supporters became wards of the state. A very small number of these women worked in state administrative agencies in positions that did not require expertise and literacy. These social service programs helped to increase the standard of living in areas of housing, education, and health care for the members of the traditional working class.

The Impact of Oil Production on the Sex Roles among Beduin Women from 1960 to 1988

Traditionally, beduin women were "self-sufficient," contributing to the fulfillment of their own needs and those of their families. The impact of oil wealth led them to abandon the productive part of their roles to men and the state. The tasks that these women had formerly performed, such as spinning and weaving rugs and tents, were no longer needed after beduin households were transferred to permanent dwellings provided by the state through its housing programs. At the same time, the beduin household lost its traditional economic functions, including food production, weaving clothes, manufacturing some households goods, and raising animals for transportation, warfare and urban markets. Thus beduin women ceased participating in economic production while men obtained employment similar to that obtained by their working urban counterparts. In the oil-based economy, the income of the Kuwaiti beduin family increased steadily.

The overall impact of oil wealth was to improve the standard of living of the beduin and to lead beduin males to become sedentary. As for females, the young entered schools while the older women were relegated to traditional urban upper-class roles that emphasized seclusion, segregation, and veiling. Prior to settlement, beduin women contributed to the household economy as had urban working-class women. Traditional forms of beduin production are currently considered outmoded by Kuwaitis. Through free education, beduin sons have become technocrats and administrators. Between the early 1950s and the end of the 1970s, the numbers of beduin performing traditional roles, such as herding for men and housekeeping and weaving for women, shrank considerably as a consequence of upward social mobility.[21]

Oil, Services, and Social Mobility: Need or Just Symbols?

A large number of foreign female migrants are employed as nannies and servants in all sectors of Kuwaiti households. These servants perform household tasks that were previously performed by poorer Kuwaiti women, such as cooking, cleaning and child rearing. In most households where women are not employed outside the home, the role of Kuwaiti women has been reduced to supervising the servants. Needless to say, such women are not only unemployed, they are also a burden on society at large. In an economy that suffers from an endemic labor shortage, any role abandoned by women leads to a concomitant loss of the knowledge, expertise, and skills that are gained from work. Increasingly, Kuwaiti society relies on foreign labor markets to fulfill its needs.

It is possible that the spread of the phenomenon of servants during the 1950s and 1960s was an attempt by women of the other social strata to emulate the condition of women among wealthy households. Servants were one of the manifestations of wealth and prosperity that working-class and beduin women were keen to adopt in order to achieve status and esteem. What created this attitude is the obsession in Kuwait with spending on symbols, such as servants that drain the family budget and waste human energy.

Most of Kuwaiti society is comfortable with the existence of an almost completely idle labor force whose members can work if they so desire but are free to refuse to do so and whose refusal is condoned and even commended by society at large. This prevalent attitude is a result of the ideological background against which oil wealth has been used to bring about conditions of social change.[22] Such conditions have brought about the destruction of the pastoral sector and urban working classes, which have been replaced by nonproductive groups dependent on state salaries. Since their jobs are "make work," little if any significance has been accorded to their physical and mental abilities. Despite this, the overall standard of living has improved and social services have expanded.

As this chapter has demonstrated, the status of women in Kuwaiti society reflects the traditional Arab patriarchal ideology and the social organization of the means of production. The changes taking place in Kuwait as a result of the influx of oil wealth have had their most dramatic impact on women through the provision of free and equal education. Although sex roles have changed somewhat in the area of employment of women outside the household, this change has been limited in scope and has not been followed or accompanied by any significant change in the patriarchal ideology and social value system. Thus in Kuwait, really significant social change has yet to occur. It is still difficult to predict the future of gender relations in Kuwaiti society. This important topic requires further empirical research and analysis.

NOTES

1. Noura al-Falah, *al-taghayur al-ijtima‘i fi-duwal al-muntija li-l-naft (mujtama‘ al-kuwayt)* [*Social Change in Oil-Producing Countries: Kuwaiti Society*], 11, no. 57, *Annals of the Faculty of Arts* (Kuwait: Kuwait University, 1988), 33.

2. Halim Barakat, "*al-nidham al-ijtima‘i wa ‘alaqatuhu bi mushkilat al-mar’a al-‘arabiya*" ["Social Organization and its Relationship to the Problematic of Arab Women"] in *al-mar’a wa dawruha fi-l-wihda al-‘arabiya* [*The Role of Women in the Development of Arab Unity*] (Beirut: Center for Arab Unity Studies, 1982), 58.

3. Ibid., 58.

4. See ‘Abd al-‘Aziz Husayn, *muhadarat ‘an al-mujtama‘ al-‘arabi fi-l-kuwayt* [*Lectures on Arab Society in Kuwait*] (Cairo: Matba‘t Ma‘had al-Dirasat al-‘Arabiya al-‘Aliya, 1960).

5. See Ahmad Abu Hakima, *tarikh al-kuwayt* [*The History of Kuwait*] (Kuwait: Government Press, 1965).

6. al-Falah, *Kuwaiti Society*, 33–35, 39–40, 45–55.

7. Yusif al-Qana^{c}i, *safahat min tarikh al-kuwayt* [*Pages from the History of Kuwait*] (Kuwait: Government Press, 1968), 77.

8. Ibid.

9. al-Falah, *Kuwaiti Society*, 45–55.

10. Ibid., 29–61.

11. State of Kuwait, Task Force on Women's Affairs, *khasa'is al-mar'a al-kuwaytiya fi-l-ta^{c}adudat* [*Kuwaiti Women in the Census*] (Kuwait: Ministry of Planning, 1980), 332.

12. Ibid., 50.

13. Ibid., 45.

14. State of Kuwait, Central Statistical Administration, *al-majmu^{c}a al-ihsa'iya al-sanawiya* [*Annual Statistical Survey*] (Kuwait: Ministry of Planning, 1980), 8.

15. See State of Kuwait, *nidham al-musa^{c}adat al-ijtima^{c}iya* [*Ordinance of Social Welfare*] (Kuwait: Department of Social Affairs, 1955).

16. al-Falah, *Kuwaiti Society*, 64.

17. See Basin Sarhan et al., *malaf ma^{c}lumat hawla al-^{c}amala al-ajnabiya fi aqtar al-khalij al-^{c}arabi* [*Data File on Foreign Labor in the Arab Gulf Countries*] (Kuwait: Arab Planning Institute, 1983).

18. State of Kuwait, *Ordinance of Social Welfare*.

19. al-Falah, *Kuwaiti Society*, 53.

20. Nuriya al-Sadani, *al-masira al-tarikhiya li-l-huquq al-siyasiya li-l-mar'a al-kuwaytiya fi-l-fatra min 1971–1982* [*The Historical Development of Women's Political Rights in Kuwait, 1971–1982*] (Kuwait: Dar al-Siyasa Press, 1983), 78.

21. al-Falah, *Kuwaiti Society*, 22–62.

22. Ibid.

7. Contemporary Trends in the Study of Folklore in the Arab Gulf States

Muhammad Rajab al-Najjar

It is obvious that the tremendous influx of oil wealth into the Arab Gulf has exposed the local culture to what may be called a "cultural revolution" involving rapid social change. In the Arab Gulf states of Iraq, Kuwait, Saudi Arabia, Qatar, Bahrain, the United Arab Amirates, and ʿUman, this change is reflected in the transformation of the values governing economic production and the traditional structure of social, political, and cultural life that existed prior to the discovery and extraction of oil resources. Caused by a variety of endogenous and exogenous factors, this social change has destroyed certain aspects of Gulf folk culture.

This destructive change has had the most noticeable impact on the old forms of production that depended on the sea as a source of livelihood. There followed in the fifties a decline in the production of tools, crafts, and small industries (sinaʿat shaʿbiya) as well as a disappearance of the customs and traditions associated with them. A significant result of this social change was the disappearance of the traditional Gulf home along with its furnishings and simple traditional tools, which could not compete with modern electronic appliances. Naturally, under these circumstances, the peoples of the region began to abandon a large part of their popular culture, which, in both its material and its spiritual form, was unable to withstand, conform to, or accommodate the new social change. At first, no one noticed how rapidly the local culture lost its identity and began to be destroyed. The local citizenry took their share of wealth believing that they were receiving God's gift: "that which is granted by God." They were overwhelmed by the material aspects of the new culture, which included, at the same time, the elements that threatened local culture with violent and savage disintegration and extinction.

It is essential to identify here some of the elements that have undermined the core of popular culture in the Arab Gulf. The most important of these is the introduction of modern technology, which has affected virtually every home in the region. The most profound material and ideological change has occurred as a result of mass communications. This technology involves customs, ideas, knowledge, and aesthetic forms derived from more advanced industrialized countries that often contradict the values embodied in the traditional local culture and deeply held religious beliefs. When these modern means of communication arrived, societies fell captive to blind imitation of the West. Of greatest concern here is the fact that the masses who were tied to popular culture fell under the control of what might be called "packaged culture." In other words, the populace of the Arab Gulf became the "receivers" of culture rather than "participants" in cultural production. As a result of neglect by Gulf inhabitants, the innovative nature of tradition was weakened. Among the generation born after the onset of oil wealth, traditional culture even came to be despised.

Migrant Labor and Arab Gulf Culture

The packaged culture transmitted by modern Western means of mass communication that has asserted itself over the intellect and consciousness of the inhabitants of the Gulf has not been the only form of imported culture. Migrant labor has brought many other cultures to the Arab Gulf states from Arab and non-Arab countries, such as Pakistan, India, and the East Asian states. This migration has constituted a second element of cultural dislocation, creating many sharp and powerful social cleavages. In most instances, the number of migrants has often exceeded that of the native populaces. Living as separate expatriate colonies among the Gulf Arabs, these migrant laborers have continued to preserve in a living, functional manner the culture and traditions that they brought with them, despite variety and diversity. This situation has formed another pressure on and threat to the traditional culture of the native inhabitants of the Arab Gulf. Inevitably the local culture, the behavior of the inhabitants, and the indigenous dialects have been affected.

Oil Wealth and Forms of Production

A third element that has been changed by the introduction of oil production is the relationship of Gulf inhabitants to traditional forms of production. Prior to the onset of oil production, the lives of the majority of Gulf Arabs were tied to the sea, primarily through pearl diving, trade, and transport. As a result, sea arts figured prominently in the region's folk tradition. However, the influx of an immense amount of oil wealth led the peoples of the Gulf to abandon the strenuous working conditions associated with seafaring and pearl diving, and to exchange them for more comfortable white-collar employment in the air-conditioned offices of the state bureaucracy. The last generation to work at sea are now grandparents, and the folk tradition has almost disappeared. As for the inhabitants of the desert, the state attempted through education and civil service employment to entice them to settle in urban areas. Thus the desert tradition also was threatened with extinction.

Oil Wealth, Institutional Change, and Alienation

A fourth impact of oil wealth appears in the institutional and organizational changes that affected the region. The more natural and simple forms of social organization, such as the primary unit of the tribe that characterized the Arab Gulf states, were transformed into more complex forms. Gulf societies came to be dominated by modern cultural, educational, and state institutions, such as primary and secondary schools, the university, the legal system, labor codes, and the social welfare system. These institutions replaced the traditional and culturally transmitted institutions and organizations, such as the Qur'anic schools, and the patron-client relationships between merchants and seamen. As it no longer had a role in transferring experience, accumulated knowledge, and the results of social experimentation, the traditional indigenous culture was eroded still further.

Although oil wealth provided Arab Gulf societies with material wealth and modern conveniences, it also created a great deal of anxiety and alienation. The main dilemma facing the peoples of the region became how to reconcile modern or contemporary forms of life with an authentic national tradition derived from the past.

Oil Wealth and Political Change

In addition to its significant impact upon material conditions in the Gulf, oil wealth has undermined the region's political stability. All of the Gulf states have become political, economic, and military targets for neighboring countries as well as the superpowers. Our interest here is not so much the overt political threats faced by Gulf states but rather the cultural dimensions of this problem. The continued existence of external conspiracies has threatened the region's sense of national identity. Aware of this problem, the Arab Gulf states have attempted to maintain the political unity of their populaces by promoting nationalism and social solidarity in order to confront not only military aggression but also efforts intended to undermine the indigenous culture. As a result, there is the need not only for military security but also what might be called "cultural security."

In sum, oil wealth led to change in the material environment and also, though to a lesser extent, in the intellectual realm. The inhabitants of the Arab Gulf found that the values previously derived from the past were being replaced by newly created values that sometimes conflicted with their traditional value system. Given the magnitude of cultural change, the situation facing Arab Gulf societies was one of life or death. Either they could submit to domination by foreign cultures and alien value systems, thereby allowing their own national identity to disintegrate or become deformed, or they could take refuge in the past and reaffirm their national identity and sense of social solidarity by struggling to preserve traditional values.

As the people of the Gulf faced this choice, the appreciation of the value of national heritage (*al-turath*) in general and popular culture (*al-turath al-sha'bi*) in particular increased, especially because a large portion of the life-styles associated with the past had already disappeared. The state began to direct its efforts toward preserving folk traditions not just because they were part of the civilization and culture of the region but also because of their political significance as a "a stabilizing element and safety valve" in confronting the dangers stemming from rapid social change. In other words, popular culture (*al-turath al-sha'bi*) came to be considered an element of social unity and cohesion that could be used to offset the hostile designs of both external and internal enemies.

Nationalism and the Revival of Folklore

To discover the origins of the interest in popular culture in the Arab Gulf, it is necessary to study the role of Arab nationalism in the region. After the introduction of oil wealth, many committed nationalists warned against neglecting popular culture, taking a condescending attitude toward it, or taking it for granted. They called for collecting and preserving what remained of the indigenous culture before it disappeared. On the grounds that popular culture is the most integral part of an individual's thought and behavior, nationalists argued that it had to be nurtured in order to repair the damage resulting from the tremendous material and cultural change that had affected Arab Gulf inhabitants. Such change, they pointed out, could lead to the destruction of society by undermining the social bonds that hold people together because societies are in dire need of this heritage when faced with a crisis that threatens their very existence.

As a result of national independence and the spread of Arab nationalist consciousness in the region, these appeals engendered a positive response both from the state and from society at large. In addition to political independence and the rise of nationalism that coincided with the onset of oil production, the political awareness of the average citizen in Arab Gulf countries increased. This consciousness served to further strengthen nationalism among many Arab intellectuals in the Gulf. Some began to search for an authentic popular tradition in existing written Arab tradition. Nationalist intellectuals also began collecting oral tradition. The number of intellectuals interested in popular tradition began to increase steadily along with the appreciation in nationalist circles of the value of this tradition.

Although it was feared that the introduction of Western technology and values would destroy Arab Gulf culture, popular culture proved to be much more resilient than expected. In a number of ways it provided a refuge from the alienation many Gulf Arabs felt. First, it continued to serve as a basis for reaffirming and authenticating ethical, social, and ideological values that allowed the populace to confront the tension that often existed between traditional and more contemporary life-styles and patterns of production. Second, it served as a source of entertainment. Third, it served an educational function through which the older generation was able to transmit knowledge to the younger generation. This was especially important given that most of the Gulf Arabs were illiterate.

The Scientific Study of Popular Culture in the Arab Gulf

Despite dire predictions, many aspects of Arab Gulf culture stubbornly persisted in the face of rapid social change. This fact prompted the awareness that it was not enough to simply collect, preserve, and nurture popular cultural production. Arab intellectuals recognized the need for a more scientific study that would help determine or predict under what conditions forms of popular culture would persist and under what conditions they would disappear. In Western countries the science of folklore as a branch of the humanities had already been well established for a century

and a half. Folklore was recognized as a scientific field of endeavor by the educated elite as well as by formal, cultural, and
educational institutions that supported such studies financially and
intellectually.

After a similar struggle, the study of folklore based on the Western model achieved formal recognition at Kuwait University and
at research centers affiliated with other Gulf universities. This occurred in the mid-1980s after political leaders and those in charge
of the educational system realized that folkloric studies represented
not only a scientific but also a national obligation. In striving to
meet the essential requirements of a modern state based on science
and technology, Arab Gulf states have realized that "modernity"
does not mean shedding their national heritage.

The Manifestations of Progress in the Folkloric Movement

The concern for the unitary relationship of language, land, history,
belief, economy, and popular culture stems not only from a political rationale grounded in nationalism, but also from an intellectual impulse that seeks to comprehend that which is original or
authentic in the cultures of peoples or nations. As ʿAbd al-Hamid
Yunis, the dean of Arab folklorists, has stated, the value of folklore is most apparent as "the sum total of popular culture that is
alive, dynamic and has accumulated from ancient times. It accompanies the history of a people and is concerned with their
progress. Folklore is that which preserves the foundations of
authenticity. Rather than resisting scientific and technological progress, it supports it by providing accurate knowledge about human nature and the relationship between the individual and his
social framework."[1]

The prevailing nationalist and ideological outlook in the Gulf
has contributed a great deal to interest in and encouragement of
Arab folk heritage. During the 1970s and 1980s this support increased immeasurably. Scientific gains have led to great progress
in uncovering, studying, and classifying many aspects of this heritage. Through organized efforts, both individualistic and coopera-

tive, folklore has increasingly become the concern of scientific and academic institutions. In turn, these institutions have used folklore to further both nationalist and scientific ends.

Arab Gulf states have played a crucial role in the institutionalization of the study of folklore by establishing national committees and associations for the study of popular culture and by founding historical and cultural museums. Departments of folklore and ethnology have concentrated on collecting folkloric materials and displaying them in prominent exhibitions. The Joint Exhibition of the Antiquities of the States of the Gulf Cooperation Council was hosted by Kuwait on November 25, 1984, under the banner "A Single Tradition and a Shared History." The exhibit consisted of little more than archaeological artifacts, which are common Gulf folkloric materials. Gulf states support the study of folklore by encouraging authors to write on folkloric subjects, fully subsidizing publication costs and providing generous stipends. University graduates and researchers are sent abroad by governments to be trained in folkloric research. Students have been sent on scholarships to Egypt, for example, to earn masters' and doctoral degrees in folklore. In addition, festivals for popular folk arts are conducted annually, and participation in international fairs and festivals is supported.

Another important manifestation of state supervision of the study of folklore and popular culture is the careful attention each Arab Gulf state takes to establishing information centers for folk culture and cultural agencies that deal with folk arts and crafts. Gulf states sponsor Arab symposia and conferences on folklore, and prizes and grants are allocated to encourage the study and collection of folkloric materials. Folk artists and groups are given financial and intellectual support.

The State and the Study of Folklore in Iraq

Following the July 1958 revolution, Iraq devoted a noticeable effort to the support of folk culture. The state established a special section specializing in folk culture and arts in the Ministry of Information and began to issue a series of valuable books under the title "Folkloric Studies." Since its founding in 1969 the Iraqi journal *Majallat al-Turath al-Sha'bi* (*Journal of Folk Culture*) is perhaps the sole specialized scientific journal of its type to have survived in the Arab world. In addition, the Iraqi government established a number of specialized museums concerned with folk culture, such as the Museum of Customs and Traditions and the Museum of Popular Dress in Baghdad. State support was also given to the important task of encouraging traditional handicraft production and the establishment of craft centers in most of the country's provinces to train people in popular crafts and handicraft production. A law enacted in 1971 established the Iraqi Folklore Center, and, in 1980, the Center for Arab Gulf Studies at Basra University founded The Center for the Study of Folklore, which was entrusted with the scientific study of folklore. One of the center's goals has been to upgrade itself to a department or scientific institute that would compile the results of folkloric knowledge and research throughout the Arab world.

The State and the Study of Folklore in Kuwait

The Kuwaiti state has exerted similar efforts to assist popular folk production. In 1957 Kuwait established The Center for the Preservation of Folk Culture, the first official Arab center concerned with folklore.[2] This center first assumed the responsibility of collecting and documenting Kuwaiti sea traditions. The Kuwait National Museum also focused on folkloric material, especially material culture, such as household implements. A number of more specialized museums were established, such as the Bayt Sadu al-Kuwayti (The Beduin Tent Museum). The state also acted to preserve examples of old Kuwaiti houses, such as the "Bayt al-Badr," which exemplify the folk (*sha'bi*) idiom in traditional architecture along with its furniture and utensils. In addition to research centers and museums, the state established the "Fishermen's Diwaniya,"[3] the "Diwaniya of Nabati Poets," and folk coffeehouses (*al-maqahi al-sha'biya*) in accordance with traditional institutional forms. A dramatic increase in the number of publications concerned with folklore and the past paralleled the state's interest. State-sanctioned studies sponsored by the Ministry of Information appeared in books and in scholarly and specialized journals published by the ministry. How highly the state considered folklore can also be seen in the fact that it created the National Council for Culture, Art and Literature, which reported directly to the Kuwaiti Council of Ministers.

The increased interest in folklore was evident in the number of articles in Kuwait's large and diversified press that dealt with the subject of popular culture, particularly that of the Arab Gulf. Indeed, the creation of an entire folk quarter in Kuwait City based on the old traditional style of architecture has even been proposed. Such a project would represent the concept of an "open museum" paralleling Saudi Arabia's efforts to build a complete village according to traditional architecture and style. Further evidence of societal concern with folklore came in 1984 when the Kuwaiti Foundation for Scientific Progress dedicated its largest award to the study of Kuwaiti and Arab folklore. For the study of local folklore, the recipient was Professor Ahmad al-Bishr al-Rumi, one of the pioneers in the study of Kuwaiti folk heritage. For the study of Arab folklore, the prizewinner was the great folklorist, Dr. ʿAbd al-Hamid Yunis.

Kuwait University has the distinction of being the first Gulf university to recognize the need to study "al-turath al-shaʿbi." In 1982 a course on folk literature was introduced in the Department of Arab Languages. This was followed in 1986 by a course in anthropology and folklore in the Department of Sociology in the Faculty of Arts. At present, similar efforts are being exerted in Saudi Arabia, Qatar, ʿUman, the United Arab Amirates, and Bahrain. While space limitations do not allow an elaborate discussion of all these efforts, it is necessary to point out that the establishment of the Arab Gulf States Folklore Centre in Qatar demonstrates that a serious concern for the need to preserve and study folklore and folk heritage scientifically has been firmly institutionalized in the region. The establishment of this center deserves detailed scrutiny because it represents a watershed in the history of the study of folklore in the Arab Gulf.

The Arab Gulf States Folklore Centre

Established in 1982 by the United Arab Amirates, Bahrain, Iraq, Kuwait, Saudi Arabia, ʿUman, and Qatar, the permanent head-quarters of the Arab Gulf States Folklore Centre is located in the Qatari capital of Dawha. The center rapidly acquired a reputation as an autonomous regional institution specializing in the scientific study of folklore. The center's main focus has been the study of the forms and content of Arab popular expressions (*al-taʿbir al-shaʿbi*) as well as the broader dimensions of contemporary and historical Arab Gulf culture. The board of directors is composed of the ministers of information of the founding states who approved the center's first five-year research program.

Officials of the center began their activities by convening four research seminars dealing with the theoretical and applied dimensions of the four basic elements of folk production in the Arab Gulf. The first of these, held in November 1984, was concerned with planning for the collection and documentation of folk literature. The seminar included a number of topics: establishing a conceptual framework for comprehending popular literature; delineating the various types of popular literature in the Gulf and the Arabian Peninsula and the types of expression associated with them; methods of collecting, classifying, and storing the basic elements, variants, and styles of regional folk literature; and methods of training researchers and field workers native to the region. The next month, following a similar format, the center held a seminar concerned with the collection and documentation of folk dance and music.

In January and February of 1985, two additional conferences were held. The first dealt with the collection and documentation of folk customs, traditions, and knowledge of the Arab Gulf and attempted to relate them to the life cycle (*dawrat al-haya al-insaniya*) of the region to study their relationship to folk literature, music, song, dance, and arts and crafts. Rather than viewing folklore as something static, conference themes emphasized such topics as "unity and diversity," "correspondence and variation," and "continuity and change," indicating a dynamic conceptualization. The sociopolitical dimension of folklore was perhaps most evident in the conference's focus on what was referred to as a "cultural attack" (*ghazw*) stemming from Western culture.

Whereas the previous concern had been "living folklore," the focus of the February research seminar was on collecting and documenting material culture and popular arts and crafts. In other words, the seminar was most concerned with artifacts associated with regional marine, desert, and agricultural environments. The question of origins was also on the minds of the seminar organizers as they directed their attention to those elements that inspired folk art in the Gulf, to the use of popular culture in everyday life, and to what could be considered authentic popular culture. In addition to origins, the organizers studied the social and economic utility of popular culture and the manner in which it could used to further sociopolitical development. In all of the seminars, methodologies for collecting and classifying folk materials and problems of field work were discussed. Efforts were made to compile descriptive guides to the folk culture of the Gulf as well as bibliographies of Arab and foreign references containing information pertinent to the study of folklore.

Through its seminars, the Arab Gulf States Folklore Centre sought to benefit from the expertise of local Arab intellectuals and those in the Arab world at large. It also sought to learn from non-Arab scholars specializing in the study of popular culture drawn from anthropology, history, linguistics, geography, music, and the visual arts in addition to literary figures and nonprofessional intellectuals interested in the heritage of the region. The aim of the center was to gather, classify, and analyze popular Arab traditions from a proper scientific perspective in order to determine precisely the theoretical and applied dimensions of the science of folklore. This objective could be accomplished only through a clear conceptualization of the theoretical frameworks, concepts, methodologies, and research strategies (*ussus ʿilmiya*) as core areas of study corresponding to the center's five research departments: folk literature, music and dance, folk customs, traditions and practices, and arts and crafts.

The accomplishments of the newly established center extended

to other areas of vital importance. During 1985 a cooperative
agreement with UNESCO was concluded whereby the agency
would undertake to assist the center in economic development,
basic research, public administration, manpower training and
development—especially scientific and technical skills, libraries
and documentation centers, publications, and the promotion of
regional and international cooperation. According to the terms of
this agreement, UNESCO began providing consultants, training
programs, and scholarships. UNESCO also helped to implement
"The Gulf Agreement for the Protection of Folkloric Expression"
as a result of work conducted by a committee of regional experts
established by the organization. The purpose of these activities
was to protect forms of folkloric expression from exploitation by
implementing a set of model rules adopted for all Arab countries.
UNESCO formulated the laws providing the basis for this
protection.

The activities of the Arab Gulf States Folklore Centre are based
on the premise that folklore is a form of expression that deserves
to be protected by guarantees normally accorded to intellectual
production in most states of the world. Arab Gulf states have considered this protection to be indispensible. It is seen as an important means to encourage the continued growth of folklore as well
as its preservation and dissemination within Arab Gulf countries
and outside the region without harming any of its intrinsic integrity. The value of such protection becomes clear when considering the exploitation and distortion of national heritage and folk
culture by corporations that control radio, television, and cinema.
Often development or trade arguments are used to justify the production of films, plays, and music that distort and commercialize
a region's national heritage. What corporations ignore is the proper
scientific and artistic respect for the cultural interests of the indigenous societies that produced this folklore, which forms a living
cultural heritage and which was conceived and developed by both
communities and individuals to express their hopes and aspirations.

During the nine years it has been in existence, the center has
published a number of important scholarly and scientific studies,
including: *Folktales in Qatar, Kuwaiti Songs,* and *Colloquial Gulf*

Poetry: Texts of Folk Literature and the Arabian Peninsula.[4] Other center publications are: *Forms of Women's Folk Dress, Ceramic Ornamentation in the Gulf, Folk Poetry in the Kingdom of Saudi Arabia,* and *The Encyclopedia of Kuwaiti Folk Riddles.*[5] The center also issues a specialized scholarly journal entitled *Folk Heritage* (*al-ma'thurat al-sha'biya*).

In cooperation with UNESCO, the center is currently undertaking the establishment of a central documentation unit that would contain a folklore archive that includes visual and vocal records. The unit would contain a library specializing in cultural heritage. The center is also engaged in the process of compiling a bibliography of all folkloric studies pertaining to the Arab Gulf and the Arab world both by Arab and non-Arab scholars.

A long-standing dream of many Arab folklorists is an endeavor supported by the center called "The Project for Collecting, Indexing, and Classifying Folkloric Elements in the Most Famous Ancient Arab Texts Dealing with Turath."[6] This comprehensive survey is aimed at indexing and classifying written folkloric heritage. This project is especially important because much of this folklore is still alive and has been functioning since the period of written documentation first began in the ninth century A.D. Currently a considerable amount of folklore has not been gathered together. It is therefore ignored, and loses much of the sought-after authenticity and vitality. This project will make material available in a systematic way to a wide variety of researchers from differing theoretical and methodological perspectives.

I have devoted a great deal of space to describing the center for two reasons: First, its creation and activities underscore the fact that the official view of folklore has changed. The field of folklore has come to be viewed as a science and not just as a source of information. There is a great difference between the two views. Of necessity, the scientific perspective requires the application of a systematic and methodologically sound approach to the study of folklore. No longer does a scientific perspective merely entail a search for the remains of a distant past in the form of sediments and fossils. It has surpassed the historical objective that searched haphazardly for a cultural or civilizational dimension in an ancient text, an inscription, or a religious temple. Instead, the scientific study of folklore has become the study of humanity, as culturally constructed, in a particular time and space. In this sense, folklore has become an integral part of the social order in which we live, both interacting and benefiting from it.

Second, from a nationalistic perspective, the founding of the center indicates that those who control the state do not believe that Arab heritage can be comprehended completely from that which is written and documented. Rather, it should also include all the folk production of common people in Arab society, be it words, symbols, rhythms and movements of daily life, or material production. The fact that the state has come to adopt this enlightened view indicates the triumph of the scientific view of folkloric production in the Arab Gulf.

From both a scientific and a nationalistic point of view, the center shoulders a great responsibility: In the near future it might become a truly Arab folkloric studies center and not just a regional one. The center has the potential to meet this responsibility given the enthusiasm of its supporters and its commitment to serving the Arab world's cultural heritage without chauvinistic or regional biases. Instead, the center is characterized by a strong commitment to Arab nationalism and a keen desire to enlighten the outside world objectively. The center's intellectuals aim to establish the authentic national character of the Arab Gulf as reflected in the behavior, customs, traditions, artistic expression, and literature that compose popular culture.

Modern Trends in the Study of Arab Folklore

Although interest in the the study of folk culture in the Arab Gulf began relatively late—no more than twenty or thirty years ago—a perceptive researcher can discern two distinct and rival trends in its study and development. This situation derives from the differing conceptualizations of folklore, both as an object of study and in terms of method, held by Arab researchers. The dualism that has affected Arab researchers parallels exactly the history of the study of folklore in the West. Thus folklorists in the Gulf states have followed in the steps of folklorists in those countries where folklore has held a prominent position among the social sciences for more than a century and a half.

The first of these tendencies is the Anglo-American approach. Followers of this approach emphasize the study of folk literary creativity, especially its verbal dimension. Consequently most of their efforts have been directed at collecting and studying different forms of myths and folktales as well as folk poetry, proverbs, riddles, folk songs, and other forms of oral expression sometimes referred to as "oral arts." Egyptian folklorists, the majority of whom were specialists in Arabic literature, originally championed this approach. Some of the most prominent of these pioneers were Ahmad Taymur, Ahmad Amin, Shaykh Amin al-Khuli, Suhayr al-Qalamawi, ʿAbd al-Ahwani, ʿAbd al-Hamid al-Yunis, Rushdi Salah, Shaykh Jalal al-Hanafi in Iraq, and many of their students and followers in Egypt and throughout the Arab world. When folklore first began to be studied in the Arab world, this approach confined the field to the study of literature and folk dialects.

A second trend, which appeared soon after the first and incorporated Franco-German influences, emphasized a holistic approach to the study of folklore. Borrowing from ethnological and sociological paradigms, it was based on the premise that folklore can be understood only as part of total or integrated cultural production that is carried on from generation to generation. As a result, adherents of this approach have studied a wide range of folk customs, traditions, beliefs, and practices as well as folk literature, material culture, and folk arts. This approach, which has been especially championed by cultural anthropologists, is one of the most common among Arab folklorists for a simple reason: It currently represents the dominant international paradigm in folkloric studies. This is true even in the United States, where this approach has gained support.

Despite the fact that the cultural approach is dominant among folklorists in Arab universities and research centers devoted to the study of popular culture, Arab researchers prefer the literary approach. This is the most likely explanation for the large number of publications and studies that are measured against those in other areas of folklore. Thus it is no surprise then that today Arab scholars are attempting to compensate for the shortcomings of this trend by encouraging their students to study other dimensions of folklore while simultaneously calling for the implementation of a holistic theory of popular culture.

In regard to indigenous theoretical and methodological trends that prevail in contemporary Arab folkloric studies, it is premature to attempt to speak about theories and methods that have originated in the Arab Gulf because, with the exception of Kuwait University, most universities still have not recognized folklore as a science. Unfortunately, folklore is not considered an essential branch of human knowledge that should be accorded its proper place in the university curriculum.

Nevertheless, Arab researchers, especially those from Egypt, have been able to draw upon prevailing international theories and methods in the science of folklore. Arab students of folklore were also exposed to the publications of foreign scholars, some of which had been translated into Arabic. Initially they were exposed to classical theory in a variety of forms: the mythological school, the anthropological school, the Eastern European diffusionist school, the historical school, the ideological school, and the psychological and structural schools. More recently Arab scholars have become acquainted with the theories of the ethnology of communication, comparative culture, and folk culture. It is no exaggeration to say that most of these theories appear in contemporary Arab folkloric research.

Arab researchers have attempted to incorporate the positive aspects of these theories while avoiding their shortcomings. Some, such as Dr. Muhammad al-Jawahiri, dean of the Faculty of Arts at Cairo University, have stressed the necessity of synthesizing four methodological approaches from these theories in order to combine them into a single unit that would constitute a unified approach. This unified approach would allow the researcher to gain a comprehensive scientific understanding of the prevailing relationship between people and folk culture. While these four approaches that comprise the folkloric method might vary from case to case, they exhibit four perspectives: historical, ecological, sociological, and psychological. The absence of any of these perspectives would prevent a comprehensive understanding of a phenomenon.[7]

Despite criticisms that this proposed holistic Arab approach is simply an attempt to synthesize a number of currently dominant methodologies or, in the view of scholars of folk literature, that it is deficient in analyzing the structure of literary texts, a number of new, younger researchers have accepted and successfully applied it. Thus the methods applied today in the study of Arab folklore are multifaceted and diverse, according to the researcher's theoretical and cultural inclinations. Nevertheless, those concerned with the development of the modern folkloric movement in the Arab Gulf will notice two prominent phenomena. First, in many significant publications dealing with folkloric subjects, materials have not been collected and classified scientifically because most authors are enthusiastic amateurs. Their primary concern is to preserve the folklore of the Gulf, which is threatened with destruction by the processes of social transformation currently engulfing the region.

Second, while there is an immense amount of existing popular culture, there is little scientific research in relation to it. This characteristic is linked to the nature of the field of folkloric studies on the pan-Arab and Gulf levels. The studies that have been published to date, especially in Iraq and Kuwait—the first two Gulf states to concern themselves with the study of folklore at both the official and popular level—concentrate on two distinct trends, one social and the other historical.

The Regional Social Trend

Those who adhere to the regional social trend have adopted a synchronic perspective, striving to collect and record aspects of folk culture that are prominent in a particular country or region and to study them from the premise that they represent collective production and reflect prevailing social conditions in that country. For the most part, these studies are descriptive rather than analytic. According to many of these amateur researchers, they have attempted to describe and understand folklore "as they practiced it in their childhood and lived with it until recently." In the words of the famous Kuwaiti historian Sayf Marzuq al-Shamlan, they have all been careful to describe and explain as well as to dedicate their books to the "new generation of indigenous Kuwaitis who resided in Kuwait prior to oil during the era of pearl diving and seafaring . . . so that they might come to know the games that their fathers, mothers and grandparents played." These works are also dedicated "to the upcoming generation in order that they can live the childhood of their fathers and grandfathers in which the natural order of things was devoid of all complications with the intention of returning to those beautiful and sweet memories of childhood and to the happy days of an age gone by, and the memories themselves that evoke a yearning for that past and the desire to return to it . . . and to become acquainted with the heritage (*al-turath*) of their fathers."

In addition, these studies seek to highlight "the primordial visions and conditions in the psyche of our people and what traces of the past these contained that could reflect upon social life, some of which has been destroyed and some of which is being pursued and destroyed by time." They are dedicated to "all those who were nurtured on this good earth" and presented "in order that they will remain in touch with their past, whose essence has been scattered and is close to becoming extinct, especially since what has replaced it is not necessarily beneficial as it comes from foreign environments which have introduced strange notions in the name of urbanization, civilization and progress. We have embraced these ideas eagerly and enthusiastically and with great conviction despite their conflict with the precepts of our native religion and our authentic Arab customs and morals," according to Ayub Husayn in his three studies of Kuwaiti popular culture. In the introduction to *The Concise Kuwaiti Encyclopedia*,[8] Hamad Muhammad al-Saʿidan dedicates his book "to the many members of this generation who know nothing of their past." He states that because "our fathers had a past, a history, literary production and a life, this life is what I am attempting to resurrect from its lethargy—it is hard for me to say from the grave—that life that represented their noble, good and wholesome society." According to folkloric researcher Ibrahim Shukri, these studies might also be seen as dedicated to "our glorious past." Much has been said in this romantic vein by other Kuwaiti and Gulf authors.

Most of these writers are natives enthusiastically committed to their primary community, to their deep-rooted heritage, to their glorious past, and to asserting their individual identity before all else. The motivations and approach that underlie their books, collections, and studies of local oral or musical folk culture of their ancestors constitute a social perspective. In addition to explaining how folklore was created in the past, these writers have tried to explain and assert the true place and utilitarian function of folklore within the local culture and community that carries this heritage—and to emphasize its role today in promoting stability and change. In this sense, these studies represent a sociological trend.[9]

The Nationalist Historical Trend

Those who adhere to the nationalist historical trend adopt a diachronic perspective based on a return to Arab recorded history and heritage and a search for folkloric elements that still persist in local folklore. In this approach, folklore is considered part and parcel of the general heritage (*al-turath*) of the Arab nation. Concern with the past is not simply limited to the search for roots and cultural authenticity, which extend back over many centuries from the Atlantic Ocean to the Gulf, but also derive from an affirmation and promotion of national identity and an exposition of Arab national character and ethos. This group of writers concentrates on "excavating" the folkloric elements or material recorded in the sources of Arab heritage, such as linguistic dictionaries, ancient encyclopedias, biographies, travelogues, and historical analysis. Through this process these writers aim to isolate and identify the historical factors, both local and foreign, that shaped the structure of *turath* as it developed over time by comparing it with the form that it takes in the present. The purpose is to create a dynamic, living picture of the folkloric phenomenon as a subject that is simultaneously both evolving and static.

The gathering of this vast amount of folklore becomes difficult because most *turath* is not annotated in manuscript form and much is unknown. Despite their serious efforts, adherents of this trend have not yet been proved successful except in certain limited areas in folk literature.[10] Perhaps the most significant results that the followers of the nationalist historical approach have achieved have been to demonstrate the unity of Arab popular culture despite regional differences and variations. This approach has not served to obscure the commonalities and holistic nature of Arab *turath* but instead has demonstrated that its peripheral functions always serve, despite their numbers, to preserve the core and authentic, pure Arab character of *turath*.

These trends complement one another, one concentrating on demonstrating the vitality of the national character in the present and the other demonstrating its historical continuity. The approaches must be combined in order for us to comprehend changes in the folk tradition (*al-turath al-sha°bi*) in both the past and present. This dynamic view of the manner in which the folk tradition has changed enhances our ability to predict future trends. The lack of qualified researchers limits the number of works employing both perspectives. However, a number of studies do exist that have synthesized a diachronic and synchronic approach by incorporating oral as well as written documented materials and by comparing such materials from more than one Arab region.[11]

It is important to note that folklore, in its literary interpretation, entered Egyptian universities as a topic of study during the early 1950s under the rubric of "national folk literature." Folklore became part of the curriculum of Kuwait University, which was founded in 1967, in the early 1980s under the title "Arab folk literature." These developments are significant for two reasons: first, the predominance of the nationalistic view of folklore, which is championed first and foremost by academic folklorists, and second, the very enthusiastic student response despite the fact that folklore has been considered a science only very recently and has been a part of the Kuwait University curriculum for only a few years. Another significant consideration is that all the workshops and conferences on folklore held under the auspices of the Arab League, or the Arab Organization for Education and Cultural Sciences (ALESCO), in Egyptian universities or at regional scientific and cultural institutions have, without exception, focused on the question of national folk culture or folk tradition and the common elements thereof.

Goals and Objectives

In light of the preceding analysis, it is possible to see the folkloric movement in the Arab Gulf as having undergone two stages or cycles. The first entailed a nationalistic concern to collect the region's folklore to protect it from extinction. Those involved in this stage were motivated by nationalistic feelings and a strong sense of pride in the past. Despite their noble intentions, their works were tinged with a romanticization of the past. With the increased interest of the state and educational institutions in folk production, the folkloric movement entered a more scientific phase characterized by greater intellectual rigor. During this latter phase, Arab folkloric studies manifested two distinct trends, one social-regional, the other nationalist-historical. The adherents of each of these trends used a variety of theories and methodologies, but applied them with limited success to a very small number of seminal studies of Gulf folklore. The most important element linking the adherents of both these trends is the commonality of the goals expected of this young science.

As for the future, the Arab Gulf will no doubt continue to contribute to the study of folklore both empirically and theoretically. What is especially important from an empirical standpoint is the tremendous oral tradition of the region. Prior to the discovery of oil, most of the people who worked at sea or in the desert expressed themselves through oral production. A continued study of this production will help to provide better comprehension of the social change that has occurred, particularly developments in the nationalist consciousness and in morals and values that created the content of folk culture. Theoretically, the study of Arab folklore can contribute to a better understanding of the comparative dimensions of folk production. The Gulf is ecologically unique in

linking the sea and the desert. Further, it occupies a strategic location as it constitutes a crossroads between two continents and three
major religions. This unique environment allows the region to express itself in both Arab and more international terms. Future studies will no doubt add to an understanding of the contributions of
the Arabs of the Gulf to a larger world culture.

In terms of practical application, the science of folklore could
contribute to a better understanding of the scope and direction of
cultural change sweeping the region and its implications for both
stability and change. This is a matter of vital importance for those
who are responsible for planning local political, economic, social,
and educational policies. Folklore could thus be used to support
the process of development. The study of regional folk culture
should be scientifically based. While this has not been accomplished yet, now is the time to implement it. We need to approach
folklore from an objective, scientific perspective that neither con-
descends nor treats it in a social vacuum, that neither glorifies it
nor becomes partisan. All this is necessary to enable us to review
our folk heritage (*al-turath al-sha°bi*) after having studied it, to
preserve and develop that which is worthy of preservation, and to
resist that which shows degeneration and contradicts the givens of
the era of modern science and scientific thinking. If this can be
accomplished, then we will not be left merely with artifacts of the
past to be placed in museums and in archivial registries. In this
manner, we will control the rhythmic structure of cultural evolution. Better understanding of the dynamics of folk culture will aid
in establishing our civilization on a solid foundation that cannot be
shaken by sudden crises such as those carried to the Arab Gulf by
the "winds of oil."

A scientific approach will assist students of folklore in establishing a firm and decisive position in confronting the problem of cultural authenticity (*al-asala*) and modernity (*al-mu°asara*), or to put
it differently, to reconcile heritage (*al-turath*) and progress. The
Arab world, especially the Arab Gulf, is currently experiencing
this difficult adjustment. We must guide our future according to a
delicate formula that is sensitive to the needs of retaining tradition
while striving for progress. In no way can this delicate balance be

accomplished before we comprehend—scientifically and objectively—the role of each of these two poles in controlling our lives and behavior.

Students of folklore also aim to benefit artistically from folkloric material after it has been classified and studied. To accomplish this end, that which is authentic must be separated from the inauthentic to establish an artistic essence correct in terms of both form and content for the arts of the region.[12] This endeavor would serve to strengthen and deepen the aesthetic and intellectual work of prior generations. It would also counteract the distortion to which regional folk arts have been subjected by the communications media in the Gulf itself, a distortion caused in some cases by an ignorant notion of progress and in others by commercial reasons. This artistic inquiry would foster an acquaintance with the Gulf folk genius as expressed in its original creative thrust. Unless such a revival is based on indigenous folk production, a true artistic revival in the Arab world cannot be achieved; for that matter, neither can an international or universally humanistic revival occur. The national art of any nation should be based on the folk production from which it necessarily develops and from which individuals draw their inspiration to produce form and content. Furthermore, viewing the development of national art according to scientific principles provides an escape from the constraints of foreign artistic trends that currently besiege us through the modern mass communications media. A greater sense of our artistic heritage in the Gulf would serve to abolish feelings of inadequacy in the face of Western arts. In fact, greater sensitivity to our artistic heritage would greatly improve our ability to generate creative artistic innovations and encourage contemporary Arab artistic expression to penetrate a broader international consciousness while maintaining its fundamental Arab character and authenticity.

These are the scientific goals and objectives linked to the new folkloric science in the Arab world. Despite its vitality and national importance, folklore has not yet achieved its potential aspirations for two reasons. First, the official and popular concern with folk culture (al-turath al-sha'bi) is not yet matched by an ability to implement the desired goals. The science of folklore is still in its infancy and suffers from a paucity of specialized researchers. Second, this new science still faces vicious opposition from the partisans of classical Arab culture, especially in their objections to folk culture under the pretext of linguistic, religious, and national taboos. While the science of folklore and those Arab researchers specializing in it declare themselves innocent of all such accusations, this is perhaps the most important obstacle that stands in the way of the future development of folklore in most of the universities of the Arab Gulf today.

NOTES

1. ʿAbd al-Hamid Yunis, difaʿ ʿan al-fulkur [The Defense of Folklore] (Cairo: al-Hay'a al-Misriya li-l-Kitab, 1973), 19.

2. It is not coincidental that this center preceded its Egyptian counterpart established a year later. However, it should be noted that Egyptian folklorists had a profound impact on founding the center.

3. Translators' note: a diwaniya is a men's meeting place.

4. Muhammad Talib al-Duwayk, al-qissas al-shabʿiya fi qatar [Folktales in Qatar], 2 vols. (based on his doctoral thesis); Yusuf Farhan Dukhi, al-aghani al-kuwaytiya [Kuwaiti Songs] (a 503-page volume based on his doctoral thesis); and ʿAli Shuʿayb al-Manaʿ, ed. and annotator, mawawil min al-khalij: nusus min al-adab al-shaʿbi fi mantiqat al-khalij wa-l-jazira [Colloquial Gulf Poetry: Texts of Folk Literature in the Gulf], 2 vols. All were published in Qatar by the Arab Gulf States Folklore Centre in 1984. These three works represent the center's initial field work.

5. Najat al-ʿUza, anmat min al-azya' al-shaʿbiya al-nisa'iya [Forms of Women's Folk Dress] (1984); Muhammad ʿAli ʿAbdallah, al-zakhrafa al-jibsiya fi-l-khalij [Ceramic Ornamentation in the Gulf] (1985); Saʿd al-ʿAbdallah al-Suwayan, al-shiʿr al-shaʿbi fi-l-mamlaka al-ʿarabiya al-saʿudiya [Folk Poetry in the Kingdom of Saudi Arabia] (1985) [translator's note: This study is based on the author's doctoral thesis at the University of California at Berkeley]; Muhammad Rajab al-Najjar, ed. and annotator, muʿjam al-alghaz al-shaʿbiya fi-l-kuwayt [The Encyclopedia of Kuwaiti Folk Riddles] (1985). All were published in Qatar at the Arab Gulf States Folklore Centre.

6. I have been responsible for both proposing and supervising this project.

7. Muhammad al-Jawahiri, ʿilm al-fulkur: dirasa fi-l-anthrupulugiya al-thaqafiya [The Science of Folklore: A Study in Cultural Anthropology] (Cairo: Dar al-Maʿarif, 1977), 1:183–88.

8. Hamad Muhammad al-Sa^{c}idan, *al-mawsu^{c}a al-kuwaytiya al-mukhtasara* [*The Concise Kuwaiti Encyclopedia*], 1st ed. (Kuwait, 1970), 1:9–10.

9. While I might be exaggerating if I claim that these studies adhered to a sociological perspective as a primary tool in research and analysis, this does not negate the fact that these studies contain a great many sociological insights. Consequently I have chosen to refer to these types of studies as the "sociological trend." The published examples in Kuwait of this trend include: *Introduction to Kuwaiti Folklore* (1968); *Studies in Kuwaiti Folk Poetry* (1984); *al-Nabati Poetry* (1981); *Selections from the Kuwaiti Folk Dialect* (1982); *With Our Kuwaiti Memories* (1972); *With Children in the Past* (1969); *Kuwaiti Folk Games* (1970); *A Selection of the Customs and Traditions of Weddings in Kuwait* (1966); and *Folk Dance in Kuwait* (1978).

10. Examples of this school or approach in the Gulf include: *al-malhuna aw al-sha^{c}biya* [*Non-Classical Poetic Arts*], 3 vols. (Iraq, 1977); *al-muwashahat al-^{c}iraqiya min bidayatiha ila nihayat al-qarn al tasir ^{c}ashar* [*Iraqi Muwashahat from their Origins to the End of the Nineteenth Century*] (Iraq, 1981); and *mawali* [*Baghdadi Monologues*] (Iraq, 1974).

11. Examples of this genre include: *Comparative Kuwaiti Proverbs*, 4 vols. (1978–84); and *al-Ghawati or Kuwaiti Folk Riddles and Their Origins in Folk Culture* (1985). I have been one of the most enthusiastic proponents of this integrated approach. Examples of my work, in which I tried to synthesize oral and historical materials, are: *Juha the Arab: His Personality and Philosophy in Deed and Expression* (1978); *Stories of Villains and Vagabonds in Arab Heritage* (1981); *The Art of Folk Medicine [nabawiyat]: A Journey in Time, Place and Consciousness* (1985); *The Art of Riddles in Arab Heritage* (1985); *The Cloak of al-Busiri: A Folkloric Reading* (1985); *Dictionary of Kuwaiti Folk Riddles* (1985); *The Folkloric Elements in the Encyclopedia of Subh al-^{c}Asha* (1985); and *al-Ghawati or Kuwaiti Folk Riddles: An Artistic and Empirical Study* (in press). I am currently annotating the oldest Arabic manuscript to have reached us, *al-i^{c}jaz fi-l-ahaji wa-l-ghaz [The Wondrous Nature of Puzzles and Riddles]*, which was compiled in 1177 by the Baghdadi writer Abu al-Ma^{c}ali Sa^{c}d bin ^{c}Ali al-Kathiri (d. A.H. 586, A.D. 1177). I am also supervising a project entitled "The Collection, Indexing, and Classification of Folkloric Elements in the Most Famous Books and Encyclopedias of Ancient Arab Heritage," being conducted under the auspices of the Arab Gulf States Folklore Centre.

12. The subjective essence of Gulf artistic expression does not contradict but rather complements Arab national arts because it enriches and fortifies them.

8. The Sociopolitical Context of the Iraqi Short Story, 1908–1968

Muhsin Jassim al-Musawi

Despite the increased interest in modern Arabic literature, very little has been written to assess this literature within the context of culture as a "dynamic force" of social change. While writings on Egyptian culture always recognize the literary as well as political significance of the contributions by Taha Husayn, Lutfi al-Sayyid, and others, such is not the case for other Arab cultures. In fact, rarely do other Arab writers view literature within its broader context as capable of stimulating change and transformation in sociopolitical life. Rather than indicating the inability of literature to affect social change, such a tendency stems from the very narrow perspective of Arab writers themselves. Mostly attracted to the political happening as either a single project or a spontaneous reaction, such historians are bound to overlook not only the eddies in political life but also the currents of public unrest, which often are shaped or provoked by writings of social protest. In this chapter I will attempt to demonstrate how the evolution of the Iraqi short story can help us not only to better understand sociopolitical change in modern Iraq but to understand the role of intellectuals in that change.

Two Camps

The primary reason for the growth of a one-sided approach to the study of Iraqi (and other Arab) literature can be traced to the distrust that has separated two camps throughout the period prior to the fall of the monarchy in 1958: the intellectuals and underground political movements, on the one hand, and the politicians and the state, on the other. To be sure, these attitudes are reflected in the broader history of the Arab world.[1] As most Arab political systems during the early part of the twentieth century were either under League of Nations mandates or military control, there was little or no space for intellectuals to practice their ideas and principles. This drove many intellectuals to withdraw from political life, rejecting state policies whenever those policies required blind subordination to political regimes.

Six years before the fall of the monarchy in July 1958, for example, the Iraqi writer Shakir Khusbak published a short story entitled "Years of Terror," which dealt with the lives of the underprivileged and the exploited. The narrator associated rejection of involvement with the state with the ability to establish a sense of personal security and peace of mind. He states: "We have been living in security and peace, as we have no dealings with the government. Everybody is on terms with himself as with his state of things. But time changes, the government gets involved in people's affairs, and people interfere with the government."[2] More important than criticizing exploitation and underprivilege here is the idea that there are always two antagonistic sides, the state and the people. As spokesmen for the latter, short story writers, poets, and essayists developed a sense of distrust, which they rechanneled into attitudes of opposition and protest throughout the period under discussion.

Beginnings

During the early part of the twentieth century, the Iraqi short story lacked artistry and depth. Influenced by Arab or Turkish writings that were in turn heavily influenced by the *Arabian Nights*, the contents of the short story also reflected the impact of the 1908 Ottoman Constitutional Reform, the consequences of World War I, and of the 1920 national uprising in Iraq. Despite the fact that historical events influenced the perspectives of short stories and even shaped the interests expressed in them, these historical events could not help develop the short story as an art form because the stories lacked proper channels or mediums for expression. Usually this medium took the form of daily journalism. Stories of national- ist commitment continued to appear alongside essays and editorials in the daily press. While the movement for constitutional reform in the Ottoman empire led to the consolidation of the Ottoman policy against the Iraqi national movement, short story writers and journalists advocated progress and social reform as a means of es- caping domination and backwardness. It is essential to note that the short story provided, on many occasions, only indirect means for awakening nationalist consciousness. For example, whether in his newspaper *al-Iqadh* (*The Awakening*) or in his so-called *Novel of Awakening* in 1919, Sulayman Faydhi's main concern was to propagate a sense of identity and revolt—as he asserts in his 1952 book, *fi ghamrat al-nidal* (*Amid the Struggle*).

Important as such works are for any assessment of the role of writing in promoting nationalist consciousness, there are others that are more in line with the genealogy of the short story as a genre that has gained in momentum and impact. One example is ᶜAta Amin's "visionary" experience, which appeared in the journal *Dar al-Salam* (*The Abode of Peace*), entitled "kayfa yartaqi al-ᶜiraq" ("How Iraq Can Make Progress").[3] In this "visionary" experience, the narrator wanders along the Tigris River at night. Upon falling asleep later in the evening, he imagines himself in a beautiful and well-defended city. In contrast to women in the rural areas, its women are well "respected." The city happens to be Babylon dur- ing Nebuchadnezzar's reign. The narrator asks the priest Pirous for a prophecy concerning his country's future. The priest regrets that Baghdad has been experiencing so much suffering and pain. However, he foresees a better future awaiting the city that has experienced past glories, emphasizing that it will regain "wealth, dignity and power. There will be no more poverty or humiliation. Education will spread throughout the country and Baghdad will become another London." Rather than mere wishful thinking, the priest's prophecy expresses itself in a number of practical ways as he hands the dreamer books, seeds, and tools that presumably symbolize agricultural and industrial reform along with education and science. In this vision of the future, as in a number of similar writings, the author poses as a social reformer espousing a cause that requires action.

Important as well for our purposes is the same writer's short story, "A Stand by Diyala River," which appeared in the daily *al-ʿIraq* in May 1921. Although ostensibly dealing with a romantic affair of a beloved in distress, recaptured by the enemy to be freed later by her own native lover, the story has definite political overtones in which the beloved symbolically represents a country under foreign domination. In this as in a large number of short stories, a persistent political theme signifies the Iraqi writer's preoccupation with political freedom and change. Thus Iraqi writers resisted, though indirectly, the establishment of treaties that placed their country under British domination during the period when Iraq was under British mandatory control (1921–30).

While appreciating the realistic and the reformist aspects of writings by non-Iraqi Arab writers such as Qasim Amin, Shibli Shumayyil, Taha Husayn, Salama Musa, and ʿAbbas al-ʿAqqad, together with the writings of some Turkish and Russian realists, Iraqi writers of the 1920s, such as Mahmud Ahmad al-Sayyid, rejected the sentimental tendency in the writings of the Egyptian Mustafa Lutfi al-Manfaluti and the Lebanese Jubran Khalil Jubran. In his lengthy narrative *jalal khalid*, al-Sayyid touches mostly on the making of an intellectual in an environment of potential social change. In this as in similar writings of the period, a significant amount of social material provides the basis for an understanding of the "cultural development of intellectuals," as a contemporary writer—ʿAbdul Ilah Ahmad—provided in his account of the background of the Iraqi short story.[4] When viewed within an intellectual framework, such preoccupations represented a search for change. This search did not always bear fruit. When the poet al-Zahawi, for example, called for women's liberation, he created so much protest that he was forced to leave Baghdad.

Marching for Reform

No matter how important such preoccupations with the shaping of intellectuals in an environment of political and social change are for a critical assessment of the role of writers, they ought not blind us to the fact that, aside from political issues, most of the social material in the Iraqi short story prior to the 1940s deals with issues of social protest. Thus, when reading the "Resident of the Palace" by Saʿid ʿAbdul Ilah, it is not surprising to find the writer concentrating upon the rich man who beats an old woman asking for her sick son's wages, without trying to delve into the implications of exploitation in an urban society.[5] So is al-Sayyid's handling of the son's revenge upon his father. In a story entitled "Revolting Against His Father," the son writes a letter to his father, explaining that the father's neglect of him, his only son, is caused by the elder man marrying a second wife. This second wife, who turns out to be a lesbian does not even love the father, yet the man's preoccupation with her causes him to neglect his only son.[6] The social issue is obviously subordinated to al-Sayyid's newly developing interest in the psychological aspects of behavior. He is more adept, however, in other stories that deal with purely social rather than psychological material.

Iraqi writers began to question traditional values in the changing modern cities. This questioning, which is due to alienation, formed the background of writers in the 1930s. In urban Iraqi society, which during the 1920s and the 1930s was still based on tribal or even medieval customs and ways of thinking, people not only held onto these customs but also succumbed to the implications of ambiguity, metaphors, and puns that were typical of the language of the period. Demanding the listener to be fully attuned to such indirect and allusive language is far from employing a rhetorical style. The masses were thus addressed with a language imbued with inflammatory language, as was the case throughout the 1920s following the al-Najaf uprising of March 19, 1918, against the British occupation and in other uprisings that preceded the 1920 Iraqi Revolution. Thus the *Euphrates Daily* wrote in its second issue (August 1920): "The Iraqi Revolution, similar to the Irish and Egyptian Revolutions in every detail, is provoked by protest, inflamed by despotism and spread by the loss of liberty." Another newspaper, *Independence*, wrote in October 1920 that "The Nation unsheathed its sword in the face of the forces of occupation . . . intent on expelling them from every piece of its land. . . ."

At times the short story writer preferred an indirect style in addressing the mind without losing contact with reality. For example, in "Two Events," an essay included in al-Sayyid's 1929 collection *The Vanguards*, the writer concentrates on an ironic situation created by the implications of allusive language. In the "Joke of a Turban," al-Sayyid portrays a man's remark to his turbaned colleague that some dirt is stuck to his headdress. The man with the turban leaves for a while only to encounter a similar remark when returning later. He leaves again but by this point the second remark has driven him to anger; he shouts that he has already murdered his wife and sister, leaving alive only his elderly mother. The man obviously took the remark to refer to some disgraceful behavior, associating the turban with honor as is common in allusive language.

More urban in outlook is al-Sayyid's other story, "*shahama*," ("Valor and Nobility"). As with many parvenus, Safwat Beg enjoys spending the evening with a group of people, drinking and gossiping. They mention in passing their colleague's mother who makes money from prostitution. So drunk as to be unable to follow their remarks, Safwat thinks that they refer to his niece, who lives alone on a mysterious income. Returning home and fetching a knife, Safwat seems determined to kill her. However, as the niece lives in another house, his wife's screams attract many neighbors. Put to bed, Safwat is soon fast asleep, and remembers nothing the next morning. The writer's satire makes obvious fun of the new parasites who appear as an affluent class that is devoid of rational ethics and any sense of social obligations.

The 1930s

A similar interest in issues of love, honor, and prostitution can be found in the writings of the 1930s. In "A Suffering Murderer," Wadi⁶ Juwayda concentrates upon Hasan, the young man who participates with his brothers in killing their own sister because she is in love.[7] On her way from the farm, they attack her. She is surprised to see Hasan, the narrator in the story, among them. "Even you, Hasan," she murmurs. The writer later returns to Hasan, who is under stress, after leaving prison and feeling abandoned and left to fare alone in the world, haunted by the image of his dying sister. Although borrowing Shakespearean material in the murder scene and endowing the villager with a degree of urban intellectualism, Juwayda indicates an early awareness of the psychological element in characterization. The short story badly needed this to escape the limitations of descriptive narratives that dealt solely with the ordinary manifestations of behavior.

In a similar vein, Yusif Matta explores the many dimensions of social evil in his short story "Ruin."[8] Visiting a brothel with a number of young men, the protagonist is surprised to see the woman with whom he was once was in love. Amazed, he asks her to explain the reasons for her present condition. She expresses her agony at her situation but stresses her need to make a living. The author implies that her statement should be seen within the context of the poverty and sickness that entrapped Baghdad's large poverty-stricken population during the 1930s. It was during this period that prostitution attracted the attention of many social reformers. As for the short story itself, we know that torn between the love he feels for the ideal in her and his lust, the protagonist decides not to succumb to the needs of the flesh, accusing the woman instead of misbehavior. She strikes him on the face, driving him out of the brothel, only to undergo herself more agony and pain. Despite concluding with a stock ending, "Ruin" obviously demonstrates a search for a realistic approach to this urban issue.

Ja'far al-Khalili wrote a number of short stories in the psychological vein. In his writings, however, the social issue is always linked to illiteracy, and, as such, his characters are always overshadowed by superstitions. Khalili was drawn to the petite bourgeoisie, the underprivileged official, or the newly emerging working class. A similar interest may be found in later writings, especially in the short stories of Edmund Sabri published during the 1950s.

However, during the 1930s, the most prominent advocate of social reform was Dhu-l-Nun Ayub, a prolific short story writer and
essayist with a keen interest in political and social change. In fact,
Ayub had a long career of political involvement. He used narratives for the sole purpose of exposing evils or to criticize state institutions. Angered by the actions of the state and by the difficult
social conditions of his time, he developed a rebellious attitude.
He says to this effect: "Many social contradictions in life as in the
dealings of statesmen are due to basic factors influencing every
aspect of our life. This excites me, driving me to express this sense
of revolt. Suddenly and almost unwillfully I found myself expressing my opinions, experiences, and criticisms in low-priced pam-
phlets that tend to entertain and to instruct. It is natural for me
then to copy down my feelings, impressions, expectations and
opinions in a lucid narrative that aims both to teach and entertain.
These stories deal with no specific individuals, but with types and
general attitudes."[9] Ayub goes on to argue that: "The uncommit-
ted writer is no more than a passing image with no wisdom or
reason, for ideas and their purpose tend to ensure the artist's im-
mortality. While styles change, correct ideas are the stones upon
which civilizations are built."

Since Ayub concentrates upon ideas and categories of writers,
his writings can be described as social treatises. When dealing with
prostitution, he sees it as a result of social oppression. In his story
"Honor" he looks upon revenge as backward, while in "Behind
the Veil" he explains that veiling women is against progress. In
another story, "Last Term Grades," the writer exposes the social
pressures exerted on teachers. In his collection of short stories,
burj babil [The Tower of Babylon], Ayub blames the state's corrupt administrative system for many of society's evils.[10]

Seen within their temporal context, Ayub's writings are of no
minor significance. In fact, his impact on both common readers
and intellectuals can hardly be overestimated. In an essay on
Ayub's impact on young writers, ʿAbd al-Malik Nuri recognized
this impact, drawing attention to Ayub's ideas and sketches that
demonstrate a tremendous sense of rebellion and revolt against
social and political corruption.[11] As he was mainly a reformer,

Ayub placed little emphasis on the search for refinement in style and manner. A survey of the modernist trend in the 1940s and 1950s indicates that he represents a line of traditional thought that provoked a revolt in the 1940s. Such political and social concerns, problems of urban life, dominate much of twentieth-century Iraqi story telling. While advocating agricultural reform or calling for the elimination of the "feudal" system (*al-nizam al-iqta'i*), these writers had no accurate knowledge of rural life during the period in question. They were inclined to overlook rural Iraq or to place their own protagonists—mostly intellectuals—within unrealistic rural settings, as Ayub himself had done in *The Hand, the Land, and Water*.[12] In that novel we are confronted with intellectuals who take upon themselves the responsibility of cultivation and land reform. This tendency to intellectualize the rural setting continued until the 1950s, when Mahdi 'Issa al-Saqr attempted to investigate not only the social side of rural life but also its psychological aspects, touching on love and depravation, expectation and frustration, happiness and suffering. This new trend in the short story corresponded to a broader preoccupation with the underprivileged as people whose inner lives also deserved attention.

It was considered a change for the better when writers of the late 1940s and 1950s, such as 'Abd al-Malik Nuri and Mahdi 'Isa al-Saqr, turned their attention to the individual. In "fatuma," which gained the *al-Adib* journal prize for short story writing in December 1948, Nuri comes upon a peasant woman waiting desperately for her husband. As she waits, she describes her suffering and her yearning for love.[13] At the point of high expectations and mounting emotions, the woman is almost paralyzed to see her husband happily returning with a large new family of his own, including a new wife and children. In this story, Nuri feels no need to demonstrate the suffering women undergo under such a social system. It is enough for him to draw the reader's attention to the peasant's wife as a human being with hopes, expectations, and rights that have to be acknowledged.

In this short story as in those by Fu'ad al-Tikirli, al-Saqr, and Shakir Khusbak, the authors display their developing interest in internal characterization that involves not only a basic recognition of people as individuals rather than social types or groups, but also new ways of expression that put an end to generalization and rhetoric. The interest in characters as individuals should not be seen as separate from the suddenly emerging interest in people as individuals rather than as masses. The painter Jawad Salim saw people as attractive and craved to reproduce their shape, whereas Nuri chose names of people, mainly women, as titles for his stories. At this time, Iraqi intellectuals were drawn to names of national significance, such as leaders of the national government—for example, the four colonels who led the 1941 uprising against the British. Although executed, these leaders soon became a source of national commitment and pride. Their sacrifices paved the way for the drive for democracy that led to the state's 1946 recognition of political parties. Increasingly during this period, individuals were able to influence politics and social change. Henceforth, as shown in the widespread demonstrations of 1947 and 1948, political activity as well as demonstrations would take the form of organized action with identifiable leaders and organizers. This sociopolitical change was reflected in a corresponding shift in writing away from traditional styles and the constraints they had imposed.

Many historians of literature saw the craving to escape the traditional and the restrictive as a reaction to World War II, to the abortive 1941 uprising in Iraq, and to the nationalistic upsurge that gained momentum in reaction to the Zionist and international conspiracy against Palestine, its people and land. Others minimized the impact of the war but recognized instead the subsequent mobility and modernization. In fact, Salim, one of the prominent figures of the modernist trend in Iraqi art, suggested that mobility was as significant in bringing about a change in Iraqi artists' ways of thinking and painting. He pointed to the Polish painters' stay in Iraq during the mid-1940s as a consequence of the war.[14] It is highly significant that Polish artists encouraged not only the native element in Iraqi art but also a strong attachment to one's own country. According to Salim, an influential critic among this group argued that great art is impossible without a basic attachment to one's own country.

A Sense of Democracy

In addition to a rising sense of attachment to their own country, a number of Iraqi poets and short story writers have felt since the mid-1940s that modern political doctrine and activism were not compatible with traditional modes of expression. Such traditional modes of expression employ and greatly emphasize a rhetorical structure at the expense of context. The ultimate example of such modes of expression is the classical *qasida* (poem). This attachment to a rhetorical mode of expression is not to be equated with social treatises that are fundamental to great art, and are structurally more complex. More important, however, is the fact that such a drive to escape the traditional and the restrictive is urban. Whether concentrating on the psychological dimensions of reality, attaching itself to the individual, or depicting the new manifestations of urban life and interests, this modernist trend represented a change in outlook that emerged in the arts as well as in poetry and short story writing. Although gaining recognition only during the mid-1950s, this trend has continued to influence Iraqi writing and painting.

While emphasizing color, the individual, and action in painting, in poetry the modernist attitude demonstrated a search for a unity of topic in developing themes of social and political interest. Whether concentrating on women in distress or pointing to issues of national or pan-Arab interest, poets during the 1950s tended to situate such themes within a general context that provided the reader with a better insight into social and political affairs. Although short story writers were no less involved in this endeavor, they manipulated the space available to them to develop scenes and situations that sought to draw the reader's attention to the unconscious side of reality, or to the "hidden stream" alluded to by Nuri.[15] Along with Fuad al-Tikirli, Shakir Khusbak, Mahdi ʿIsa al-Saqr, ʿAbd al-Samad Khanaqa, Muhammad Rasmanchi, Nizar Salim, and ʿAbdallah Niazi, ʿAbd al-Malik Nuri searched for a way in which to draw the reader into a situation where a revelation or epiphany that brought new awareness and understanding could be attained. While these writers were all interested in exposing political and social evils (e.g., political oppression, prostitution, traditional ways of thinking), they tended to view them through a rather personal prism that allowed space for each individual's inhibitions, inclinations, and expectations. In political action as in social life, their characters are hardly mere pawns in a chess game.

In the "Deaf Wall," Nuri depicts his protagonist as capable of change and resilience at the moment of defiance and love. When deprived of his freedom by the state, the protagonist is forced to make a choice between freedom and love, and in doing so he turns against the state. A similar attitude can be found in al-Tikirli's "The Others." While the story depicts a day of demonstrations against the rulers' servility to the British, its main focus is a girl's hard choice whether to join the demonstrations despite her sick mother's need for attention and care. Even when a writer of this group decided to depict a situation with political implications, as in the court scene of al-Saqr's "The Anger of the City," the purpose was to demonstrate the state's fear of the people. Faced with a huge crowd, the trial committee is wary lest a demonstration develop. Set within the broader context of city life, the court becomes the microcosm of social and political life during the 1950s. Demonstrating the antagonism between the rulers and the ruled and exposing suffering and poverty, the court is meant to stand for a society whose people "are crushed by horror, pain and boredom," as the narrator himself explains. Such a trend continued to manifest itself in a large number of short stories, especially in the writings of Shakir Khusbak, ʿAbd al-Majid Lutfi, ʿAbd al-Razzaq Shaykh ʿAli, Ghayb Tuma Farman, and Edmund Sabri. In these writings the emphasis is placed on issues that call for social and political reform. Especially in Farman's and Shaykh ʿAli's stories, there is always a tendency to expose evils, to criticize the ruling class, and to demand change. Through less direct methods other writers pointed to such evils without necessarily becoming politically involved.

While the late 1950s concluded on a note of strife and antagonism, some stories of the time anticipated social change intellectually. Ennui continued to manifest itself throughout the 1960s. Fearing persecution but driven nevertheless to frustration, intellectuals resorted to ambiguity and allusion during the late 1950s. Although advocating revolution and social change, these types of ambivalent intellectuals found themselves reluctantly pushed into political action. Such is the case with Ghanim al-Dabbagh's protagonist in *Noise in the Alley*, a novel that also documents the 1956 political demonstrations in Iraq in support of Egypt. A similar situation can be found in Nazar ʿAbbas' "New Waters." In this short story, the protagonist finds himself driven to join in a demonstration despite his disillusioned frame of mind and ambivalent attitude toward his city, which he both loves and detests. Without a job, he vents his anger on the insulting boss despite the fact that this boss could be the one in charge of giving him back his job. He warns the boss that he and similar administrators will be swept away by a flood that differs from biblical tides. "It will be brown human beings, swarming with hatred out of every city, every alley, corner and school, springing out of every place, sweeping clean away our town, endowing it with a new life."[16]

Politics and Urban Life

No matter how fluctuating the attitudes were toward city life, the short stories of the 1950s also evince a new sense of place that is not devoid of relevant implications according to circumstance and time. As noted earlier, the Iraqi short story is an urban product that failed to accommodate itself to the rural setting. Its urbanism is steeped in the political context of Iraqi life that began to be focused on city centers, especially Baghdad since the 1950s, as Rizq Allah Augustin rightly noticed in 1954.[17] In fact, readers of Iraqi short stories are bound to notice two conspicuous aspects that became established during the 1950s: the attachment to city life and simultaneously an avowed hatred for it.

Aside from the political action directed against cabinets accused of total dependence on the British, the flood of rural migrants that swept the outskirts of Baghdad, economic restlessness, and the increasing call for efficient use of wealth to develop city and rural life drew writers' attention to urban issues. One such writer, ʿAbd al-Razzaq Shaykh ʿAli, mysteriously disappeared in 1957. Like Khusbak and Farman, Shaykh ʿAli concentrated on sociopolitical issues, such as unemployment, poverty, and illiteracy. In his short stories Shaykh ʿAli places emphasis on the urban context that elicited both attachment to city life and rejection of its evils. There is no better evidence of this attachment than the recurrent mention of the city in numerous titles of short stories and published collections: Examples include al-Tikirli's "The Road to the City" written in 1954; al-Saqr's 1959 collection is named, "The Anger of the City"; Ghanim al-Dabbagh wrote "A Job in the City" in 1959; while Musa Kiraydi entitled his 1968 collection, *Voices in the City*. The other aspect related to this urban attachment is the protagonist's delicate relationship with the surrounding urban outside world, with its conflicting enticements and taboos, its appeal and repugnance, its peace and oppression. Although most modern Iraqi short stories are set within a political or a social framework, this relationship with urban themes distinguishes them.

Whereas writers of the 1950s saw this relationship in light of their critical assessment of Iraqi society, later writers were bound to develop a different viewpoint. During the 1950s writers still looked on themselves as advocates of change, as Nuri's numerous letters to his friend and colleague Fu'ad al-Tikirli indicate. al-Tikirli himself never assumed that their endeavors lacked social or political purpose. Writing later in "My Experience as a Short Story Writer," al-Tikirli explains how he and other writers felt their commitment toward their people was reflected in their choice of style, a style that was not applicable to the period following the July 1958 revolution.[18] Whether dealing with intellectuals at a moment of choice and action, concentrating on people under stress, such as Salima the prostitute in al-Tikirli's "Green Eyes" and Nuri's Fatuma in the story bearing the same name, or coming upon a protagonist in a moment of revolt against city life, as in al-Dabbagh's "Job in a City," writers of the 1950s were interested either in attitudes or in the marginalized elements of society rather than in the intellectual as an outsider.

Regarding the sociopolitical implications of city life, the Iraqi short story reflects a number of attitudes as a consequence of the July 1958 revolution. In so far as migration to Baghdad is concerned, for example, writers had a sympathetic understanding for

those peasants who flooded the city's suburbs in search of a livelihood. Driven from rural areas either by the floods or by feudal
oppression, peasants desperately searched for sustenance in cities,
especially Baghdad, where the ghettos continued to challenge and
frighten numerous governments. Whether fearing them as a symbol of poverty or as a center for radical politics, successive governments looked upon such ghettos with suspicion; this view is
reflected in the pejorative term *sharagwa*, or "coming from the
East" (as underprivileged, uncultivated, and poverty-stricken) used
by the privileged classes and their associates to refer to the migrants. It is as an urban issue, however, that writers interacted
with these migrants. In a short story entitled "al-Shaykh," the writer Gha'ib Tuʿma Farman dealt with one of the hardships that confronted these peasants. The old man in the story finds a sign on his
door that he cannot decipher. Someone reads it for him. Although
it tells him to leave the area, the old man refuses to leave. Instead,
he prepares himself for the approaching trouble, remaining vig-
ilant despite being physically feeble.

The individual is bound to encounter a number of problems in
city life. Expecting to be able to take advantage of city privileges,
Hamada in Shakir Khusbak's "Dark Night" searches for a doctor
to accompany him to the poor suburbs to treat his sick wife. Rejected by all, he decides to bring her to the city in a carriage (automobiles were rare at the time). However, the carriage he finds
gets stuck in a muddy alley. Hamada has to carry his wife on his
back during a rainy night. After experiencing such hardships, the
poor wife cannot survive. These issues demonstrate the short story
writer's concern with problems of accommodation and adaptation
to city life.

Another issue that attracted short story writers' attention during
the 1950s was the rights and feelings of the marginalized elements
of society. This interest, influenced by Dostoyevski, acquired a native flavor.[19] As city life overflowed with these marginalized elements, writers came to see them as worth studying and analyzing.
They were depicted as having special whims but no fantasies. As
such ʿAbbud in Nuri's story of the same name reacts passionately

to his dog while undergoing a number of stimulating experiences. The writer views ʿAbbud's suspicious caresses from another angle, the dog's, internalizing its reactions in a monologue that expresses the dog's astonishment and surprise at ʿAbbud's shameless behavior in an open square. In "The Train of the South" Nuri deals also with a recurrent situation, but he reproduces portions of the whole scene from the cock's viewpoint. The cock internalizes his reaction while being pressed hard to the woman's lap lest he escape. While introducing such a scene in a new light, Nuri never loses sight of the social problem: The woman comes with her blind daughter to the city to sell the cock in order to acquire the services of a certain priest supposedly capable of bringing back her daughter's eyesight. In the past the mother herself had expressed her aspirations for the future in interior monologues. Her utmost desire is to strive to guarantee a suitable husband for her blind daughter.

No less intricate is al-Tikirli's treatment of the marginalized, eccentrics, and young officials. While ʿAbbud in the "Road to the Town" attempts to meet his social obligations, al-Tikirli makes fun of the whole issue. He not only presents the sister ʿAbbud is expected to murder as retarded, but also depicts ʿAbbud himself as a human being who cannot be turned into an animal by such customs and obligations.

Even when it comes to issues of incest, marriage, and sex, al-Tikirli, who had contact with foreign literature, never succumbs to traditional values and methods. Rather he begins to look at such issues with suspicion, searching for real meaning behind the superficial façade. As such, "The Oven" depicts a villager, who is accused of murdering his brother's wife, defending himself in the court. The man retells the story in numerous ways from different perspectives not to save his own life but to defend his sister (from his mother), with whom he is in love. A similar intricate approach is discernible in "The Other Side." Rather than being an outsider, Muhammad Jaʿfar, the short story's protagonist, passes through a process of meditation upon social and moral obligations. Should he continue living with his wife who was blinded after her aborted

pregnancy? Should he return to his small town? Should he succumb to his lust? Finally he decides to act, regardless of any expectations held by others, when an old woman pushes him aside
in order to step ahead of him in a bus and when the horse that he
passes along the way to his small town is about to die.

No less important are "The Crow" (1962) and "The Extinguished
Lantern" (1954) by al-Tikirli. "The Crow" explores a husband's
sense of righteousness and revenge when his wife discovers his ex-
tramarital relationship. Instead of criticizing himself, he is driven
to murder his wife by his sense of shame, on the one hand, and his
fear of exposure, on the other. In the second story, a father rapes
his son's young wife when he sees that the young man is reluctant
to sleep with her. The entire scene is depicted through the son's
eyes. The influence of Dostoyevski, Sartre, and Camus on Iraqi
writers is evident in these and other short stories of the 1950s. The
authors reach conclusions regarding responsibility and choice that
were at variance with long-standing complacent or fatalist approaches to life in Arab culture.

The Disillusioned Intellectual of the 1960s

Although it is impossible to draw clear-cut distinctions between
the writings of the 1950s and the 1960s, the political nature of the
latter writings can be noted. Disillusioned with the 1958 revolution
and its aftermath, the Iraqi short story writers of the 1960s developed a somewhat rejectionist attitude toward life and politics despite their attachment to earlier technical achievements as well as
their appreciation of existentialist literature. As such, they concentrated on portraying protagonists in action, resorting to interior
monologues or to flashbacks and stream-of-consciousness tech-
niques to depict true-to-life characters. They also tended to concentrate on situations that required choice or action. They were
more inclined, however, to identify with the newly emerging Arab
intellectualism, which began in the mid-1960s to distinguish itself
from both the Western liberal tradition represented in the journals
Hiwar, Mawaqif and *Shi'r*, as well as from the existentialist phi-

losophy that was in vogue at the time. These three journals that adopted liberalism patronized Arab intellectuals by increasingly emphasizing experimentalism and innovation and disregarding ideology and politics. However, there soon developed an intellectual perspective that called for change and systematic thinking with a tinge of revolutionary idealism, represented, for example, by Muta° Safadi's protagonist in his novels *Professional Revolutionary* and *Generation of Fate*.[20] Following the 1952 Egyptian revolution, the 1956 aggression against Egypt and the July 1958 Iraqi revolution, an activist line of political thought developed that called for the nationalization of oil, land reform, and democratic freedoms. Disillusionment with military involvement in domestic politics was also evidenced. Hence the call for political activism was no longer identical with military coups; writers had begun to become disenchanted due to the coups' bloodshed, especially in the aftermath of Iraq's 1958 revolution. Ideologies flourished again during the 1960s, to be sure, with intellectuals posing as reformers and with an increasing search for a reconciliation between "scientific socialism" and nationalism. Despite the aspirations for political reform and modernization in Arab societies that still suffered from poorly developed social thought and behavior, intellectuals continued to look on party politics and military involvement in political affairs with suspicion. Given the political situation at the time, intellectuals were bound to suffer at the hands of politicians and their supporters.

As such the most distinctive aspect of Iraqi writing during the 1960s is disillusionment and doubt. Whether expressed bluntly, as in the works of °Abd al-Rahman Majid al-Ruba°i or in the short stories of both Sargon Bulos and Yusif al-Haydari, or more indirectly, as in the refined writings of both Muhammad Khudhayir and Musa Kiraydi, disenchantment and ennui are very conspicuous. Mostly passive, prone to thinking and meditation, the protagonists in these stories seem to be overwhelmed by the outside world with which they cannot cope. Hence, in "Morning Complex" Musa Kiraydi's Mahmud behaves indifferently upon finding his wife leaving the house without explanation despite his effort to find her a doctor to relieve her labor pains. Although there are no narrative explanations, the reader is drawn to the conclusion that the wife is leaving to express her mounting anger toward her husband's indifferent attitude throughout their marriage. Thus we see how the Iraqi short story writer attempts to convey the impact of the larger social and political world on the family and gender relations.

The sociopolitical context of Kiraydi's short stories differs significantly from that of Sargon Bulos. Both depict their characters as intellectuals who are under stress due to the incompatibility they feel with city life. Unable to adapt and incapable of revolt, they lead a life of disillusionment and alienation.

Although less refined as short story writers, both al-Ruba'i and al-Haydari care more for the marginalized and political defeatists who experience suffering and fear due to their political views. Such writings fit well into the sociopolitical context of the 1960s. Due to a number of military coups d'état and persistent internal conflict, political strife became a characteristic aspect of daily life that breathed distrust and hatred into the personal lives of ordinary Iraqis. It is not surprising to find Iraqi writers stressing an interior monologue as the most appropriate form with which to express their protagonists' fears. Thus one of al-Ruba'i's outcasts has the following dialogue with himself: "They are besieging the city, sweeping it clean from all that relates to you. What are they up to? He sets out towards al-Nahda Square where people gather. But seeing one of his compatriots, he moves away stealthily, vanishing into the alley since he has no idea of what that man thinks of him."[21]

No less disillusioned are al-Haydari's characters, who are withdrawn, hollow, and spiritually dead. They mostly project their own feelings onto whatever they encounter and see. As such the world is just as hollow in their eyes. In al-Haydari's "Ghost," for example, we read the following: "Shops are closed, while people are enclosed in their dwellings. Few still wander as he does. . . . Dragging his feet in these empty roads, he feels that he is only a stranger, a mere piece of dust swept by a merciless wind. So wretched and hollow is he."[22]

A better depiction of the sense of loss, betrayal, and deceit can be found in a number of 'Abd al-Sattar Nasir's short stories, especially "Secret Rooms," "The Smell of City Houses," and "A Short Biographical Sketch of Shaykh Nadir." This consistent note of fear develops into a feeling of paranoia that expressed well many an Iraqi writer's sense of insecurity during the 1960s. In "Secret Rooms" the young protagonist is driven by curiosity to explore the secrets of some closed rooms. In a pattern characteristic of an *Arabian Night* tale, such unwarranted curiosity is bound to be punished. In the "Short Biographical Sketch of Shaykh Nadir," the protagonist undergoes moments of terror that make the story one of the few that deal brilliantly with paranoia within a social environment characterized by feelings of oppression and hatred. The writer is much more effective when dealing with a larger social setting in "The Smell of City Houses." The narrator depicts life in the Beggars' Alley where both Nawaf, the Jewish merchant, and the mysterious Manhal spread their control over others' lives. Nawaf's drugs cause paralysis and pain, while Manhal's schemes are geared toward implicating everyone, including the narrator as a boy, in his lecherous dealings. Although concentrating on character portrayal, the writer develops a view of the alley with its miserable living conditions that reminds the reader of Najib Mahfuz's *zuqaq midaq* [*Midaq Alley*].

In contrast to many other writers of the period, Muhammad Khudhayir is less fatalistic and thus more sophisticated in his approach to portraying the personal in the larger social environment. While investigating the minds of his protagonists and assessing their inner response to the outside world, Khudhayir never looks upon life as lacking in compassion or possible redemption. In the short story "Minaret," for example, the evening call to prayer touches the wife's heart on her way home after a disillusioning visit to her mother's home. In a desperate search for old sources of comfort and love, she had visited her mother, only to experience more frustration and agony as her mother's avowed love smacks of a false emotion. Her mother seems only a "frog" on a piece of wood hewn from "an old tree." Freed from sentimentalism, Khudhayir encounters new social issues that require fresh consideration, especially in giving more attention to the psychological element in life.

While deeply concerned with the social dimension of city life and social attitudes, Khudhayir always associates the social with the personal, intensifying both with objective correlatives or with recurrent references to images of relevant meanings. In "A Monkey's Wish" two girls relax during weekends, spending most of their time cleaning or resting. One of them loves to look at a picture hanging on the wall that depicts a wounded lioness surrounded by dark-complected men who are riding horses and holding spears. While looking down on the street through the opened window, she sees a gypsy who tells her of his monkey's peculiar inclination to imitate the sultan's wife in a ridiculous sexual position with her legs wide apart. The implication is not hard to fathom as the girl draws back to her bed waiting like the wounded lioness to be conquered. Obliquely, Khudhayir is referring not only to sexual repression but also to the terrible complications involved in appeasing sexual desires.

Although there had been a great deal of talk about restoring control over national wealth, especially oil, during the 1960s, in fact little changed for the better. Consequently, Iraqi society could develop only slowly. Disease, poverty, and illiteracy, which continued to characterize the sociopolitical context of the 1960s, formed the fabric of the lives of the writers themselves. Mostly underprivileged, their alliance with the mass element of society ultimately gave them the right to speak of their own personal careers as representative of society at large. This can be seen in Nuri's short stories during the 1960s as well as in those of Yusif al-Haydari's and others. There were other reasons behind the emphasis on sexual repression and similar issues. Due to the lack of radical transformation, closed societies develop their own lines of secrecy, frustration, and fear. Such are the characteristics of the short stories of Musa Kiraydi and ʿAbd al-Sattar Nasir. In al-Nasir's short story entitled "A Short Biographical Sketch of Shaykh Nadir," sexual repression leads to incest, prostitution, and persecution, thereby becoming a metaphor for social repression writ large that dwarfs the individual and his ideas. It is not surprising, therefore, that the idea of the little man, the downtrodden and the underprivileged is the most conspicuous aspect of the Iraqi short story during the 1960s.

It is debatable whether the 1967 Arab defeat caused a radical change in the general outlook of writers in the late 1960s and the early 1970s. The most obvious literary response to this defeat was an increased sense of frustration rather than alienation. Its most salient impact on Iraqi politics manifested itself in the July 1968 revolution in Iraq. As a political event, the defeat was most influential in promoting the normalization of relations among political parties and social groups and socioeconomic change. Culturally the revolution began to influence literature, especially poetry and criticism. Expressing the feelings and radical aspirations of the period, both genres developed a sense of the immediate. Prior to the late 1970s the short story was only partly affected by this. Following the nationalization of oil, on the one hand, and the plans to employ rising oil prices for development, on the other, urban society began to experience significant social change. Its impact was felt even by the marginalized peasantry that had migrated in large numbers to urban centers.

Sudden expansion and affluence were bound to introduce new themes into the Iraqi short story. Along with the Iraq-Iran War, which broke out in 1980, this new sense of affluence entailed a number of radical changes not only in the social structure of the urban centers but also in the behavior and thought of the groups being treated in the short story.[23]

Despite the significant impact of oil wealth prior to 1975, it began to have real influence on Iraqi life only once oil prices began their meteoric rise later in the decade. Along with persistent efforts to popularize literacy and improve education and health programs, the Iraqi government introduced development plans in every field leading to radical changes in social structure. Better opportunities for peasants were part of the overall rising expectations of the nation and drove large numbers to flood the cities, preferring daily wages to the unforeseen vagaries of rural life.

The influx of new migrants only enlarged the already sprawling cities, a fact that drove the state to impose modern architectural designs upon some older districts and suburbs, thereby reshaping larger areas and sweeping away older ones. Such changes caused some writers to capture this moment; in Mahmud Jandari's "A

State of War" (1984), the protagonist decides to move to the city
despite his handicap. Once there, he finds himself overwhelmed
by the urban surroundings and new architectural changes. Time
no longer represents a series of frustrations or alienation but rather
a number of lines of demarcation that sharply punctuate life and
put an end to older, traditional ways of living. In poetry, as in
Sami Mahdi's collection *min awraq al-zawal* [*From the Papers of
Extinction*], a rather romantic view of social change predominates.
In that collection, the monologue of "The Event" reveals the speaker
under a stress who finds himself dwarfed and rejected:

> Who is he
>   among millions of his race
> Who is he?
>   Afraid of what he sees
>   or hears,
>   of overwhelming buildings
>   store windows,
>   people's fury,
>   noise of buses
>   and their horns . . .[24]

Money itself has attracted the attention of the storyteller, who
focuses here on its penchant to cause both good and evil. Whenever it indicates an improvement in the quality of life, material
wealth bestows some comfort on the writer, as is the case in Lutfiya
al-Dulaymi's short story "Returning from Abroad." The story deals
with the feelings of joy that overcome the female protagonist when
encountering her new surroundings: "Embarking from a speedily
driven car, streets washed by justice, joy upon the faces, the city
no longer rejects its dwellers."[25]

Rather different is Ghazi al-'Ibadi's approach to the changing
material conditions of urban life caused by the impact of oil
wealth. While signifying improvement and welfare for al-Dulaymi,
to al-'Ibadi, they point to the end of the values of virtue and honesty. The writer sees the impact of wealth on the newly moneyed
classes as substituting appearances and images for reality and driv-

ing the nouveaux riches to callously overlook the needs and lives of others. In "A Source of Danger" the protagonist pushes the filthy young laborer away so hard, lest he stain him, that a passing car runs the worker down and kills him. The pernicious impact of money on the prevailing value system is also treated in "Termination," where a young girl looking for a seat away from a group of nasty boys feels the well-dressed, middle-age man on the bus is no cause for suspicion. She is shocked, however, to feel his hand delve smoothly beneath her skirt to touch her body. In other words, the new wealth of the 1970s while causing material improvement of Iraqi society, also served to disrupt and confuse social values.

Iraqi writers as such were mostly journalists whose channels of expression were usually subliterary, driven by the continuous demand of the daily newspapers, on the one hand, and the attractive superficial side of change, on the other. In other words, it was inevitable that "pure" literature would retreat to become a private and individualistic pursuit devoid of public interest. Both poetry and the short story are becoming more similar to daily reporting, dealing with public issues and touching on the superficial side of transformation. The exception is war literature, where the monologue, dramatic or otherwise, has become a channel for projecting internal modes of feeling and experience. Here, as in the literature from 1908 to 1968, space gains greater significance, not only because of its conspicuous nature but also due to the sense of time that manifests itself only temporarily in war situations where the fleeting moment assumes greater significance in the face of imminent death. Otherwise, money negates time because it imposes its materialistic values that, by their very nature, drive away sense of the spiritual. This overwhelming line of thought dominates the Iraqi short story.

Viewed within a socioeconomic context, such a regard for the materialistic and the external is to be expected. Overwhelmed by rapid social change and hard-pressed for meditation, the writer is bound to capture the fleeting and the conspicuous. Although still expressing some love for better times or a few quiet moments, short story writers are no different from poets: Both react spontaneously to issues and developments of current interest.

NOTES

1. On Iraqi literature and politics, see ʿAdbul Ilah Ahmad, *nash'at al-qissa wa tatawwuruha fi-l-ʿiraq* [*The Emergence and Growth of the Short Story in Iraq*] (Baghdad: Shafiq Press, 1969); Raphael Butti, *al-sahafa fi-l-ʿiraq* [*Journalism in Iraq*] (Cairo: 1955); and Ibrahim al-Waʿli, *thawrat ʿishrin fi-l-shiʿr al-ʿiraqi* [*The 1920 Revolution in Iraqi Poetry*] (Baghdad: Imaʾ Press, 1968).

2. See Shakir Khusbak's collection, *al-ʿasr al-jadid* [*The New Era*] (Cairo: Muʿasir Bookshop, 1951).

3. ʿAta Amin, "*kayfa yartaqi al-ʿiraq*" ["How Iraq Can Make Progress"], *Dar al-Salam* [*The Abode of Peace*], nos. 17/18 (1919).

4. Ahmad, *The Short Story in Iraq*, 95, n. 37.

5. Saʿid ʿAbdul Ilah, "*sakin dhalik al-qasr*" ["Resident of the Palace,"], *al-Hasid*, no. 32 (February 1931).

6. Mahmud Ahmad al-Sayyid, "*thawra ʿala abihi*" ["Revolting Against His Father"], *al-Hasid*, no. 15 (30 May 1929), p. 6.

7. Wadiʿ Juwayda, "*qatil yataʿalam*" ["A Suffering Murderer"], *al-Hasid*, no. 29 (February 1932), 18.

8. Yusif Matta, "*hutam*" ["Ruin"], *Utarid*, no. 1 (August 1934), 9.

9. *al-Adib* (February 1954), 78.

10. Dhu-l-Nun Ayub, *burj babil* [*The Tower of Babylon*] (Baghdad: al-Ahali, 1939). Both "*min wara' al-hijab*" ["Behind the Veil"] and "*sharaf*" ["Honor"] appeared in *al-Hasid*, 912–19, (September 1936), and *Modern Journal* (15 June 1937).

11. ʿAbd al-Malik Nuri, "*akhbar al saʿa*" ["The News of the Hour"], *Akhbar al-Saʿa*, 2 April 1953.

12. Dhu-l-Nun Ayub, *al-yadd al-ard wa-l-ma'* [*The Hand, the Land, and Water*].

13. ʿAbd al-Malik Nuri, "*fatuma*" ["Little Fatima"], *al-Adib*, January 1948.

14. ʿAbd al-Malik Nuri, "*kana fanan shab: dhikrayat jawad salim*" ["The Artist as a Young Man: Jawad Salim's Memoirs"], *al-Hiwar*, no. 8 (January–February 1964), 99–101, 103, 108.

15. Nuri's phrase in "The News of the Hour."

16. Ghanim al-Dabbagh, *al-ma' al-ʿadhib* [*Sweet Water*] (Baghdad: al-Adib Press, 1969); Mahdi ʿIsa al-Saqr, *mujrimun tayibun* [*Good Criminals*] (Baghdad: al-Rabita Press, 1954); ʿAbd al-Malik Nuri, *zuqaq al-fi'ran* [*Rat Alley*] (Baghdad: Ministry of Information, 1972); Nuri, *nashid al-ard* [*The Song of the Land*] (Baghdad: n.p., 1954); Fu'ad al-Tikirli, *al-wajh al-akhar* [*The Other Side*] (Baghdad: n.p., 1960); al-Saqr, *ghadab al-madina* [*The Anger of the City*] (Baghdad: n.p., 1960); Gha'ib Tuʿma Farman, *kitab min al-ʿiraq* [*A Letter from Iraq*], *al-Thaqafa al-Misriya*, April 26, 1950, 600. See also ʿUmar al-Talib, *al-qissa al-qasira fi-l-ʿiraq* [*The Modern Short Story in Iraq*] (Musul: Musul University Press, 1979).

17. Rizq Allah Augustin, *"al-tawasu^c al-maradi li madinat baghdad"* ["The Unhealthy Expansion of Baghdad"], *Four Seasons* (Autumn 1954), 81–89.

18. See Fu'ad al-Tikirli, *"khibrati ka katib qissa"* ["My Experience as a Story Writer"], *al-Adib*, no. 7 (July 1973): 69.

19. On Dostoyevski's impact, see the author's *al-tayar al-mu^casir fi-l-qissa al-^ciraqiya al-qasira* [*The Modernist Trend in the Iraqi Short Story*] (Baghdad: al-Mu'assasa al-^cArabiya, 1984), along with the documentary material. References are made to correspondence between Nuri and al-Tikirli.

20. No study has appeared to date regarding Safadi's impact. The *al-Adib* monthly may be a good source for any research on this issue. Regarding intellectualism in Syrian Arabic literature, see Hisham al-Khatib's *tabi^cat al-ta'athur al-ajnabi ^cala al-qissa al-suriya al-mu^casira* [*The Nature of Foreign Influence on the Modern Syrian Story*] (Damascus: Arabic Studies Institute, 1973.)

21. On the writings of ^cAbd al-Rahman Majid al-Ruba^ci, see Musa Kiraydi, *"mutarad"* ["The Chased"] in *^cuyun al-hilm* [*The Eyes of a Dream*] (1974) and *"^cuqdat al-nahar"* ["The Day's Knot"] in *adwa' fi-l-madina* [*Lights in the City*] (Beirut: Modern Press, 1968); see also Muhammad Khudayir, *"bayt fi dahiyat al-madina"* ["A House in a Suburb"] in *al-farara* [*The Whirlwind*] (Baghdad: Dar al-Rashid, 1979). Nasir's "A Short Biographical Sketch of Shaykh Nadir," and "The Smell of City Houses," appeared in *al-Adib*, no. 6 (June 1970) and no. 4 (April 1973). ^cAbdul Ilah Ahmad, *bibliugrafiyat al-qissa al-qasira fi-l-^ciraq* [*A Bibliography of the Iraqi Short Story*] (Baghdad: al-Hurriya Press, 1973), provides exact dates of publication in daily newspapers and monthly journals until 1970.

22. Yusuf al-Haydari, *"al-shabah"* ["The Ghost"] in *huna yajufu al-bahr* [*Here is Where the Sea Dries Up*] (al-Najat: Dar al-Kalima, 1967), 104.

23. On the impact of war on the Iraqi short story, see the author's *al-haqiqa wa-l-khayal* [*The Seen and the Imagined*], 2 vols. (Baghdad: Cultural Affairs Press, 1987).

24. Sami Mahdi, *min awraq al-zawal* [*From the Leaves of Extinction*] (Baghdad: al-Adib Press, 1985), 91, 49–50.

25. Lutfiya al-Dulaymi, *"al-^ca'id min al-safar"* ["Returning from Abroad"] in *al-bishara* [*Tidings*] (Baghdad: Ministry of Information, 1974), 42.

9. Economic Relations among Social Classes in Algerian Proverbs

Abdel-Malek Mortad

The study of Arabic literature in Algeria should, in my view, promote progressive social values and goals.[1] Unfortunately, the development of this perspective is yet to be achieved. A progressive perspective implies the analysis of literature from a sociopolitical or sociological perspective. Since literature is a product of imagination and thus has an elusive character, this is not an easy task. Metaphorically speaking, literature's elusiveness is like trying to grasp the sun as it travels from east and west between dawn and dusk. The study and analysis of literature then is not comparable to formal social science research that deals with such "concrete" subjects as rural-urban migration, illiteracy, endemic poverty, and international migration. These subjects are much more concrete than literature because they can be more easily subject to causal analysis.

The Popular Oral Tradition

Embedded in a complex and nuanced structure of thought that is the product of both emotion and intellect, literary production represents a creative form whose boundaries are often (self-consciously) ambiguous. Given this quality and the fact that every type of literature is governed by a myriad of genres and rules that are often linked to age-old traditions, it is difficult to subject literature to rigorous scientific analysis.

As a man of letters (*adib*), I am not concerned with these rules or traditions when studying literature. Traditional rules were formulated to suit the needs of earlier epochs, whether epistemological, social, political, or economic. An analogy can be made with architecture, which represents an old and respected tradition in Algeria. Contemporary Algerian architecture should develop rules that are geared toward modern needs, such as providing suitable housing for the masses rather than the construction of monuments, as was the case in the past. Another analogy could be made with the construction of mosques. The construction of tall minarets in the past was intended to enable the *mu'adhdhin* (caller to prayer) to reach as many people as possible from a high vantage point. Today, the development of modern electronic communications has rendered obsolete the need for tall minarets. Instead of building tall minarets, architects should be more concerned with building mosques suitable to accommodating the large number of people that inhabit our rapidly growing cities.

Thus my concern is not to reproduce the accomplishments of my predecessors, for people, including writers, should live synchronically in their own age. This means that just as architects should focus on the utilitarian aspects of construction instead of monuments, writers should likewise strive toward accomplishing social and political goals through literature rather than reproducing traditional genres. Whatever form of literature that is being studied, whether the short story or the proverbs and riddles of the oral tradition, one should focus on its social, political, and economic content. Accordingly, even its philosophical ramifications should be viewed in terms of their nationalist goals. In focusing on literature's sociological content, I am implying neither that other dimensions such as epistemological concerns are not proper fields of study nor that other dimensions do not exist.

I am also aware that, in focusing on sociological or sociopolitical dimensions alone, our holistic understanding of literature might be weakened. However, ours is just one type of analysis, which needs to be complemented by stylistic, artistic, and epistemological analyses of literary production.

The collection of popular proverbs from western Algeria that is analyzed here contains a relatively large number dealing with economic relations that bind people to society and to one another. These proverbs usually deal with wisdom, socialization and education, ethics and life experiences. Most of these proverbs encourage social cooperation, glorify self-reliance, and advise people to cooperate and support one another. Other proverbs urge people to lead a virtuous life. What we might refer to metaphorically as the "folk wise man" views social relations as reflecting the relations of production embedded in society's economic system. Thus the wise man did his best to elucidate the rules that govern such relations and to gear them toward constructive social values, such as cooperation and self-reliance. Every proverb in this small collection upon which our study is based is full of wisdom, and every piece of wisdom reflects centuries of human experience.

Popular Algerian proverbs contain didactic as well as moral messages. By extrapolating these messages, we seek to demonstrate that these proverbs contain an authentic worldview so pure, "innocent," and noble that it embodies the very essence of popular consciousness. The analysis of such proverbs is not limited to the identification of social problems such as poverty, but transcends it so as to provide, solutions for the problems. The common folk of Algeria are more likely to accept and understand this identification of the problems and the concomitant solutions through the study of folk proverbs. This is so because the material such proverbs contain is drawn from a popular source, popular literary production, which belongs to the people and is thus authentically Algerian, as such proverbs are used and coined in everyday life. Whether sociological or otherwise, the sentiments that are being decoded by the analyst are socially pertinent and thus acceptable to the common people. Such sentiments are purely Algerian, embedded in the very essence of folk wisdom that is constantly produced and utilized among the people. In my view, the role of the researcher is to identify social concerns and provide solutions. Such concerns and solutions should be moral and in synchrony with nationalist aspirations. By identifying problems and providing solutions, the researcher can play a progressive role in the process of building a modern nation from the ruins of colonialism based on principles and values that are truly Algerian.

In the proverbs that are analyzed here, a number of social problems and solutions are identified as "themes."[2] All themes have poverty as a common denominator. The first theme is that of social class. Earlier in the century when Algeria was dominated by colonial rule, the poor were depicted as a social class. This class, which comprised most Algerians, was exploited, persecuted, deprived, and constantly humiliated. It should not be surprising that class conflict is subsumed within the themes of poverty and social class. A pitfall of exploitation and poverty is envy. A common characteristic of those who are deprived is a desperate attempt to fulfill illusory expectations in order to cope with the degradation that results from poverty and deprivation. Envy is identified in proverbs and people are admonished not to succumb to its evils.

Besides identifying the source of contemporary society's problems that remain an obstacle to nation-building, this chapter also seeks to identify possible solutions. Interestingly, these solutions, which place a heavy emphasis on self-reliance, are embodied in the same proverbs as the problems of poverty and envy themselves. In Algerian proverbs self-reliance is essential in combating poverty and envy, especially when compared to a complementary theme, cooperation. Furthermore, other solutions include thrift as opposed to extravagance as well as contentment as opposed to self-pity. Self-reliance discourages the manipulation of neighbors and relatives. The proverbs chastise the exploitation of rural workers and instead emphasize the efficient management of resources. Dependence is deplored as are escapism and the use of superstitions and magic in solving problems. Instead, these proverbs urge the use of modern science and rational thinking, and identify and encourage honesty and trust in economic transactions.

All of these themes in popular Algerian proverbs portray the poor as they really are in society, the butt of discrimination (*manbudhun*), deprived, pressured, despised, and neglected. As a popular proverb so eloquently states: **"The words of him who has no money are unsalted."**

This proverb depicts the large gap between classes that has afflicted society. It stresses the importance of social class, a sign of the times in colonial Algeria. The proverb does not provide a solution for the situation; it does not analyze the prevailing conditions, nor does it condemn the class exploitation (*al-tabaqiya*) that it portrays. Instead, it draws a realistic picture of the condition of the poor in Algerian society under French colonial rule: The poor are downtrodden and despised. The proverb presents the exploitation of the deprived class by the rich and opulent class, the bourgeoisie.

The deprived class was persecuted in the name of various principles that the rich alone understood well. When the wealthy spoke, the words they spoke were sweet and delicious. The wealthy "salted" every word they pronounced. Quite often, the wealth of the rich veiled their shortcomings so that they did not manifest themselves or were nearly obscured. If the rich wanted people to laugh, they made them laugh. If they wanted people to cry, they caused them to cry. Even if the rich wanted to resurrect the dead, they would. The rich possessed esteem and whatever else elicits the respect of the poor. Such qualities the rich took with them wherever they went. In contrast, when the poor talked, their words were cold and heavy. They possessed nothing that impressed society. If the poor even wished to laugh, people laughed at them. If the poor wished to make people sad or cause them to understand the conditions of poverty, what they would get in return is negligence, pity, and aggression. The rich would victimize, ridicule, belittle, and neglect the poor.

There is no equal to that person whose pocket or sock is full of money that people envy and wish to possess. On the other hand, those who do not possess riches that cause the greedy to drool and attract sycophants count for nothing. According to the proverb, the poor are forbidden to converse about current affairs, for society has condemned them to a fatal destiny.

We may conclude that this proverb also deals with a society full of class conflict, a society with values in constant conflict and one with principles and contradictions vying for dominance. Some of the rich reign supreme, victorious, but others prevail through tyranny. We may also assume that the person who coined this proverb was himself poor and deprived. He offered his wisdom to transmit his feelings when trying times had exhausted him and reduced him to skin and bones. The poor man must have composed the proverb after a trying experience or as a result of learning a hard lesson from life. He had developed a gloomy outlook on life and expected calamity. This dark outlook resulted from persecution of the poor. If we assume for the sake of argument that persecution did not exist in Algerian society, we cannot assume that this proverb did not express neglect and contempt. A poor person whose speech lacks "salt" (eloquence) and who is unable to express himself to attract listeners suffers because he lacks money. Material deprivation elicits contempt, and contempt is a form of moral deprivation. Under such conditions, a person would refuse to have his honor disparaged through insults. The worst insult is for a person to be neglected while speaking to a group that chooses not to listen to him and to avoid him, giving him the cold shoulder and despising him. This proverb clearly expresses the impact of class relations. It seems to have been composed in an environment of poverty. Its depiction of class struggle is deliberate. It portrays two distant classes in conflict. One class has wealth, honor, status, power, and acts in a tyrannical fashion. Oppressed and exploited to the limit, the lower class is burdened with poverty and deprivation. Pushed to the breaking point, this class is about to revolt.

As they refer to economic relations among people, the envy of others, and reliance on wealth instead of hard and productive work, some Algerian folk proverbs demonstrate that obsessive envy is an illusion that leads to false expectations. For example, another proverb strongly affirms the exclusive rights of individuals to their own property. It says: "**People's (goods) belong exclusively to them.**"

Living in a fog, a certain individual may constantly imagine that he will someday gain control over some of the wealth of his friend, brother, or dear neighbor. Such a person gains nothing but bitter disappointment and experiences nothing but deprivation.

A large number of Algerian proverbs deal with some aspect of economic relations and urge people to be content. The underlying assumption is that what people possess is theirs exclusively. These proverbs regard as an ugly habit the greediness that causes people to wish they have what does not belong to them. Such a desire causes vain and unacceptable behavior, for what people own is theirs alone. To become attached to something that does not belong to you is illusory. If this proverb advises contentment, it also encourages the poor to work hard in order to gain wealth, which in turn might save them from need and deprivation. From this perspective, the proverb not only makes greed appear ugly; it also urges work and perseverance. This exhortation is indirect, however, because it is embedded in the description of bitter reality.

Other proverbs deal more directly with greed and depict as natural the socioeconomic dimension of social relations. An Algerian proverb says, for example: **"He who is dressed in other people's clothes is naked."** Similarly another proverb states: **"He who depended upon his neighbor went to bed without supper."**

The person who borrows people's garments to clothe himself will inevitably revert to nakedness when he returns what he has borrowed. The person who is hungry and expects to obtain some of his neighbor's food is destined to go to bed on an empty stomach.

An analysis of these proverbs has a bearing on the understanding of the socioeconomic conditions in Algerian society. In present-day Algeria, ignoring the wise teaching of the proverb that uses clothes symbolically, some people refuse to accept painful reality. Such people depend on borrowing and taking loans to make themselves presentable in order to gain respect and to appear as if they possess high status. The two proverbs just mentioned deserve consideration here for their relevance to the implications of self-reliance and content. Algerian women of poor means, for example, resort to borrowing when faced with the burden of planning family wedding festivities. Such women do not hesitate to borrow luxurious clothes and even jewelry in order to adorn themselves for the wedding ceremony. In such attire, a poor woman would appear proper and dignified. So that it will not be said that a poor woman does not own jewelry, she borrows it, knowing quite well that all the people present will know it is borrowed. All the people of the neighborhood and even the village know that such women are poor and that the jewelry adorning their breasts, necks, and wrists is not theirs. In fact, this jewelry resembles the adornment of the "old hag" who uses beauty powders and ointments to obscure reality.

There is no escape from being poor, even if a poor woman has covered herself with diamonds, agates, and rubies. The painful reality is not erased by just escaping from it momentarily and rejecting it. On the contrary, escaping that reality requires hard work to change circumstances through noble and legitimate means. Facing up to reality would be better than trying to escape it. The prevalent custom among poor people of borrowing jewelry ignores the values expressed in the folk proverbs discussed earlier. The custom has spread among Algerian brides; in some regions mothers of brides refuse to allow their daughters to leave the family house in simple jewelry that befits their own and their husbands' social status. These mothers absolutely refuse to face social reality. Instead, they approach their neighbors, relatives, and friends to borrow jewelry in such quantity that it burdens their daughters' necks, hands, fingers, and heads. The brides are covered with jewelry. No one renounces this custom, even though all the women present know that most of the jewelry adorning the bride is borrowed. Even stranger is the fact that the husband knows all this himself and when asked would not even deny it!

Such customs require a great deal of unwarranted energy and should be condemned by Algerian society. A woman should only adorn herself with what she owns. A man should not use his friend's car, among other things, if he does not own one himself because this could lead him to face problems with which he could not cope. For example, a man could borrow a car from a friend and drive it feeling very happy and showing off. However, consider his sorrow if he finds himself in a traffic accident.

Clearly, as the proverbs already discussed suggest, Algerian folk society disdains spurious economic relations that produce social conflict leading to hatred and enmity. Such enmity might lead people to envy what others own or, under the best of intentions, to try to enjoy what they do not own and to engage in theft and crime. Popular or folk literature (*adab sha*ʿ*bi*), as exemplified in proverbs with economic themes, does not oppose social cooperation. Quite the contrary, it often proposes such cooperation and urges people to follow it, as shown in the following proverb: "**Help even the Christians, cooperation is never a loss.**"

This proverb rejects economic relations that do not entail work and that rely on dependence in the hope of acquiring what belongs to other people out of envy. What belongs to other people is in reality theirs alone. The literature of folk wisdom, including the proverbs, does not reject poverty, which is, after all, part of social reality. Rather folk wisdom considers poverty something inevitable that cannot be eliminated. Proverbs repeatedly acknowledge the existence of poverty.

The following proverb refers to an inevitability that cannot be rejected: **"Blessed is the small amount."** A small amount should never be considered trivial or inconsequential. When preserved, utilized, and managed well, a small amount will quite often bring a great return resulting in wealth and satisfaction. Such is the meaning embedded in this folk proverb, especially in the word "blessed" (*baraka*). When wasted, plenty amounts to nothing at all in any economic order. Such thought must have encouraged the people to echo the same sentiment in other proverbs, as for example: **"If you divide the river, you will get a large number of irrigation ditches."**

Huge and full of water, a river could become nothing but a number of small ditches if it is divided and partitioned. Of course, this folk proverb speaks of hard reality and not about human effort that might attempt to divide a river. It draws its metaphor from the physical world. Thus if one misused money and spent it extravagantly, he would render it nothing but a trivial amount.

The following proverb presents a worthy reminder: **"Even the sultan who wears a crown can be in need!"** The folk worldview illustrated here recognizes that need or indeed poverty can affect even kings. From a modern economic perspective, this proverb can be explained to mean that even governments need the help of individuals. Often this help comes in the form of people's savings deposited in banks offering good returns; it is impossible for any state to maintain a sound economic base without these bank deposits that regulate its fiscal policy because the state spends the money of one person to compensate another. This cooperation pays dividends resulting in economic prosperity benefiting the populace at large. Thus need is not confined to individuals alone since it is a phenomenon that can affect governments and states, which must borrow in order to invest people's money in a safe modern banking system.

The proverbs considered here reject dependency and envy of

other people's wealth. This economic outlook, despite its roots in folk society, appears to be sound in that it encourages a social order devoid of dependency and free of the evils of envy. In the ideal sense, such a society would indeed be healthy. Under such a social order, work would become the standard by which people measure their success and the means by which they earn their living and accumulate the wealth that enables them to achieve some of their goals in life.

Many other Algerian proverbs reject dependency and portray the envy of the possessions of others as a nasty habit. These proverbs deserve consideration because they illustrate economic relations between varied social classes. The following proverb is attributed to Shaykh ʿAbd al-Rahman al-Majdhub: **"You who plant al-dum [an edible wild plant], the benefits of al-dum are many. Blood does not benefit blood. Woe to him whose hand fails him."**[3]

This popular wisdom rejects dependence not only on nonrelatives but also on relatives, such as brothers, in-laws, and cousins. A person who loses his strength, whose hands have failed him, and who is unable to work and till the soil is destined to poverty and nothing else. This is so only because relatives formed through genealogical descent and affinity do not count for anything in the dictionary of social relations. Hard work is the sound economic course for individuals and groups, not dependence based on vain hopes and deceptive greed. The inability to work because of some misfortune results in dire poverty and miserable living conditions. Clearly the proverb expresses a sense of desperation because relatives are often not dependable in time of need. The wisdom of current folk proverbs repudiates dependence upon relatives. Another proverb calls for the avoidance of greed: **"Relatives are like scorpions (al-aqarib ʿaqarib)."**

In Algerian folk literature, the innocent and pure worldview of the people—a worldview that has dealt with harsh daily reality—compares relatives to poisonous and deadly scorpions to emphasize the fact that they are jealous of one another and competitive. No wonder that the proverb's author and those who believe in it consider themselves wise and experienced—they place their trust only in their own possessions.

The worldview depicted by these folk proverbs explicitly

portrays the connection between cultivating the soil and its benefit and between greed and deprivation. Every pointed utterance in these insightful proverbs evokes deep psychological symbolism. Tilling, the foundation of all economic and agricultural wealth in rural areas, is discussed first. Most (domesticated) living plants are connected with this activity. It is impossible for any peasant in possession of his full faculties to hope to make a decent and honest living without cultivating the land. Granted there are manual laborers who do not perform agricultural tasks in the rural areas, but this is because these people do not own agricultural land. In most cases, however, the tasks of laborers in rural areas are always connected to agriculture. Many agricultural tasks originate from the act of tilling. A rural laborer might spin the rope that ties a pile (*nadir*)[4] of hay. This is agricultural work. A laborer might earn a living by spinning the ropes used in making containers and sell them in the market. Another laborer might carry his sickle and go to the harvest and spend his daylight hours working. Another might offer himself on contract to work for a peasant of means (*muqataᶜa*) through the winter season as a plowman. Such a person might work all summer reaping, threshing, and collecting produce in exchange for a fixed sum of money agreed upon ahead of time. A worker might herd sheep or cows belonging to a large landlord. This type of manual labor for hire is a form of agricultural work that entails insult and belittlement.

In the Algerian countryside, past and present, there is a sense of sharp social class differentiation. The rich peasant does not spin rope; rather he uses rope made by poor country people, as his time is too precious to be wasted in such a menial task. Spinning itself is also harmful to the fingers because the fibrous plants contain sharp thorns. So too is handling ropes that are used for containers and baskets and also of the fibers, which are beaten, dried (*al-mughdara*),[5] and then soaked to be used in making nets and the like. The rich peasant who followed a traditional method of cultivation based on manual labor in the absence of machinery was obliged to employ poor laborers from the village or migrant laborers who frequented agricultural regions at seasons of high labor demand. Such laborers are called *muqatiᶜun*, or contract laborers. Poor villagers, if they were blessed with male children, would send their grown sons to work on contract as laborers for rich peasants. They would work from the beginning until the end of the harvest season, threshing and storing in exchange for a wage agreed upon in advance by both parties. In most cases, the rich peasant was cruel and stingy. These laborers endured miserable conditions and often would not own more than a single woolen *jallaba*. They would wear this garment on their bare skin without any undergarments. This *jallaba* would have to last for the entire season. If the garment became wet in the rain, the laborer could not change it. Instead he would lean against a wall wearing his dripping *jallaba* waiting for it to dry!

Herding is an integral part of the agricultural cycle. A poor father in the Algerian countryside did not send his children to school; rather he used to distribute them among the peasants of his village or in some neighboring villages to herd sheep in exchange for a very meager wage.

The conditions just described involve a social class dimension in form and in substance. Thus all proverbs involving rural work contain a class dimension. This can be seen, for example, in the proverb dealing with *al-dum*.[6] Tilling is primary in each of these proverbs; were it not for tilling, such proverbs would have little significance. *al-dum* is not mentioned in the proverb for its own sake, but rather as a symbol of cultivation, plowing, and tilling. The folk narrator referred to this plant because of the certainty of the benefits resulting from its cultivation. In modern economics, such benefits are primary. Today valuable resources are called "gold." Petroleum is known as "black gold," gas as "liquid" gold, wheat as "yellow gold," and so on. In accordance with contemporary international relations, states bargain with their natural resources, whether these resources consist of ores extracted from the earth or of agricultural resources. At the end of the twentieth century, there is no large difference between extracting gold or planting wheat. Wheat-producing countries are no less wealthy than oil-producing countries. In the modern international arena, agricultural resources are as significant as oil.

The innovator of folk proverbs refers to agriculture symbolically by using the word *al-dum*, mentioning the abundant goodness of this plant. These references possess an economic significance, because every agricultural method is based on its own established wealth-producing principles. Consequently all wealth brings riches to society. This populist economic outlook is essentially based on cultivating and sowing the land—a sound economic outlook. To a great extent, Algerian peasants each till a small piece of land. When this land receives rain and produces in abundance, it does so because the peasant has done all he could to cultivate it.[7]

In the second part of al-Majdhub's proverb, the folk narrator completes a comparison after implying that agriculture produces wealth and tilling constitutes the economic foundation in generating wealth. The thrust of the proverb then changes to say that the person who turns away from tilling and utilizing the land resorts to envy and greed. Such a person wants what is in the hands of others even if these others are his relatives, even close blood relatives. When such a person becomes lazy, dependent, and tardy, he will experience nothing but disappointment and loss. Thus this populist proverb projects two different images. The first is a fertile, rich, and productive image because it relates to work that is glorified, especially work exemplified in the service of the land. The second is a negative, miserable, dark, and poor image because it is related to laziness, dependency, and greed.

This folk proverb thus depicts two pictures. As the physicists would say, the first is positive while the other is negative. However, here the positive and negative do not have the same properties as electricity, for electrical positives and negatives generate a third beneficial image that is useful to human life. Despite outward appearances, the two pictures generated in the proverb are separate and have no connection worth mentioning. They represent two entirely different worlds, the world of serious work, investment, and self-reliance on the one hand, and the world of laziness, greed, false hopes, and dependence on the other.

Perhaps the repudiation of dependency caused the folk narrator to utter this proverb: **"Tasteless is the loaf made by ten people."** In other words, a job meant for one person, if handled by many without organization and precision, leads to waste.

A number of proverbs deal with social relations built on economic insights. The following proverb serves as an example: "**He who came and brought a gift deserves the bedding and welcome, and he who came and brought nothing deserves the barking dogs.**"

Two situations or social images appear in this proverb. The first refers to the obligation of bringing gifts to one's host and the other obliges guests not to overstay their welcome. The second image is reinforced in another proverb: "**Welcome is the one who visited and his stay was light.**" Such a person is welcomed by the people of the house and offered hospitality, the spreading of bedding, an extravagant assortment of foods, and a variety of drinks offered in an aesthetically pleasing manner. Such treatment is accorded to a welcomed guest and a respected visitor who obeys the etiquette of visiting and knows that his visit entails expenses and discomfort for the host. As for the "heavy" guest who ignores all this and who enters others' homes to stay and eat their food without bringing an offering, he deserves punishment in the form of being crowded at the guest house, not being treated with deference while consuming a meal, and being exposed to barking dogs.

Algerian beliefs, customs, and rituals are evident in the following folk proverb: "**This *sayyid*, he writes and serves lunch and even provides the ink (*sumaq*).**"[8] This highly illustrative proverb portrays the predicament of those who are inflicted with double stupidity; it also depicts the dubious craft practiced by vagabonds and deceitful beggars. It presents three themes, by describing the derelict designated as *sayyid*[9] as harmed from three vantage points without receiving any benefit in return.

According to the proverb, the *sayyid* "writes"—not literary writing (novels, stories, essays, or any other literary genre, be it administrative, clerical, documentary, archival, or even legal). Rather in its popular meaning in Algeria, especially in rural areas, and probably in the rest of the Arab world as well, the act of "writing" refers to the wise man (*al-hakim*) in the village who is primarily a writer of charms (*al-huruz*). When sick or when their sons or close ones are sick, people do not go to specialized physicians. Instead they go to the *hakim*. He takes a piece of white paper and fills it with symbols that neither he nor others understand. Sometimes he writes Qur'anic verses on this paper. At other times he writes strange non-Arabic words, which he often claims are names of evil spirits. Then the *hakim* gives this *hirz* (pl. *huruz*) to the customer who sought his help, asking him to wear it on the afflicted part of his body. The *hirz* is placed on the head for a headache, for example, on the neck for the evil eye,[10] or on the waist if the patient is pregnant or complaining of pain in her joints. For pain in the abdomen, the *hirz* is soaked in water, the ink is dissolved, and the patient is made to drink the mixture or part of it while spreading the rest on the abdomen after adding a medicinal herb called *al-fiyjal*.[11] During the French occupation, the craft of writing *huruz* almost died out. Today, however, it has again become profitable despite the rise of literacy and scientific awareness because a large minority of the populace continues to believe in it. As incomes have risen to meet the increased cost of living, people have been paying large sums of money for these *huruz*.

In many cases, people deliberately refrain from seeking the truth through science, preferring a metaphysics that anyone who is scientifically aware knows to be devoid of truth. People in the countryside do not seek a physician when a son or a bride is afflicted with the evil eye. "Magic" is used to attract a husband or to subdue an unwilling bride, or to deflect a spell caused by rivalry and competition. These forms of belief are varied and rich; some are humorous while others are indeed regrettable.

The word "lunch" (*ghadha'*) in this proverb means nourishment or the essence of feeding, not the actual food one eats. The main nutritious meal of the day is *ghadha'*, the midday meal. Customarily peasants in Algeria do not pay much attention to the evening meal (*'asha'*), as in the proverb: "**Dinner is a puzzle.**" One might go to bed without supper and never miss it, but to miss lunch is a terrible misfortune. Furthermore, the proverb mentions *ghadha'* nourishment as the pronunciation of the term to provide poetic symmetry. We will see more of this in the third part of this proverb.

The *faqih* who finds himself feeding his clients and giving them the *hirz* for free risks being considered a vagabond. If he does not charge money for them, his efforts are not worth compensating.

The famous Iraqi commentator Abu ʿUthman al-Jahidh said of a vagabond shaykh he met one day, "The elder among them is a novice of the trade." He then asked the shaykh how he felt, and the shaykh answered, "May God curse the practice of vagabonds and its people, for it is demeaning and the least rewarding of trades. It is, as you know, the type which demeans a face and belittles a man."[12] Amazingly, in Algerian society we consider this writing a craft. People who "write *huruz*" occupy special places in the market (*al-suq*) and have special rooms in their own homes[13] from where they conduct their business.

"And even provides the ink" ("*al summaq on me*"), the last part of this popular proverb, underscores the lost revenue of the *faqih* who writes for free. In addition to expending effort of the hand and the intellect, the *faqih* has also used his own ink, which is either bought or produced with great difficulty. This popular proverb is used to express the experience of a double loss. It is full of folk symbolism related to social relations and organized according to the strict artistry of poetry. As the proverb mentioned earlier scolds guests who arrive and take advantage of their host, this proverb scolds those who accept loss from both ends. It reflects the message of the ancient Arab proverb: **"He sold us bad dates (*hashf*) and cheated us with the scale."**[14]

This famous proverb describes a double loss incurred from a commercial transaction—a sale. In the Algerian folk context, this means loss from two perspectives—work and effort. When compared to the proverb dealing with the writer of charms, we note that this man was wronged and suffered a loss as a result of the work he performed. "Writing" entails an effort of sorts that should have been rewarded by payment. Feeding the client in addition was gratis. According to this proverb, social relations should operate according to principles of justice and be devoid of aggression and stealth. Such relations should be based on cooperation and a clear understanding between individuals in society. Efforts should not be wasted, and rights should not be overlooked. This is a pragmatic and realistic outlook on social relations between people so that no one appropriates the rights of others. Every laborer should have his wage and every food should bring its price. Some-how free "items" involve taking advantage of people, for, as the modern proverb indicates: **"Every servant has his wage."**

The writer of *hirz* is a man of a trade. He is a worker, and every worker should work for wages. The proverb chastises those who do not pay people just wages. It involves a dimension that smacks of social persecution. The person who loses from both ends is not only suffering from social oppression; he is also being exploited. Thus we have seen how a number of proverbs elo-quently convey a sense of the Algerian folk worldview, carefully defining just and fair economic relations in light of social condi-tions and prevailing customs. A value underlying all these proverbs is that no one should oppress others. Everyone should receive his rightful due. These proverbs reflect most strongly the economic dimension of the folk worldview. They capture with poetic care and skill the basic agricultural endeavors of cultivating the land and raising and herding animals.

NOTES

1. This chapter is based on an article by the same title published in the Iraqi journal *Majallat al-Turath al-Sha*ᶜ*bi* [*The Journal of Folk Culture*] 11, no. 10 (1980) 13–30.

2. This study is part of a larger research project dealing with Algerian prov-erbs entitled "A Study of Western Algerian Folk Proverbs."

3. Nur al-Din ᶜAbd al-Qadir, *al-qawl al-ma'thur min kalam al-shaykh* ᶜ*abd al-rahman al-majdhub* [*Proverbs from the Sayings of Shaykh* ᶜ*Abd al-Rahman al-Majdhub*] (Algiers: al-Thaᶜalibiya Press, n.d.), 6. We assume that this popular wise proverb was in use tens if not hundreds of years ago, for is attributed to Shaykh ᶜAbd al-Rahman al-Majdhub. al-Majdhub lived during the seventeenth century in the western Arab world (*al-Maghrib al-Aqsa*). He died in A.H. 976. His full name is Abu Zayd ᶜAbd al-Rahman bin ᶜIyad bin Yaᶜqub bin Salama al-Sanhaji al-Dakali. al-Majdhub is a nickname given to him by his contemporar-ies because he was well known for his wisdom, stoicism, Sufism, and dedication. See ibid., 2 and 94.

4. *al-nadir* is an agricultural expression denoting a pile of produce collected during the harvest, then carried and stashed next to *al-nuhba*, meaning *al-baydar*, the threshing floor. *al-nadir* is used to mean any kind of produce collected or piled in a designated place. It is also used to mean the hay that is collected and

piled in a specific geometric shape. Masters among the peasants pile this structure after threshing has been completed. The operation of building this structure
is called *darb al-tibn*. *darb al-tibn* does not take place unless there is a work gang
where the youth of the village gather along with the elderly. These people pass
the containers containing hay to the *darib* (builder), who in turn piles them creating a domelike structure. Stones placed at the corners of the structure are tied
with ropes to secure it from top to center. Some Andalusian books use the word
al-nadir in a different way. Written *al-andar*, it is used in this proverb: "The proof
is in the *faddan*, it is better than having regrets at *al-andar*." See Ahmad al-Zajali
al-Qurtubi, *ray al-ᶜawam wa marᶜa al-sawam fi nukat al-khasa wa-l-ᶜawam* [*The
Opinion of Commoners and the Judgment of Nobles in Dealing with the Jokes
of Nobility and Commoners*], pt. 2, 51, ed. Muhammad bin Sharifa, printed in
al-maghrib al-aqsa. The word originated in Syria, and spread to Andalusia through
some Syrian migrants.

A number of researchers dealing with folk proverbs have analyzed this proverb. Among them are: ᶜAbd al-Salam bin Suda in *amthal ahl fas* [*The Proverbs
of the People of Fas*], proverb no. 647; Muhammad Da'ud in "*alf mathal wa
mathal min amthal tuwan*," ["1,001 Proverbs of the Proverbs of Tuwan"], *Majalat
al-Bahth al-ᶜIlmi*, vol. 1, no. 2, proverb no. 903; and Ahmad Taymur, *al-amthal
al-ᶜamiya* [*Common Proverbs*], 3d ed. (Cairo: Muᶜassasat al-Ahram, 1970), 301–2.

5. Spinners use *al-mughdara* to mean a plant that is left under the sun after it
is picked to dry. This plant is then placed in a well for a period of time after
stones are placed on it to prevent it from floating. Then it is taken out of the well
and allowed to dry. It is pounded on a smooth rock (the same type used by
women to wash clothes that need beating, such as heavy woolens, *jallaba*, and
the like) with *al-razzama*. *al-razzama* is a heavy wooden paddle, cylindrical in
shape, with a handle that is held by the fingers. Peasants use *al-razzama* to pound
the dried and soaked plant *al-halfa* until it is smooth and pliable, suitable for
spinning and weaving.

6. *al-dum* is found in the forest as well as in cultivated fields. It is seasonal
and never planted, but grows naturally. Strands from this plant are taken to be
used in the making of slings, as well as strings that are used in sewing straw trays.
al-dum wood burns quickly when dry. During the rainy season, shepherds used
to dig it up and extract its edible inner part. It has a sweet taste with a trace of
delicious natural bitterness.

7. I was once told by a laborer at Oran University whom I trust that in 1937,
when working as a plowman with his father in the village of Jabala, in the dis-
trict of Tilimsan, their family was able to harvest an extraordinary amount of
produce. They collected eight hundred *talis* of barley (a *talis* is forty *qurdiya*,
which is a container that holds about five kilograms), six hundred *talis* of wheat,
two hundred tons of fava beans, and a hundred tons of millet. If we consider
that the common ten-member Algerian family would consume, at most, one *talis*
of wheat a month, the amount harvested by this family would sustain 116 families

for one year. Economically, it is obvious that the Algerian land is capable of abundant production. I have noted similar agricultural conditions. For example, a single peasant can harvest in one season enough to feed hundreds of families in the cities. The peasant in those days only had a capital of a plow, a sickle, and a pair of plow animals.

8. Among those who teach in Qur'anic schools in Algeria, the word *al-sumaq* is used to mean ink derived from the remains of wool burned in a clay skillet until the wool becomes liquified and black. Then a stone is placed on it and water is poured on the stone. A piece of wool is then placed in the container and a writing reed is dipped in it. (This is not the same *sumaq* derived from a tree. See ʿAbd al-Razzaq bin Ahmadush al-Jaza'iri, *kashf al-rumuz fi bayan al-aʿshab* [*Explaining the Symbols Pertaining to Plants*], 100.)

9. According to Algerian social customs, those who write amulets are *sayyids*; meaning those who are not "masters" of social rank but rather those who have a spiritual status characterized by piety and *baraka* (blessing).

10. The "evil eye" is an affliction or a misfortune besetting an individual, the cause of which cannot be explained logically. People in Algeria strongly believe in this. The evil eye usually afflicts only the rich, the beautiful, the new, and the like. It would not afflict the ugly, the poor, and old. Thus a beautiful car that gets into an accident, in the opinion of the populace, has been exposed to such a misfortune. If the car then is involved in an accident while in its prime, most people would agree that the cause was the evil eye. (If a bride becomes sick on the day of the wedding or soon before or after, the cause is also the evil eye.) If a boy who has a beautiful face trips while passing in front of an old lady who was staring at him, the parents of that child will no doubt say that the old lady inflicted the boy with the evil eye!

It is impossible to enumerate all the conditions under which the evil eye is believed to operate in Algeria. When people feel that the evil eye has been cast, they hurry to the village *faqih* or the neighborhood *hakim*, asking him to write a *hirz* that they can hang around their necks to offer protection against the evil eye. They call each particular affliction *ʿayn al-miʿyan*. People who become afflicted often take great precautions. Horsemen in the countryside used to hang these *huruz* around the necks of their mounts in order to prevent them from spooking or being harmed if they danced or galloped.

11. There are two kinds of *fiyjal*, a wild one that might be called *harmal* or *al-fiyjal al-ʿarabi* and a cultivated one known as *al-fiyjala*. The *fiyjal* is *al-sadhab*, pronounced as *al-sahab* (meaning "clouds"). It is among the plants that are often mentioned in the context of folk medicine. See al-Jaza'iri, *kashf al-rumuz fi bayan as-aʿshab*, 92, 1332.

12. Ibrahim bin Muhammad al-Bayhaqi, *al-mahasin wa-l-masawi'* [*The Good and Bad Deeds*], vol. 2, ed. Muhammad Abi al-Fadl Ibrahim (Cairo: Nahdat Misr Press, 1961), 410.

13. It is amazing that the writers of *huruz* consider their work a craft. In 1973

I published an article in the journal *al-Asala al-Jaza'iriya*, dealing with diseases and afflictions as they relate to the beliefs of the common people in Algeria. In my article I dealt with the writers of *huruz*, citing earlier criticisms. A number of *huruz* writers streamed to my father's house and complained to him: "How can he speak ill of our craft? This craft is the source of our income and livelihood."

14. Abu al-Fadl Ahmad bin Muhammad al-Naysaburi al-Maydani, *majma^c al-'amthal*, 1:288. *al-hashf* is the worst kind of date.

Bibliography

ᶜAbdallah, Muhammad ᶜAli. *al-zakhrafa al-jibsiya fi-l-khalij* [*Ceramic Ornamentation in the Gulf*]. Qatar: Arab Gulf States Folklore Centre, 1985.

Aglieta, Michel. *Theory of Capitalist Regulation*. London: New Left Books, 1979.

———. "World Capitalism in the Eighties." *New Left Review* 136 (1982): 5–41.

Ahmad, ᶜAbdul Ilah. *bibliugrafiyat al-qissa al-qasira fi-l-ᶜiraq* [*A Bibliography of the Iraqi Short Story*]. Baghdad: al-Hurriya Press, 1973.

———. *nash'at al-qissa wa tatawwuruha fi-l-ᶜiraq* [*The Emergence and Growth of the Short Story in Iraq*]. Baghdad: Shafiq Press, 1969.

Akhavi, Sharough. "Egypt: Neo-Patrimonial Elite." In *Political Elites and Political Development in the Middle East*, edited by Shahrough Akhavi. New York: John Wiley, 1975.

ᶜAli, Jamal Hashim. "*al-wasiti fi mahrajanahu al-thalith*" ["al-Wasiti's Third Festival"]. *al-Riwaq*, no. 15 (1985): 56–59.

al-Alusi, Hasan Muhyi al-Din. "*sura naqdiya li-l-istishraq al-taqlidi wa-l-jadid*" ["A Critical Overview of Traditional and Neo-Orientalism"]. *Afaq ᶜArabiya*, 3 February 1989.

Amin, ᶜAta. "*kayfa yartaqi al-ᶜiraq*" ["How Iraq Can Make Progress"]. *Dar al-Salam*, nos. 17, 18 (1919).

Amin, Samir. *The Arab Nation*. London: Zed Press, 1978.

ᶜAmir, Ibrahim. *al-ard wa-l-fallah* [*The Land and the Peasant*]. Cairo: al-Dar al-Misriya li-l-Tibaᶜa wa-l-Nashr, 1958.

Anderson, Lisa. *The State and Social Transformation in Tunisia and Libya, 1830–1980*. Princeton, N.J.: Princeton University Press, 1986.

———. "The State in the Middle East and North Africa." *Comparative Politics* 20 (October 1987): 1–18.

———. "The Tripoli Republic, 1918–1922." In *Social and Economic Development of Libya*, edited by E.G.H. Joffe and K.S. MacLachlan. London: MENAS Press, 1982.

al-Ansari, Muhammad Jabir. *lamahat min al-khalij al-ᶜarabi: dirasa fi tarikh al-khalij wa thaqafatahu wa rijalahu wa fulklurahu al-shaᶜbi* [*Glimpses of the Arab Gulf: Studies in the History of the Gulf, Its Prominent Men, and Folklore*]. Bahrain: al-Sharika al-ᶜArabiya li-l-Wikalat wa-l-Tawziᶜ, 1970.

————. *tahawwulat al-fikr wa-l-siyasa fi-l-mashriq al-ᶜarabi, 1930–1970* [*Intellectual and Political Transformations in the Arab East, 1930–1970*]. Kuwait: ᶜAlam al-Maᶜrifa, 1980.

Antonius, George. *al-yaqdha al-ᶜarabiya* [*The Arab Awakening*]. 6th ed. Beirut: Dar al-ᶜIlm li-l-Malayin, 1980.

al-ᶜAqabi, ᶜAbd al-Sahib. *al-mawruth al-shaᶜbi fi athar al-jahidh* [*Folk Heritage in the Works of al-Jahidh*]. Baghdad: Ministry of Culture and Information, Dar al-Hurriya Press, 1976.

al-ᶜAqqad, Salah. *al-tayarat al-siyasiya fi-l-khalij al-ᶜarabi* [*Political Trends in the Arab Gulf*]. Cairo: al-Anglo al-Misriya Press, 1965.

Arslan, Amir Shakib. *limadha ta'akhar al-muslimun wa limadha taqadama ghayruhum* [*Why are the Muslims Underdeveloped While Others Have Progressed?*]. 3d ed. Cairo: ᶜIsa al-Babi al-Halabi, 1939.

Asad, Talal. "Equality in Nomadic Social Systems? Notes Towards the Dissolution of an Anthropological Category." In *Équipe et anthropologie des sociétés pastorales* and *Pastoral Production and Society* (trans.), 419–28. Cambridge and Paris: Cambridge University Press and Maison des Sciences de l'Homme, 1979.

Augustin, Rizq Allah. *"al-tawasuᶜ al-maradi li madinat baghdad"* ["The Unhealthy Expansion of Baghdad"]. *Four Seasons* (Autumn 1954).

ᶜAwad, Luis. *tarikh al-fikr al-misri al-hadith: min ᶜasr ismaᶜil ila thawrat 1919* [*History of Modern Egyptian Thought: From the Age of Ismaᶜil to the 1919 Revolution*]. Cairo: al-Hay'a al-Misriya al-ᶜAma li-l-Kitab, 1980.

Awziran, Salih. *The Portuguese and the Ottoman Turks in the Arab Gulf*. Arabic trans., Basra, 1979.

al-Ayub, Ayub Husayn. *mukhtarat min al-lahja al-kuwaytiya* [*Selections from the Kuwaiti Folk Dialect*]. Kuwait: Maqhawi Press, 1982.

————. *maᶜ al-atfal fi-l-madi* [*With the Children in the Past*]. Kuwait: Government Press, 1969.

————. *maᶜ dhikrayatana al-kuwaytiya* [*With Our Memories in Kuwait*]. Kuwait: Government Press, 1972.

Ayub, Dhu-l-Nun. *burj babil* [*The Tower of Babylon*]. Baghdad: al-Ahali, 1939.

————. *"min wara' al-hijab"* ["Behind the Veil"]. *al-Anba'*, nos. 912–19 (September 1936), and *Modern Journal* (15 June 1937).

————. *"sharaf"* ["Honor"]. *al-Anba'*, nos. 912–19 (September 1936), and *Modern Journal* (15 June 1937).

al-Ayubi, Nazih Nasif. *"tatawwur al-hay'at al-siyasiya wa-l-idariya fi misr, 1952–77"* ["The Development of the Political and Administrative Organizations in Egypt, 1952–77"]. In *misr fi rubᶜ qarn, 1952–77* [*Egypt during a Quarter of a Century*], edited by Saᶜd al-Din Ibrahim. Beirut: Maᶜhad al-Inma' al-ᶜArabi, 1981.

Aziz, Tariq. *"al-jaysh wa makanuhu fi-l-thawra al-ᶜarabiya"* ["The Army and Its Role in the Arab Revolution"]. *al-Maᶜrifa* (July 1970).

al-Baadi, Hamid Muhammad. "Social Change, Education, and the Roles of Women in Arabia." Ph.D. dissertation, Stanford University, Stanford, CA, 1982.

al-Badawi, Rashid. *mashru^c suriya al-kubra: ^{c}ard, wa tahlil wa naqd* [*The Greater Syria Project: Exposition, Analysis, and Criticism*]. Cairo: Maktabat al-Nahda al-Misriya, 1947.

Baer, Gabriel. *Population and Society in the Arab East.* New York: Praeger, 1966.

Barakat, Halim. "*al-nidham al-ijtima^{c}i wa ^{c}alaqatuhu bi mushkilat al-mar'a al-^{c}arabiya*" ["Social Organization and Its Relationship to the Problematic of Arab Women"]. In *al-mar'a wa dawruha fi-l-wihda al-^{c}arabiya* [*The Role of Women in the Development of Arab Unity*]. Beirut: Center for Arab Unity Studies, 1982.

Baran, Paul A. *The Political Economy of Growth.* New York: Monthly Review Press, 1968.

Batatu, Hanna. *The Old Social Classes and the Revolutionary Movements of Iraq.* Princeton, N.J.: Princeton University Press, 1978.

al-Bayhaqi, Ibrahim bin Muhammad. *al-mahasin wa-l-masawi* [*The Good and the Bad*]. Edited by Muhammad Abi al-Fadl Ibrahim. Cairo: Nahdat Misr Press, 1961.

Beblawi, Hazem, and Giacomo Luciani, eds. *The Rentier State.* London: Croom Helm, 1987.

Beguinot, Francesco. "Roma e i Berberi." *Roma*, 1939.

Bell, Montague. "Britain and the Persian Gulf." *Journal of the United Empire* 6 (April 1915).

Berreby, Jean Jacques. *al-khalif al-^{c}arabi* [*The Arab Gulf*]. Arabic trans. by Najda Hajir and Sa^{c}id al-^{c}Uz. Beirut: al-Maktab al-Tijari li-l-Tiba^{c}a wa-l-Nashr wa-l-Tawzi^c, 1959.

al-Burini, Ahmad Qasim. *al-imarat al-sab^c ^{c}ala al-sahil al-akhdar* [*The Seven Emirates on the Green Coast*]. Beirut: Dar al-Hikma, 1957.

Butti, Raphael. *al-sahafa fi-l-^{c}iraq* [*Journalism in Iraq*]. Cairo, 1955.

Campbell, John C. "The Role of the Military in the Middle East." In *The Military in the Middle East: Problems in Society and Government*, edited by S.N. Fisher. Columbus: Ohio State University Press, 1963.

Chardin, John. *Travels in Persia and the East Indies.* London: Argonaut Press, 1961.

Clawson, Patrick. "The Development of Capitalism in Egypt." *Khamsin* 9 (1981): 116.

Colomb, P.H. *Slave Catching in the Indian Ocean: A Record of Naval Experience.* London, 1873.

Crozier, Michel, Samuel Huntington, and Joji Watanuki. *The Crisis of Democracy.* New York: New York University Press, 1975.

Cumming, D.D. *Handbook on Cyrenaica: History.* Cairo: British Military Administration, 1947.

Curzon, George N. *Persia and the Persian Question.* 2 vols. London: Cass, 1966.

al-Dabbagh, Ghanim. *al-ma' al-ᶜadhib* [*Sweet Water*]. Baghdad: al-Adib Press, 1969.

————. *zuqaq al-fi'ran* [*Rat Alley*]. Baghdad: Ministry of Information, 1972.

al-Dajani, Ahmad Sidqi. *libya qubayl al-ihtilal al-itali, 1882–1911.* [*Libya before the Italian Occupation, 1882–1911*]. al-Matbaᶜat al-Fanniya al-Haditha, 1971.

————, and ᶜAbd al-Salam Adham, eds. *watha'iq tarikh libya al-hadith: watha'iq ᶜuthmaniya* [*Documents of Modern Libyan History: Ottoman Documents*]. Banghazi: University of Libya Press, 1974.

Danvers, F. C. *The Portuguese in India.* 2 vols. London: Great Britain, India Office, 1892.

D'Arville. *Le golfe persique, route de l'Inde et de la Chine, Extrait de la revue des questions diplomatiques et coloniales.* Paris, 1905.

Darwazih, al-Hakam. *al-shuyuᶜiya al-mahalliya fi maᶜrakat al-ᶜarab al-qawmiya* [*Regional Communism in the Nationalist Arab Struggle*]. Beirut: Dar al-Fajr al-Jadid, 1961.

al-Da'ud, Mahmud ᶜAli. *al-khalij al-ᶜarabi wa-l-ᶜalaqat al-duwaliya, 1890–1914* [*The Arab Gulf and International Relations, 1890–1914*]. Cairo: Markaz al-Dirasat wa-l-Buhuth: al-Jamiᶜa al-ᶜArabiya, 1963.

Davis, Eric. "Between Development and Underdevelopment: Knowledge, Power, and the Study of the Third World." In *Critical Paradigms in the Study of Middle East Politics,* edited by L. Cantori and I. Harik. Forthcoming.

————. "Imagery of the Third World and the Construction of the Self in Contemporary American Society." Mimeo., Rutgers University, New Brunswick, N.J., 1987.

————. "The Political Economy of the Arab Oil-Producing Nations: Convergence with Western Interests." *Studies in Comparative International Development* 19, no. 2 (1979): 75–94.

Dawn, C. E. "The Rise of Arabism in Syria." *The Middle East Journal* 16 (Autumn 1962): 145–68.

Deeb, Marius. *Party Politics in Egypt: The Wafd and Its Rivals, 1919–1939.* London: Ithaca Press, 1979.

Delacroix, Jacques. "The Distributive State in the World System." *Studies in Comparative International Development* 15, no. 3 (1980): 3–21.

Dickson, H. R. P. *Kuwait and Her Neighbours.* London: Allen & Unwin, 1956.

al-Disuqi, ᶜAsim. *kibar mullak al-aradi al-ziraᶜiya wa dawruhum fi-l-mujtamaᶜ al-misri, 1914–1952* [*Large Landowners and Their Role in Egyptian Society, 1914–1952*]. Cairo: Dar al-Thaqafa al-Jadida, 1975.

Dukhi, Yusuf Farhan. *al-aghani al-kuwaytiya* [*Kuwaiti Songs*]. Qatar: Arab Gulf States Folklore Centre, 1984.

al-Dulaymi, Lutfiya. "*al-ᶜawd min al-safar*" ["Returning from Abroad"]. In *al-bishara* [*Tidings*]. Baghdad: Ministry of Information, 1974.

al-Duwayk, Muhammad Talib. *al-qissas al-shabᶜiya fi qatar* [*Folktales in Qatar*]. 2 vols. Qatar: Arab Gulf States Folklore Centre, 1984.

Edelman, Murray. *Constructing the Political Spectacle*. Chicago: University of Chicago Press, 1988.

Eickelman, Dale. *The Middle East: An Anthropological Approach*. Englewood Cliffs, N.J.: Prentice-Hall, 1981.

Abou El-Hajj, Rifaat Ali. "The Social Uses of the Past: Recent Arab Historiography of Ottoman Rule." *International Journal of Middle East Studies* 14, no. 2 (1982): 185–201.

Evans, Peter B., Dietrich Rueschemeyer, and Theda Skocpol, eds. *Bringing the State Back In*. Cambridge: Cambridge University Press, 1985.

Evans-Pritchard, E. E. *The Sanusi of Cyrenaica*. Oxford: Clarendon Press, 1949.

al-Falah, Noura. *al-taghayur al-ijtimaᶜi fi-l-duwal al-muntija li-l-naft (mujtamaᶜ al-kuwayt)* [*Social Change in Oil-Producing Countries: Kuwaiti Society*]. *Annals of the Faculty of Arts*, vol. 11, no. 57. Kuwait: Kuwait University, 1988.

al-Falaki, Yusif. *qadiyat al-bahrayn bayn al-madi wa-l-hadir* [*The Bahrain Issue between Past and Present*]. Cairo, 1953.

al-Farhan, Rashid ᶜAbdallah. *mukhtasar tarikh al-kuwayt wa ᶜalaqatuhu bi-l-hukuma al-baritaniya wa-l-duwal al-ᶜarabiya* [*A Concise History of Kuwait and Its Relations with Britain and the Arab Countries*]. Cairo: Maktabat Dar al-ᶜUruba, 1960.

Farman, Gha'ib Tuᶜma. *kitab min al-ᶜiraq* [*A Letter from Iraq*]. *al-Thaqafa al-Misriya*, 26 April 1950, 600.

Foucault, Michel. *The Archaeology of Knowledge*. New York: Harper & Row, 1972.

———. "Power, Sovereignty, and Discipline." In *States and Societies*, edited by David Held et al. New York: New York University Press, 1983.

Gadallah, Fawzi F., ed. *Libya in History*. Banghazi: University of Libya Press, 1968.

Gavrielides, Nicolas. "Islamic Fundamentalism and Tribalism in the State of Kuwait." Paper delivered at the American Anthropological Association Annual Meeting, Washington, D.C., 1980.

———. "Tribal Democracy: The Anatomy of Parliamentary Elections in Kuwait." In *Elections in the Middle East*, edited by Linda L. Layne, 153–213. Boulder, Col.: Westview Press, 1987.

Geertz, Clifford. "Ideology as a Cultural System." In *Ideology and Discontent*, edited by David Apter, 47–76. New York: Free Press, 1964.

Gellner, Ernest, and Charles Micaud, eds. *Arabs and Berbers*. London: Duckworth, 1973.

Gordon, David C. *Self-Determination and History in the Third World*. Princeton, N.J.: Princeton University Press, 1971.

Gramsci, Antonio. *Selections from the Prison Notebooks*. London: Lawrence and Wishart, 1971.

al-Habib, Muhsin Husayn. *haqa'iq ᶜan thawrat 14 tammuz fi-l-ᶜiraq* [*The Facts of the July 14 Iraqi Revolution*]. Beirut: Dar al-Andalus, 1981.

Hadid, Zahar Abdul-Karim. "Mass Communication and Social Change in Iraq:

Changing the Attitudes of Women." M.A. thesis, Department of Sociology, University of Durham, Durham, England, 1980.

Abu Hakima, Ahmad Mustafa. *tarikh al-kuwayt* [*The History of Kuwait*]. Kuwait: Government Press, 1967.

Hanafi, Hasan. *"limadha ghab mabhath al-tarikh fi turathina al-qadim?"* ["Why Has Historical Research Been Missing from Our Ancient Heritage?"]. *al-Fikr al-ᶜArabi* 27 (May–June 1982): 97–98.

Hasan, M.S. "The Economic Development of Iraq, 1864–1964: A Study in the Growth of a Dependent Economy." In *Studies in the Economic History of the Middle East*, edited by M.A. Cook, 346–72. London: Oxford University Press, 1970.

Hasan, Zaki Muhammad. *"malamih madrasat baghdad li taswir al-kitab"* ["The Characteristics of the Baghdadi School of Miniature Art"]. *al-Riwaq*, no. 15 (1985): 42–47.

al-Hasani, ᶜAbd al-Razzaq. *al-asrar al-khafiya fi harakat sanat 1940* [*The Hidden Secrets of the 1940 Movement*]. 3d ed. Sidon: al-ᶜIrfan Press, 1971.

———. *tarikh al-wizarat al-ᶜiraqiya* [*The History of Iraqi Cabinets*]. 10 vols. 6th ed. Beirut: Maktabat al-Yaqdha al-ᶜArabiya, 1982.

———. *al-thawra al-ᶜiraqiya al-kubra* [*The Great Iraqi Revolution*]. 4th ed. Beirut: Dar al-Kutub, 1978.

al-Hatim, ᶜAbdallah. *min huna bada'at al-kuwayt* [*Here Is Where Kuwait Begins*]. Damascus, 1962.

Hawley, Donald. *The Trucial States*. London: Allen & Unwin, 1970.

al-Haydari, Yusuf. *huna yajufu al-bahr* [*Here Is Where the Sea Dries Up*]. al-Najaf: Dar al-Kalima, 1969.

———. *"al-shabah"* ["The Ghost"]. In *hina yajufu al-bahr* [*Here Is Where the Sea Dries Up*]. al-Najaf: Dar al-Kalima, 1967.

al-Hisnawi, Habib. *al-riwayat al-shafawiya wa-l-tarikh li-harakat al-jihad al-libi: mulahazat manhajiya* [*Oral Narrations and the History of the Libyan Liberation Movement: Methodological Notes*]. Actes du IIème séminaire sur l'histoire du mouvement national: Sources et methodes de l'histoire du mouvement national tunisien (1920–1954). Tunis: Imprimerie Officielle de la République Tunisienne, 1985.

Hobsbawm, Eric J. "The Social Function of the Past." *Past and Present* 55 (1972): 3–17.

——— and Terence Ranger, eds. *The Invention of Tradition*. Cambridge: Cambridge University Press, 1983.

Hoskins, Halford. *British Routes to India*. London: Octagon Books, 1928.

Hudson, Michael. *Arab Politics: The Search for Legitimacy*. New Haven, Conn.: Yale University Press, 1977.

Huede, William. *A Voyage up the Persian Gulf and Journey Overland from India to England in 1817*. London: Longmans, 1819.

Husayn, ᶜAbd al-ᶜAziz. *muhadarat ᶜan al-mujtamaᶜ al-ᶜarabi fi-l-kuwayt* [*Lec-*

tures on Arab Society in Kuwait]. Cairo: Matbaᶜt Maᶜhad al-Dirasat al-ᶜArabiya al-ᶜAliya, 1960.

Husayn, Mahmud. *Class Struggle in Egypt, 1945–1970*. Arabic trans. Beirut: Dar al-Taliᶜa, 1971.

Husayn, Saddam. *hawla kitabat al-tarikh* [*On the Writing of History*]. Baghdad: Ministry of Culture and Arts, 1979.

———. *al-turath wa al-muᶜasara* [*Heritage and Modernity*]. Baghdad: Ministry of Culture and Arts, 1977.

Ibrahim, Hasan Ahmad. *al-matamiᶜ al-urubiya fi-l-khalij al-ᶜarabi min mutlaq al-qarn al-sadis ᶜashar hatta muntasaf al-qarn al-tasiᶜ ᶜashar: mu'tamar dirassat tarikh sharq al-jazira al-ᶜarabiya* [*European Designs on the Arab Gulf from the Beginning of the Sixteenth until the Mid-nineteenth Century: A Conference on the Study of the History of the Eastern Arabian Peninsula*]. Qatar, 1976.

ᶜAbdul Ilah, Saᶜid. *"sakin dhalik al-qasr"* ["Resident of the Palace"]. *al-Hasid*, no. 32 (February 1931).

al-Jabiri, Muhammad ᶜAbid. *al-kitab al-ᶜarabi al-muᶜasir: dirasa naqdiya tahliliya* [*Contemporary Arabic Writing: An Analytical and Critical Study*]. Beirut: Dar al-Taliᶜa, 1982.

al-Jahidh, Abi ᶜUthman ᶜAmru bin Bahr. *al-bukhala'* [*The Misers*]. Annotated by Taha al-Hajiri. Cairo: Dar al-Maᶜarif, n.d.

———. *al-bursan wa-l-ᶜurjan wa-l-ᶜumyan wa-l-hawlan* [*The Lepers, the Lame, the Blind and the Cross-eyed*]. Edited and annotated by ᶜAbd al-Salam Muhammad Harun. Beirut: Dar al-Taliᶜa li-l-Tibaᶜa wa-l-Nashr, 1982.

al-Jarari, Muhammad Tahir. *"hawla tahrir al-tarikh min al-fikr al-istiᶜmari"* ["On Liberating History from the Colonial Mentality"]. *Majallat al-Buhuth al-Tarikhiya* 1, no. 2 (1979).

———. *"limadha markaz buhuth wa-dirasat al-jihad al-libi?"* ["Why the Center for the Study of the Libyan Struggle?"]. *Majallat al-Buhuth al-Tarikhiya* 1, no. 1 (1979).

al-Jawahiri, Muhammad. *ᶜilm al-fulklur: dirasa fi-l-anthrupulugiya al-thaqafiya* [*The Science of Folklore: A Study in Cultural Anthropology*]. Cairo: Dar al-Maᶜarif, 1977.

al-Jaza'iri, ᶜAbd al-Razzaq bin Ahmadush. *kashf al-rumuz fi bayan al-aᶜshab* [*Uncovering the Meaning of Symbols in the Study of Plants*]. N.p., n.d.

Juwayda, Wadiᶜ. *"qatil yataᶜalam"* ["A Suffering Murderer"] *al-Hasid*, no. 29 (18 February 1932).

Kamal, Safwat. *min ᶜadat wa taqalid al-zawaj fi-l-kuwayt* [*Marriage Customs and Traditions in Kuwait*]. Kuwait: Ministry of Information, Center for the Protection of Folk Arts, 1966.

———. *madkhal fi dirasat al-fulklur al-kuwayti* [*Introduction to Kuwaiti Folklore*]. Kuwait: Government Press, 1968.

ᶜAbd al-Karim, Samir. *adwa' ᶜala al-haraka al-shuyuᶜiya fi-l-ᶜiraq* [*Perspectives on the Communist Movement in Iraq*]. 5 vols. Beirut: Dar al-Mirsad, n.d.

al-Kathiri, Abu al-Maᶜali Saᶜid bin ᶜAli. *al-iᶜjaz fi-l-ahaji wa-l-alghaz* [*The Wonderous Nature of Puzzles and Riddles*]. MS, 1177 A.D.

Kelly, John. *Britain and the Persian Gulf, 1795–1880*. Oxford: Clarendon, 1968.

al-Khafaji, ᶜIssam. *al-dawla wa-l-tatawwur al-ra'smali fi-l-ᶜiraq, 1967–1978* [*The State and Capitalist Development in Iraq, 1967–1978*]. Cairo: Dar al-Mustaqbal al-ᶜArabi, 1983.

al-Khalil, Samir. *Republic of Fear: The Politics of Modern Iraq*. Berkeley: University of California Press, 1989.

al-Khatib, Hisham. *tabiᶜat al-ta'athur al-ajnabi ᶜala al-qissa al-suriya al-muᶜasira* [*The Nature of Foreign Influence on the Modern Syrian Story*]. Damascus: Arabic Studies Institute, 1973.

Khazᶜal, Husayn Khalaf al-Shaykh. *tarikh al-kuwayt al-siyasi* [*The Political History of Kuwait*]. 5 vols. Beirut: n.p., 1962, 1972.

Khudhayr, Muhammad. "*bayt fi dahiyat al-madina*" ["A House in a Suburb"]. In *al-farara* [*The Fugitive (Female)*], 329–32. Baghdad: Dar al-Rashid, 1979.

———. *al-rajul alladhi tarakatahu al-madina* [*A Man Rejected by the City*]. al-Najaf: al-ᶜUzi Press, 1969.

Khusbak, Shakir. *al-ᶜasr al-jadid* [*The New Era*]. Cairo: Muᶜasir Bookshop, 1951.

Kiraydi, Musa. "*ᶜuqdat al-nahar*" ["The Day's Knot"] In *adwa' fi-l-madina* [*Lights in the City*]. Beirut: Modern Press, 1968.

Krasner, Stephen. *Defending the National Interest: Raw Materials, Investments and U.S. Foreign Policy*. Princeton, N.J.: Princeton University Press, 1978.

Landen, R.G. *Oman since 1856: Disruptive Modernization in a Traditional Arab Society*. Princeton, N.J.: Princeton University Press, 1967.

Lapidus, Ira M., ed. *Middle Eastern Cities: A Symposium on Ancient, Islamic, and Contemporary Middle Eastern Urbanism*. Berkeley: University of California Press, 1966.

Laroui, Abdallah. *The Crisis of the Arab Intellectual: Traditionalism or Historicism?* Berkeley: The University of California Press, 1976.

Longrigg, S.H. *Syria and Lebanon under the Mandate*. Beirut: Librarie du Liban, 1968.

Lorimar, J.J. *dalil al-khalij* [*Guide to the Persian Gulf*]. Arabic trans. 14 vols. al-Dawha: Matabiᶜ al-ᶜUruba, 1967.

Magdoff, Harry. *The Age of Imperialism: The Economics of U.S. Foreign Policy*. New York: Monthly Review Press, 1969.

Mahdi, Sami, *min awraq al-zawal* [*From the Leaves of Extinction*]. Baghdad: al-Adib Press, 1985.

ᶜAbd al-Majid, Ahmad. "*qira'a fi jaridat al-wasiti*" ["A Reading of the Journal of al-Wasiti"]. *al-Riwaq*, no. 15 (1985): 53–55.

Makkiya, Muhammad. "*turath al-rasm al-baghdadi*" ["The Heritage of Baghdadi Drawing"]. *al-Riwaq*, no. 15 (1985): 29–41.

Maksoud, Clovis. *azmat al-yasar al-ᶜarabi* [*The Crisis of the Arab Left*]. Beirut: Dar al-ᶜIlm li-l-Malayin, 1960.

ᶜAbd al-Malik, Anwar. *Egypt: Military Society*. Arabic trans. Beirut: Dar al-Taliᶜa, 1974.

al-Mallah, ᶜAbd al-Ghani. *tarikh al-haraka al-dimuqratiya fi misr* [*The History of the Democratic Movement in Egypt*]. Beirut: al-Mu'assasa al-ᶜArabiya li-l-Dirasat wa-l-Nashr, 1980.

al-Manaᶜ, ᶜAli Shuᶜayb, ed. and annotator. *mawawil min al-khalij: nusus min al-adab al-shaᶜbi fi mantiqat al-khalij wa-l-jazira* [*Colloquial Gulf Poetry: Texts of Folk Literature in the Gulf and the Arabian Peninsula*]. 2 vols. Qatar: Arab Gulf States Folklore Centre, 1984.

Mann, Major Clarence. *Abu Dabi: Birth of an Oil Sheikhdom*. Beirut: Khayats, 1964.

Marlowe, John. *The Persian Gulf in the Twentieth Century*. London: Cresset Press, 1962.

Matta, Yusif. "*hutam*" ["Ruin"]. *ᶜUtarid*, no. 1 (August 1934).

al-Maydani, Abu al-Fadl Ahmad bin Muhammad al-Naysaburi. *majmaᶜ al-amthal* [*The Encyclopedia of Proverbs*]. Vol. 1. Cairo: al-Maktaba al-Hijaniya al-Kubra, 1956.

Michalak, Laurence. *Cruel and Unusual: Negative Images of Arabs in American Popular Culture*. Washington, D.C.: ADC Research Institute, 1988.

Migdal, Joel S. *Strong Societies and Weak States: State-Society Relations and State Capabilities in the Third World*. Princeton, N.J.: Princeton University Press, 1988.

Miles, Samuel. *The Countries and Tribes of the Persian Gulf*. 2 vols. London: Harrison & Sons, 1919.

Miliband, Ralph. *The State in Capitalist Society*. New York: Basic Books, 1969.

Mitwalli, Mahmud. *al-usul al-tarikhiya li-l-ra'smaliya al-misriya wa tatawwuruha* [*The Historical Roots and Development of Capitalism in Egypt*]. Cairo: al-Hay'a al-Misriya li-l-Kitab, 1974.

Mommsen, Wolfgang J., and Gerhard Hirschfeld, eds. *Social Protest: Violence and Terror in Nineteenth and Twentieth Century Europe*. London: Macmillan, 1982.

Mortad, Abdel-Malek. "*al-ᶜalaqat al-iqtisadiya bayn al-tabaqat al-ijtimaᶜiya fi-l-amthal al-shaᶜbiya al-jaza'iriya*" ["Economic Relations among Social Classes in Algerian Proverbs"]. *al-Turath al-Shaᶜbi* 11, no. 10 (1980): 13–30.

Musa, Salama. *tarbiyat salama musa* [*The Education of Salama Musa*]. Cairo: Dar al-Kitab al-Misri, 1948.

al-Musawi, Muhsin Jassim. *al-tayar al-muᶜasir fi-l-qissa al-ᶜiraqiya al-qasira* [*The Modernist Trend in the Iraqi Short Story*]. Baghdad and Beirut: al-Mu'assasa al-ᶜArabiya, 1984.

———. *al-haqiqa wa-l-khayal* [*The Seen and the Imagined*]. 2 vols. Baghdad: Cultural Affairs Press, 1987.

————. "al-ishtishraq al-siyasi: fardiyatuhu wa-istintajuhu" ["Political Orientalism: Its Hypothesis and Conclusions"]. Afaq ⁿArabiya, nos. 1–3 (January–February 1987, 1989).

ⁿAbd al-Muⁿti, ⁿAbd al-Basit. "al-tharwa wa-l-sulta fi misr" ["Wealth and Authority in Egypt"]. Majallat al-ⁿUlum al-Ijtimaⁿiya [Journal of the Social Sciences] 10 (3 September 1982).

al-Nafisi, ⁿAbdallah Fahd. majlis al-taⁿawun al-khaliji: al-itar al-siyasi wa-l-istratiji [The Gulf Cooperation Council: The Political and Strategic Dimensions]. London: Ta Ha Advertising, 1982.

al-Najjar, Muhammad Rajab. al-ghatawi aw al-alghaz al-shaⁿbiya al shafawiya: dirasa faniya wa mawduⁿiya [al-Ghatawi or Kuwaiti Oral Folk Riddles: An Artistic and Empirical Study]. Forthcoming.

————. al-ghatawi aw al-alghaz al-shaⁿbiya fi-l-kuwayt wa usuluha fi-l-turath al-shaⁿbi [al-Ghatawi or Kuwaiti Folk Riddles and Their Origins in Folk Culture]. Kuwait: al-Rubayⁿan Co., 1985.

————. juha al-ⁿarabi: shakhsiyatuhu wa falsafatuhu fi-l-hayat wa-l-taⁿbir [Juha the Arab: His Personality and Philosophy in Deed and Expression]. Kuwait: National Council of Culture, Art, and Literature, 1978.

————. hikayat al-shuttar wa-l-ⁿayarin fi-l-turath al-ⁿarabi [Stories of Villains and Vagabonds in Arab Heritage]. Kuwait: ⁿAlam al-Maⁿrifa Series, National Council on Culture, Arts, and Literature, 1981.

————, ed. and annotator. muⁿjam al-alghaz al-shaⁿbiya fi-l-kuwayt [The Encyclopedia of Kuwaiti Folk Riddles]. Qatar: Arab Gulf States Folklore Centre, 1985.

al-Naqeeb, Khaldoun Hasan. Preliminary Studies in Social Stratification in Arab Countries. Annals of the College of Arts, vol. 1, monograph 5. Kuwait: Kuwait University, 1980.

Nasir, ⁿAbd al-Sattar. rasm mukhtasar li-hayat shaykh nadir ["A Short Biographical Sketch of Shaykh Nadir"]. al-Adib, no. 6 (June 1970).

————. "buyut al-madina laha ra'iha" ["The Smell of City Houses"]. al-Adab, no. 4 (April 1973): 20.

Nawfal, Sayyid. al-awdaⁿ al-siyasiya fi imarat al-khalij wa junub al-jazira al-ⁿarabiya [Political Conditions in the Gulf Amirates and the Southern Arabian Peninsula]. Cairo: Maⁿhad al-Buhuth wa-l-Dirasat al-ⁿArabiya, 1960.

Nawwar, ⁿAbd al-ⁿAziz. tarikh al-ⁿarab al-muⁿasir: misr wa-l-ⁿiraq [Contemporary Arab History: Egypt and Iraq]. Beirut: Dar al-Nahda al-ⁿArabiya, 1973.

New York Times, 8, 14, 16, 17 October 1990.

al-Nishaymi, Muhammad Ahmad. al-zawaj qadiman fi-l-kuwayt [Marriage in Kuwait in the Past]. Kuwait: Dar al-Taliⁿa, 1974.

Nordlinger, Eric A. On the Autonomy of the Democratic State. Cambridge, Mass.: Harvard University Press, 1981.

al-Nuri, ⁿAbdallah. al-amthal al-darija fi-l-kuwayt [Common Proverbs in Kuwait]. 2 vols. Beirut: Qalfat Press, 1976.

al-Nuri, ⁿAbd al-Malik. "fatuma" ["Little Fatima"]. al-Adib, January 1948.

———. *"akhbar al-saᶜa"* ["News of the Hour"]. *Akhbar al-Saᶜa*, 2 April 1953.

———. *"kana fanan shab: dhikrayat jawad salim"* ["The Artist as a Young Man: Jawad Salim's Memoirs"]. *al-Hiwar*, no. 8 (January–February 1964): 99–101, 103, 108.

Palgrave, A.G. *Narrative of a Year's Journey Overland from Central and Eastern Arabia, 1862–1863.* 2 vols. London: Macmillan, 1865.

Panetta, Ester, ed. *L'Italia in Africa: Studi italiani de etnografia e di folklore della Libia.* Roma: Ministero degli Affari Esteri, 1963.

Polk, William, and Richard Chambers, eds. *Beginnings of Modernization in the Middle East: The Nineteenth Century.* Chicago: University of Chicago Press, 1968.

Pool, David. "From Elite to Class: The Transformation of Iraqi Political Leadership." In *The Integration of Modern Iraq*, edited by Abbas Kelidar, 63–87. New York: St. Martin's Press, 1979.

ᶜAbd al-Qadir, Nur al-Din. *al-qawl al-ma'thur min kalam al-shaykh ᶜabd al-rahman al-majdhub* [*Proverbs Spoken by Shaykh ᶜAbd al-Rahman al-Majdhub*]. Algiers: al-Thaᶜalibiya Press, n.d.

al-Qadu, Dirar. *"madrasat al-musul li-l-taswir"* ["The Musul School of Representational Art"]. *al-Riwaq*, no. 15 (1985): 48–52.

al-Qanaᶜi, Yusif. *safahat min tarikh al-kuwayt* [*Pages from the History of Kuwait*]. Kuwait: Government Press, 1968.

al-Qashshat, Muhammad Saᶜid. *sada al-jihad al-libi fi-l-adab al-shaᶜbi* [*The Impact of the Libyan Struggle on Popular Literature*]. Beirut: Dar Lubnan li-l-Tibaᶜa wa-l-Nashr, 1970.

Qasim, Jamal Zakariya. *al-khalij al-ᶜarabi: dirasa li tarikh al-imarat al-ᶜarabiya, 1840–1914* [*The Arab Gulf: A Study of the History of the Arab Emirates, 1840–1914.*] 2 vols. Cairo: Matbaᶜat Jamiᶜat ᶜAyn Shams, 1973.

al-Qaysi, Nuri Hamudi. *al-shiᶜr wa-l-tarikh* [*Poetry and History*]. Baghdad: Dar al-Hurriya li-l-Tibaᶜa, 1980.

Qurayshi, Muhsin. *al-malhuna aw al-shaᶜbiya* [*Non-Grammatical or Folk Poetry*]. 3 vols. Baghdad: Ministry of Information, 1977.

al-Qurtubi, Ahmad al-Zajali. *ray al-aᶜwam wa marᶜa al-sawam fi nukat al-khasa wa-l-aᶜwam* [*The Opinion of Commoners and the Judgment of Notables in Dealing with the Jokes of Nobility and Commoners*]. Edited and annotated by Muhammad bin Sharifa. *al-Maghrib al-Aqsa*: n.p., n.d.

Rafiq, ᶜAbd al-Karim. *al-ᶜarab wa-l-ᶜuthmaniyun, 1516–1916* [*The Arabs and the Ottomans, 1516–1916*]. Damascus: Maktabat al-Atlas, 1974.

Ramadan, ᶜAbd al-ᶜAzim. *al-jaysh al-misri fi-l-siyasa, 1882–1936* [*The Egyptian Army in Politics, 1882–1936*]. Cairo: al-Hay'a al-Misriya al-ᶜAmma li-l-Kittab, 1977.

al-Rashid, Yaᶜqub ᶜAbd al-ᶜAziz. *al-kuwayt fi mizan al-haqiqa wa-l-tarikh* [*Kuwait on the Scale of Facts and History*]. Kuwait: n.p., 1963.

al-Rawi, Nuri. *"madrasat baghdad fi-l-taswir al-islami"* ["*The Baghdadi School in Islamic Representational Art*"]. *al-Riwaq*, no. 15 (1985): 4–19.

———. *"al-wasiti bayn al-ramz wa-l-haqiqa"* [*"al-Wasiti Between Symbol and Reality"*]. *al-Riwaq*, no. 15 (1985): 2–3.

Richmond, J.C.B. *Egypt, 1798–1952: Her Advance Towards a Modern Identity.* London: Methuen, 1977.

al-Rihani, Amin. *muluk al-ᶜarab* [*The Arab Kings*]. 2 vols. 4th ed. Beirut: Dar al-Rihani, 1924, 1960.

Rizq, Yunan Labib. *al-ahzab al-misriya qabla thawrat 1952* [*Egyptian Political Parties before the 1952 Revolution*]. Cairo: Center for Political and Strategic Studies, al-Ahram, 1977.

Rostow, Dankwart A. "The Military in Middle East Politics." In *The Military in the Middle East,* edited by S.N. Fisher, 3–20. Columbus: Ohio State University Press, 1963.

al-Rubaᶜi, ᶜAbd al-Rahman Majid. *"mutarad"* ["The Chased"]. In *ᶜuyun al-hilm* [*The Eyes of a Dream*]. N.p.: n.p., 1974.

al-Rumayhi, Muhammad Ghanim. *al-bahrayn: qadaya al-taghayur al-siyasi wa-l-ijtimaᶜi, 1920–1970* [*Bahrain: The Issues of Political and Social Change, 1920–1970*]. Kuwait: Mu'assasat al-Wihda li-l-Nashr wa-l-Tawziᶜ, 1976.

———. *al-judhur al-ijtimaᶜiya li-l-dimuqratiya fi mujtamaᶜat al-khalij al-ᶜarabi al-muᶜasira* [*The Social Roots of Democracy in Modern Gulf Societies.*] Kuwait: Sharikat Kadhima li-l-Nashr wa-l-Tarjama wa-l-Tawziᶜ, 1977.

———. *al-khalij laysa naftan: dirasa fi ishkaliyat al-tanmiya wa-l-wihda* [*The Gulf Is Not Oil: A Study of the Problematic of Development and Unity*]. Kuwait: Sharikat Kadhima li-l-Nashr wa-l-Tarjama wa-l-Tawziᶜ, 1983.

al-Sadani, Nuriya. *al-masira al-tarikhiya li-l-huquq al-siyasiya li-l-mar'a al-kuwaytiya fi-l-fatra min 1971–1982* [*The Historical Development of Women's Political Rights in Kuwait, 1971–1982*]. Kuwait: Dar al-Siyasa Press, 1983.

Saᶜid, Amin. *al-khalij al-ᶜarabi: dirasa li tarikhahu al-siyasi wa nahdatahu al-haditha* [*The Arab Gulf: A Study of Its Political History and Its Modern Renaissance*]. Beirut: Dar al-Kitab al-ᶜArabi, n.d.

———. *al-thawra al-ᶜarabiya al-kubra* [*The Great Arab Revolt*]. Vol. 2. Cairo: al-Salafiya Press, 1935.

Said, Edward. *Orientalism.* New York: Pantheon, 1978.

al-Saᶜid, Rifᶜat. *al-asas al-ijtimaᶜi li-thawrat ᶜurabi* [*The Social Basis of the ᶜUrabi Revolution*]. Cairo: Maktabat al-Madbuli, 1966.

al-Saᶜid, Shakir Hasan. *"al-mawqif al-thaqafi li yahya bin mahmud al-wasiti"* ["The Cultural Perspective of Yahya Bin Mahmud al-Wasiti"]. *al-Riwaq*, no. 15 (1985): 24–28.

al-Saᶜidan, Hamad Muhammad. *al-mawsuᶜa al-kuwaytiya al-mukhtasara* [*The Concise Kuwaiti Encyclopedia*]. Vol. 1. Kuwait: al-Matbaᶜa al-ᶜAsriya, 1970.

al-Salami, Muhammad Bin ᶜAbdallah, and Naji Asaf. *ᶜuman tarikhun yatakalam* [*Uman's History Speaks*]. Damascus: n.p., 1963.

———. *tuhfat al-aᶜyan bi sirat al-ᶜuman* [*The Gem of Notables Is among the Biographies of the People of ᶜUman*]. Cairo: n.p., 1961.

Salman, ʿIsa. "al-madrasa al-ʿarabiya fi-l-taswir al-islami" ["The Arab School in Islamic Representational Art"]. al-Riwaq, no. 15 (1985): 20–23.

Samara, A. Rashid. mawalat baghdadiya [Baghdadi Monologues]. Baghdad: Ministry of Information, 1974.

al-Samaraʾi, Majid Muhammad. al-tayyar al-qawmi fi-l-shiʿr al-ʿiraqi al-hadith, 1939–1967 [Nationalist Trends in Iraqi Poetry, 1939–1967]. Baghdad: Ministry of Culture and Information, Dar al-Hurriya li-l-Nashr, 1983.

al-Saqr, Mahdi ʿIsa. mujrimum tayibun [Good Criminals]. Baghdad: al-Rabita Press, 1954.

———. ghadab al-madina [The City's Anger]. Baghdad: n.p. 1960.

Sarhan, Basin, et al. malaf maʿlumat hawla al-ʿamala al-ajnabiya fi aqtar al-khalij al-ʿarabi [Data File on Foreign Labor in the Arab Gulf Countries]. Kuwait: Arab Planning Institute, 1983.

al-Sayyid, Mahmud Ahmad. "thawra ʿala abihi" ["Revolting Against His Father"]. al-Hasid, no. 15 (30 May 1929).

Scarce, Jennifer M. The Evolution of Culture in Kuwait. Edinburgh: Her Majesty's Stationery Office, 1985.

Seal, Patrick. The Struggle for Syria. Arabic trans. Beirut: Dar al-Kalima, 1980.

Segre, Claudio G. Fourth Shore: The Italian Colonization of Libya. Chicago: University of Chicago Press, 1974.

al-Shaykh, al-Tali. dawr al-shiʿir al-shaʿbi al-jazaʾiri fi-l-thawra, 1830–1945 [The Role of Algerian Popular Poetry in the Revolution, 1830–1945]. Algiers: al-Sharika al-Wataniya li-l-Nashr wa-l-Tawziʿ, 1983.

al-Shamlan, Sayf Marzuq. al-alʿab al-shaʿbiya al-kuwaytiya [Kuwaiti Folk Games]. Beirut: Dar Iʿlam al-Fikr, 1970.

———. min tarikh al-kuwayt [On the History of Kuwait]. Cairo: Maktbaʿat Nahdat Misr, 1959.

———. tarikh al-ghaws ʿala al-luʾluʾ fi-l-kuwayt wa-l-khalij al-ʿarabi. 2 vols. Kuwait: Government Press, 1975, 1978.

al-Siyabi, Salim Bin Mahmud. idah al-maʿalim fi tarikh al-qawasim [Explanation of the Characteristics of the History of Qawasim]. Damascus: n.p., 1976.

Skocpol, Theda. "Rentier State and Shiʾa Islam in the Iranian Revolution." Theory and Society 11 (1982): 265–83.

Smith, Adam. The Wealth of Nations. 2 vols. Hartford, Conn., 1811.

State of Kuwait. nidham al musaʿadat al-ijtimaʿiya [Ordinance of Social Welfare]. Kuwait: Department of Social Affairs, 1955.

———, Central Statistical Administration. al-majmuʿa al-ihsaʾiya al-sanawiya [Annual Statistical Survey]. Kuwait: Ministry of Planning, 1980.

———, Task Force on Women's Affairs. khasaʾis al-marʾa al-kuwaytiya fi-l-taʿadudat [Kuwaiti Women in the Census]. Kuwait: Ministry of Planning, 1980.

Subhi, Ahmad Mahmud. al-bahrayn wa daʿwat iran [Bahrain and the Claims of Iran]. Alexandria: n.p., 1962.

bin Suda, ʿAbd al-Salam, and Muhammad Daʾud. alf mathal wa mathal min *mathal tuwan* [*One Thousand and One Proverbs of the Proverbs of Tuwan*]. *Majalat al-Bahth al-ᶜIlmi*. Vol. 1, no. 2. n.d.

al-Suwayan, Saᶜd al-ᶜAbdallah. *al-shiᶜr al-shaᶜbi fi-l-mamlaka al-ᶜarabiya al-saᶜudiya* [*Folk Poetry in the Kingdom of Saudi Arabia*]. Qatar: Arab Gulf States Folklore Centre, 1985.

al-Talib, ᶜUmar. *al-qissa al-qasira fi-l-ᶜiraq* [*The Modern Short Story in Iraq*]. (Musul: Musul University Press, 1979).

al-Tamimi, ᶜAbd al-Malik Khalaf. "*al-khalij al-ᶜarabi: dirasa fi-l-tarikh al-iqtisadi wa-l-ijtimaᶜi*" ["The Arab Gulf: A Study in Economic and Social History"]. *Majallat al-ᶜUlum al-Ijtimaᶜiya* 9, no. 2 (June 1981).

Tarbush, Muhammad A. *The Role of the Military in Politics*. London: Kegan Paul International, 1982.

Taymur, Ahmad. *al-amthal al-ᶜamiya* [*Folk Proverbs*] 3d ed. Cairo: Mu'assasat al-Ahram, 1970.

al-Tayzini, Tayib. *min al-turath ila al-thawra* [*From Heritage to Revolution*]. Vol. 1. Beirut: Dar ibn Khaldun, 1976.

Thomson, David. *Europe since Napoleon*. 2d ed. London: Longman, 1983.

al-Tikirli, Fu'ad. "*khibrati ka katib qissa*" ["My Experience as a Short Story Writer"]. *al-Adib*, no. 7 (July 1973).

———. *al-wajh al-akhar* [*The Other Side*]. Baghdad: n.p., 1960.

Tilly, Charles, ed. *The Formation of National States in Western Europe*. Princeton, N.J.: Princeton University Press, 1975.

Tucker, Robert W. "Further Reflections on Oil and Force." *Commentary* 59 (March 1975): 45.

———. "Oil: The Issue of American Intervention." *Commentary* 59 (January 1975): 21.

———. "Using Force against Libya?" *New York Times*, 11 January 1989.

al-ᶜUmani, Sirhan Bin Saᶜid al-Azkazi. *tarikh ᶜuman* [*The History of Uman*]. N.p., n.d.

al-ᶜUza, Najat. *anmat min al-azya' al-shaᶜbiya al-nisa'iya* [*Forms of Women's Folk Dress*]. Qatar: Arab Gulf States Folklore Centre, 1984.

Vatikiotis, P. J. *The Egyptian Army in Politics*. Bloomington: Indiana University Press, 1961.

———. *The History of Egypt from Muhammad Ali to Sadat*. 2d ed. London: Weidenfeld and Nicolson, 1980.

al-Waᶜli, Ibrahim. *thawrat ᶜishrin fi-l-shiᶜr al-ᶜiraqi* [*The 1920 Revolution in Iraqi Poetry*]. Baghdad: Inma' Press, 1968.

Warriner, Doreen. "Land Tenure in the Fertile Crescent." In *The Economic History of the Middle East*, edited by Charles Issawi, 71–78. Chicago: Chicago University Press, 1966.

Watson, Robert Grant. *History of Persia from the Beginning of the Nineteenth Century to 1856*. London: Smith, Elder, 1866.

Weber, Max. *Economy and Society*. 2 vols. Berkeley and Los Angeles: University of California Press, 1978.

Winder, R. B. "Syrian Deputies and Cabinet Ministers, 1919–1959." Pt. 1. *Middle East Journal* 16, no. 4 (1962): 409–19.

Yunis, ʿAbd al-Hamid. *difaʿ ʿan al-fulklur* [*The Defense of Folklore*]. Cairo: al-Hay'a al-Misriya li-l-Kitab, 1973.

al-Zawi, Tahir Ahmad. *jihad al-abtal fi tarablus al-gharb* [*The Hero's Struggle in Western Tripoli*]. Beirut: Dar al-Fatah, 1970.

Index